"It's a fil

D0469866

The rural Irish landscape often has this effect on visitors, especially from Hollywood. A splash of sea, forty shades of green, the white homestead, the priestly collar, the village pub. Before you know it Tom Cruise and Nicole Kidman are dressed in peasant rags, playing out a torrid love affair in ridiculous accents even the deaf would recognize as Scottish. If you ask me, Hollywood's version of Ireland is always ridiculous. If the John Wayne of *The Quiet Man* came back from America tomorrow, he'd be selling mobile phones in Dublin for a living and settling his arguments over women with a flick knife.

But trust me, the view from Creeslough really was like a film set.

PRAISE FOR LAWRENCE DONEGAN'S
No News at Throat Lake

"An entertaining, enlightening account of daily life in rural Ireland—the ever-present economic hardships, but also the passion for family, politics, religion, and sports. . . . [W]onderful glimpses into what it actually would be like to live behind the picture-postcard facade that tourists see while touring Ireland."
— *The Des Moines Register*

"The style is chatty, self-effacing and revealing, Nick Hornby sharing a quiet pint with Bill Bryson, being served by barmaid Lorrie Moore."
— *Pasadena Weekly* (CA)

"[A] most entertaining book."
— *Sky* (Delta Air Lines)

BY THE SAME AUTHOR

Maybe It Should Have Been a Three Iron

For orders other than by individual consumers, Pocket Books grants a discount on the purchase of **10 or more** copies of single titles for special markets or premium use. For further details, please write to the Vice President of Special Markets, Pocket Books, 1230 Avenue of the Americas, 9th Floor, New York, NY 10020-1586.

For information on how individual consumers can place orders, please write to Mail Order Department, Simon & Schuster, Inc., 100 Front Street, Riverside, NJ 08075.

lawrence donegan

No news At THROAT Lake

In
Search
of
Ireland

POCKET BOOKS
New York   London   Toronto   Sydney   Singapore

The sale of this book without its cover is unauthorized. If you purchased this book without a cover, you should be aware that it was reported to the publisher as "unsold and destroyed." Neither the author nor the publisher has received payment for the sale of this "stripped book."

 POCKET BOOKS, a division of Simon & Schuster, Inc.
1230 Avenue of the Americas, New York, NY 10020

Copyright © 2000 by Lawrence Donegan

Originally published in hardcover in 2000 by Pocket Books

All rights reserved, including the right to reproduce this book or portions thereof in any form whatsoever. For information address Pocket Books, 1230 Avenue of the Americas, New York, NY 10020

Library of Congress Cataloging-in-Publication Data

Donegan, Lawrence
    No news at Throat Lake / Lawrence Donegan
    p. cm
    ISBN: 0-671-78544-3
    1. Donegan, Lawrence. 2. Journalists—Ireland—Biography.
    2. Creeslough (Ireland)—Social life and customs. I. Title
PN5146.D66 A3 2000
070'.92—dc21
[B]   99–089574

First Pocket Books trade paperback printing March 2001

10 9 8 7 6 5 4 3 2 1

POCKET and colophon are registered trademarks of Simon & Schuster, Inc.

Cover design by Brigid Pearson, front cover photos by Roderick Field

Printed in the U.S.A.

The frontispiece map was created by Reg and Marjorie Piggott and is used with their kind permission.

W. B. Yeats "The Great Day" and lines from "Under Ben Bulben" are reprinted with the permission of Scribner, a division of Simon & Schuster, from *The Collected Works of W. B. Yeats, Volume 1: The Poems*, revised and edited by Richard J. Finneran. Copyright 1940 by Georgie Yeats; copyright renewed © 1968 by Bertha Georgie Yeats, Michael Butler Yeats, and Anne Yeats.

For John, Francis and, of course, Bouncer

It would be much easier for everyone if today's opponents came dressed up in the old too-familiar clothes of the conqueror. But Apathy does not wear the historically hated Red Coat. Indifference does not charge in on a Calvary horse and Injustice and Charity do not come tearing down Barrack Street in black-and-tanned lorries to shoot up a town which has already surrendered to Batman and the pop press-agentry and plug boys and the whizz-kiddery of the economic jargon boys of Dublin who have assured them they have no future anyway, and don't call us, we'll call you.

Yes, but what can you do? What can we do?

John Healy
The Death of an Irish Town

Wouldn't it be fucking great if there was a paper in Donegal that would print a story, regardless of who it offended? Or that took adverts? Wouldn't it be great if that paper always took the side of the people, regardless of whether the people were right or wrong?

John McAteer, 1987

Contents

Acknowledgments

About three years ago I was standing in a phone booth in Creeslough, County Donegal, when I had the vague notion that I might one day write a book about life in rural Ireland. A huge number of people and one special book helped me turn that germ of an idea into *No News at Throat Lake*.

The book was *The Death of an Irish Town*, the late John Healy's account of the decline of his birthplace, Charlestown, County Mayo. What I have written bears no resemblance to Healy's masterpiece (if only it did!), but I hope I've captured even a little of what his book taught me: that rural Ireland is a far more complex and interesting place than the twee adventure playground so often portrayed by film and television drama makers.

If John Healy gave me the initial inspiration, the residents of Creeslough provided the encouragement and, above all, friendship that helped me complete this book. In particular, I would like to say thanks to Michael Kelly, Patricia Kelly, Noel Toye, Francie Brennan, Ciaran 'Ollie' Rodden, James Toye, Hughie McGinley, John Shiels, Johnny Shiels, Gerry Friel, Bernadette McFadden and to Bernard Lafferty and his wonderful family. Bill Gallagher, Seamus Harkin and, especially, Sarah McCaffrey were a great help to me as I struggled to learn some local history. (However, it goes without saying that the mistakes are all my own.)

I would also like to say thanks to St. Michael's GAA club, which was kind enough (some might say daft enough) to indulge my enthusiasm for the wonderful game of Gaelic football. In particular thanks to Moses Alcorn, Michael McColgan, Liam Ferry and those members of the reserve team who, often against their better judgment, passed the ball to me during games. Don't worry, lads, there's always next season. I owe a special debt of gratitude to Danny Lafferty. Not only was he a good friend and excellent guide

Acknowledgments

on matters relating to Creeslough, he also pushed me toward the wonderful world of the *Tirconaill Tribune*.

At the *Tribune*, Noel Gillespie, Declan Kerr and Kathleen McGrory were helpful and tolerant colleagues. Thanks also to Pauric Sheerin, Patrick Logue, Cattie Martin, Harald Schmidle, Anita Guidera, Sally Blake, Louis Boyce, Shaun Boyce and the McAteer family of Fanad, particularly Peggy, Deirdre, Annette, Noleen, Mairead, Brideen, Seamus and the late Annie McAteer.

Thanks to John Hamilton for the title, and also to Jonny Geller, Tony Lacey, Hazel Orme, John Colquhoun, Denis Campbell, Jeremy Ettinghausen, the staff at the *Guardian* library and to Rose Toye, who read the original manuscript and made many important corrections.

Finally, thanks to Hugh and Greta Shiels, who gave me the use of their home for a year. Not only that, they raised a wonderful daughter called Maggie. She, of course, was great.

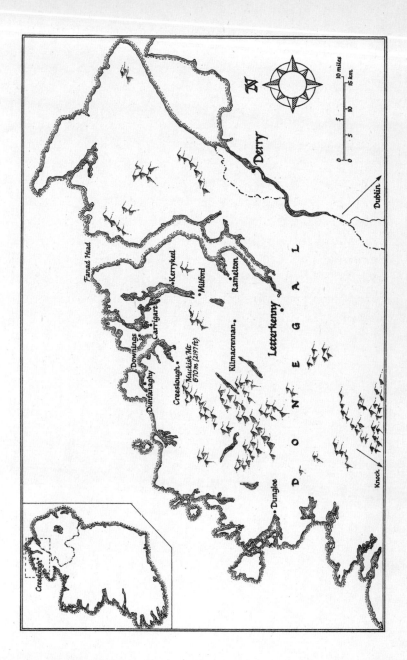

N

10 miles
15 km.

Derry

Dublin

Fanad Head

Kerrykeel
Milford
Rathmelton

Letterkenny

Downings
Carrigart
Dunfanaghy
Creeslough
Muckish Mt
670m (2197ft)
Kilmacrenan

D O N E G A L

Dunglae

Knock

Creeslough

No News at Throat Lake

Good-bye

In the summer of '91 a helicopter carrying the Richest Girl in the World floated across the big country sky over Creeslough. An elderly American woman with a face made taut as a snare drum by the plastic surgeon's scalpel peered through the Plexiglas windscreen of the cockpit. She then turned to her fellow passenger and, through bee-stung lips, sighed, "Why did you ever leave, Bernard? It's the most beautiful place in the world."

When one considers the life and times of this elderly woman—what she had seen and what she had done—her words could be construed as an enormous compliment for an Irish village as small and unassuming as Creeslough.

Doris Duke was given the epithet "The Richest Girl in the World" at the age of twelve when she inherited $200 million on the death of her father James "Buck" Duke, founder of the American Tobacco Company. She lived as varied, as opulent and as ridiculous a young life as would be expected of any obscenely rich brat. Every morning the schoolgirl Doris woke to a tape recording of her favorite waterfall before bathing in scented waters in a sunken, solid gold bath. She would dress, then hand her textbooks to a French governess, who would take them downstairs and hand them to the footman, who would give them to the butler, who in turn passed them to the chauffeur. Meanwhile, their young employer undertook the arduous task of choosing which of her eight limousines would carry her to school that day. Two private detectives were detailed to follow her to the classroom and wait outside until her lessons were over.

The young Doris eschewed the traditional childhood pleasures of dolls' houses and scrapbooks. Occasionally, she would pick up the phone and hire a circus for the evening. As you do. She liked to tinker on the piano or converse in French with her governess in order to infuriate a monolingual mother she had grown to loathe. She played the stock market with a gambler's relish that would have made Michael Milken blanch. Alas, in 1929 financial disaster struck with the Wall Street Crash, and Doris was down to her last $150 million.

Somehow she struggled on. Her young adult life was blighted by her constant fretting over the way she looked. She was not, it must be said, a beauty. After a long and fruitless search for the man of her dreams, she married an amateur boxer called Jimmy Cromwell. As a pugilist Jimmy would have lost on points to John Inman but as a gold digger he was in the Sonny Liston class. On their wedding night he carried the blushing bride to the marital bed, where his first thoughts were not sexual but financial. He asked Doris what his annual income paid from her trust fund might be. She locked him out of the honeymoon suite for starters and gave him his final answer in the divorce court a couple of years later: nothing.

Thereafter, according to her army of biographers, Doris Duke embarked on five decades of profligacy, baroque sex and quasi-mysticism. She had a series of love affairs, most famously with Errol Flynn, a Hawaiian swimming champion and a Paraguayan playboy called Porfirio Rubirosa who was afflicted—if that's the right word—with a medical condition that left him with a permanent erection.

For reasons that can only be guessed at she was particularly taken with the Paraguayan. She showered him with intimate lover's gifts, like his own B-25 bomber. But not even Porfirio and his amazing magic wand could make Doris truly happy. In her later years she grew increasingly depressed. She sought solace in the dubious attractions of alternative medicine and vaudeville spiritualists. When not being injected with her daily dose of life-elongating sheep's placenta, she would be encased in her personal magnetic rejuvenation chamber. If not having a nose job she would be huddled in a corner with Madame ZaZa and her crystal ball trying to contact the spirit of her prematurely born daughter, Arden, who'd survived only twenty-four hours.

When Doris was doing none of these things, she tended her money with the inconsistency becoming of a true eccentric. She thought nothing of lending Imelda Marcos $5 million to post bail and restock her shoe closet, yet long-serving and trusted members of her staff received jars of jam for Christmas. It was said that any servant who dropped a glass or a piece of crockery would find its replacement cost deducted from their wage slip at the end of the month.

Such parsimony might have explained why at the time of her death in 1993 Doris Duke had an array of palatial homes from Manhattan to Hawaii, her own private police force, a Boeing 737 and a bank account that clocked in just short of $1.5 billion.

There was just one person exempt from the tyrannical, paranoid grip exerted on her houschold by Doris Duke in these final years and his name was Bernard Lafferty, her homosexual, ponytailed, barefoot Irish butler. It was he who was sitting beside her as she flew over Creeslough on that balmy summer's afternoon.

Lafferty had left the village below twenty years before and never looked back. He didn't exactly dislike the place where he grew up but it was nowhere near big enough to satisfy an imagination filled with youthful dreams of becoming famous. From

Ireland, he went to Scotland and from there to Philadelphia. He worked in hotels, casinos and as personal assistant to the lounge singer Peggy Lee. He was the perfect servant, ever attentive, the very soul of discretion and feminine kindliness. He was also an excellent embroiderer. Doris Duke took him on at $500 a week plus room and board.

Before long, she came to trust her butler more than anyone else on earth. It was he who repaired her favorite ballgowns, he who knew exactly what temperature a melon should be before his mistress would eat it. It was Bernard Lafferty, dressed in his favorite gold lamé Armani jacket, who escorted Doris Duke to fashionable charity events in Los Angeles and New York. And it was he who, for old times' sake, brought her back to the Donegal village where he spent his childhood.

There is little doubt that the American billionairess and the Irish butler came to regard each other as mother and son, with all the love, joy and, let's be candid, petty disagreements that the filial relationship entails. Both are now dead, so it is with the utmost confidence, not to mention libel immunity, that I repeat here the words uttered, apocryphally, by Bernard Lafferty when the Richest Girl in the World described this tiny corner of Ireland as the most beautiful place in the world.

"Miss Duke," he said, "I think it might be time for your medicine."

I did, I confess, make a silent nod of agreement toward the memory of Bernard Lafferty as I drove past the white *fáilte* road sign that greets every new arrival to Creeslough. Nightfall had draped the village in a thick black curtain, illuminated only by the muted glow of half a dozen streetlights. A storm was blowing out of the north, buffeting my car and throwing forth white globules of rain that threatened to smash the windscreen. I felt momentarily depressed, as if I had just driven into the end of the world. It had been that kind of day.

If you ask me, there are two great benefits to being as rich as Doris Duke. Like her, you can disregard the mores of polite society and indulge your every whim, be it a well-endowed Paraguayan gentleman or an addiction to LSD and enemas. The second attraction of enormous wealth is that you need never ever experience the economic necessity that requires you to travel second class on a ferry across the Irish Sea in the company of the No. 1 Loyal Limavady Rangers Supporters' Club.

Alcohol has never been a stranger in my life. The only enticement for going to church when I was young was the thought that I might get the chance to see Father McCallum's enormous, strawberry-textured nose explode. "He's got a very bad flu," my grandmother said, when I asked about our parish priest's extraordinary facial appendage. I may have been young but I wasn't stupid. When I replied that he must have had the flu for the last four years she would shoo me away with the instruction, "Say three Hail Marys for our dear Father's soul."

The sad truth was that Father McCallum's liver, not his soul, required the Hail Marys and that three hundred, never mind three, would be nowhere near enough for salvation. As fast as Famous Grouse could make the stuff, our old priest could guzzle it. Yet even he would have blanched at the amount of alcohol consumed by the Rangers fans as the ferry made its unsteady passage from Stranraer to Belfast.

Bad weather had delayed our sailing. My fellow passengers were delighted. It increased their onshore drinking time. They were blind drunk when the ship edged out of port. And when we left the shelter of Loch Ryan for the open sea thirty minutes later, they were already on their fourteenth rendition of "We'll Guard Old Derry's Walls." By the time we reached Belfast harbor it was clear to all those on board who were still sober (me, the barmaid and the coach driver) that Derry's walls would have to look after themselves for the time being.

Belfast gleamed invitingly in the twilight rain. I resisted the temptation to explore and joined the rush-hour traffic on the motorway heading west. Housing estates quickly gave way to an unremarkable rural landscape. An uneventful journey was punctuated by a cheerless shuffle of one-street towns.

Eventually, I reached Derry and its unguarded walls. I drove over the Foyle Bridge, joined the city bypass and pressed on through the unmanned, unmarked border between Northern Ireland and the Republic. Only when the road signs became frankly surreal did it dawn on me that I was in another country. I was certain the Republic of Ireland had many attributes but on first impressions it was obvious that motorists were spectacularly ill-served by the nation's road signs. As I drove toward the cathedral town of Letterkenny it was progressively thirty-five, fourteen, seven and eleven miles away.

Creeslough, my final destination, was just a further half-hour drive away. Or, as the government's roads department would have it, fifty-seven miles due northwest.

I had been to the village before, on holiday with my girlfriend. Her father was a Creeslough man. We stayed for three weeks in a farm worker's cottage that had been passed down through generations of her family. We had a wonderful time. It hardly mattered that the cottage was a dank and dark monument to bad taste and the Irish winter. It was summer. We spent most of our days on the beach and most of our nights gazing at the stars and the moon.

"Come on, let's make ourselves a new life here in Donegal," I said, one balmy night. "It'll be like starring in *The Quiet Man*."

"You're drunk," she replied, seductively. "Shall we go to bed?"

I was smitten. This was the kind of love that happens perhaps once in a lifetime.

But Donegal does that to you, with its vast stretches of wild, unspoiled beauty (commemorated so touchingly in a local song, "Donegal, pride of all, miles and miles of sweet fuck all") and a pace of life that makes the slow rhythm of southern European summers seem manic in comparison.

I returned to Creeslough again and again. Each time I went back, the idea of making a new life there grew a little bigger and kicked a little harder.

I began to accumulate a list of reasons why I should move there. I was Irish—at least, several generations ago I was. It was a back-to-my-roots thing. London was filthy, crowded, expensive. Above all, it was inhospitable. I had lived in the same ground-floor flat for eight years and I had still to pass a civil word with anyone in the street. This wasn't healthy. Not even the friendly neighborhood busker—"Here's a song from my latest album, *Van Morrison's Greatest Hits*. I bought it this morning"—could convince me that living next door to the tube station with the worst record in Western Europe for muggings, assault and rape was a terrific idea. Even if I managed to evade the queue of villains waiting to relieve me of my wallet in the morning, I still had to endure a fifty-minute train journey of unremitting discomfort, my nose pressed against the forehead of a complete stranger.

My job was another problem. I worked as a journalist in the London office of the *Guardian* newspaper. I liked to think that I could turn out a decent story every now and then, when I wasn't picking fluff balls from my belly button or gazing wistfully in the direction of the female librarians. But I was never going to be the editor. What's more, I never wanted to be the editor. It would have meant employing people like me.

Even when I was transferred to Glasgow—a city where I'd

spent ten happy years of my life—I had little difficulty in finding compelling reasons for moving to Creeslough. I spent much of the time diving into shops and alleyways, trying to avoid old girlfriends, old enemies and people I'd borrowed money from in 1988.

One day I had lunch with an old and dear friend, who had become something big in political lobbying or some such nonsense. He was wearing a loud, expensive suit but even that was drowned out by the noise of his ambition.

"There are four types of client," he told me, leaving aside his radicchio and toasted pine nut salad while he mapped out his inevitable ascent to world domination. "Those who know who you are but don't know why they need you, those who don't know who you are but know why they need you, those who know who you are and know why they need you and those who don't know who you are and don't know why they need you."

The depressing thing is: when he finished this little soliloquy he looked deeply pleased with himself, like someone who sincerely believed he had just been speaking in English. My mind was made up. I knew then I had to escape this madness.

It was against this backdrop of fanciful dreams and deepening misery—Walter Mitty sings the Leonard Cohen songbook—that I did the unthinkable. I resigned from my job and made plans for the future. I was moving to Creeslough. My company car went back. I paid a visit to a backstreet dealer called Gary, who sold me a 1983 Nissan that had clearly enjoyed a long, chaotic life on the stock-car racing circuit. I settled all my outstanding bills and allocated what time I had left before leaving to bidding a fond farewell to those people who were proud to describe me as a really close friend (two minutes each, six minutes in total) and packing my bags (eleven days).

Isn't it amazing how much stuff you collect as you progress through life? I spent hours rummaging through a sea of junk. Occasionally, I would resurface with a Duran Duran T-shirt (among countless fashion atrocities) in my hand and the anguished cry, "Fuck me, did I spend good money on this?" I opened one cupboard door and out leapt a mauve velvet jacket, a pair of tartan bondage trousers and the three well-fingered copies of *Readers' Wives* magazine, which had nursed me through those difficult teenage years when lank hair and a lank personality made me so unattractive to the opposite sex.

I couldn't take all of it, of course. I decided to limit myself to five of each of those items I considered essential for modern life. To add a little excitement to the whole exercise I pretended I was a guest on *Desert Island Discs*. "Well, Sue, I've chosen five pairs of boxer shorts rather than the usual bog standard Y-fronts. I find that, on a hot summer's day, Y-fronts make your balls sweat like two Sumo wrestlers in a sauna . . ."

Gradually, the car filled up. Five pairs of jeans (Lee, of course), five shirts, five pairs of boxer shorts, five computer games (Wipeout 2097, Sonic, Street Fighter II, Football Manager, Mortal Kombat), five T-shirts, five golf clubs (driver, three-iron, seven-iron, sand-wedge and putter), and so on.

I had a lot of stuff but nothing that automatically commanded a leading role in the film of my new life—no wife, no kids, no Meg Ryan character from *When Harry Met Sally* (one of my five videos, if I'd been taking a video-recorder) offering platonic friendship and the promise of a romantic ending. It was surprisingly simple, really, except for the soundtrack.

I had fifteen hundred records, all carefully indexed and stacked in alphabetical order. Like Rob Fleming in *High Fidelity* (one of my five chosen books, naturally, along with *The Catcher in the Rye*, *Independence Day*, *The Lost Continent* and *Trainspotting*), my record collection was my autobiography—from the schoolboy error of Clive Dunn's "Grandad" to the desperate attempt to hang on to my youth that was *Nu-Clear Sounds* by Ash.

After four days I got it down to five singles—"Overnight Sensation" by the Raspberries, "A Girl Like You" by Edwyn Collins, "Superstition" by Stevie Wonder, "Good Vibrations" by the Beach Boys, "William It Was Really Nothing" by the Smiths—and five albums: the Velvet Underground banana album, the first Stone Roses LP, *Stranded* by Roxy Music, *Nevermind* by Nirvana and Dylan's *Blonde on Blonde*. On the fifth day, I decided to take all 1,500 records except Clive Dunn and Duran Duran.

I took a lease on the holiday cottage and made a deal with my I-can't-believe-you're-doing-this-but-I'm-calm-about-it because-it's-just-a-stupid-phase-you're-going-through girlfriend. I would leave for Ireland. She would remain at home. Hopefully, I would manage to upgrade the cottage from the hovel of our holiday memories and find a way of earning a living that would keep two adults above the United Nations' designated poverty line. I was optimistic. I'd already heard a little whisper that there might be some work on offer from a friend of a friend. Or was it the friend's second cousin? Anyway, his name was Johnny and he had a farm. I knew it was an uncertain future, I knew that I would occasionally be lonely. We agreed I would come home the moment it became obvious I had made a rash and terrible mistake.

I arose the next morning, ate a hearty breakfast and found a space under the driver's seat for Clive Dunn and Duran Duran (well, I didn't want to break up a collection). I spent an hour making a final tour of the neighborhood until it was time to go. Accompanied by my stern-faced girlfriend, I walked out of my front door for the last time.

Needless to say, it was a touching farewell. Anyone of a sensitive disposition, or who cried at the scene in *Sleepless in Seattle* when Tom Hanks put his arms round his son and confessed to American radio listeners how much he missed his dead wife, may well want to skip on to the next chapter.

"Good-bye," I said, snatching one last tender kiss. Our fingers remained entwined for a few more seconds. I broke away. "I love you."

"Good-bye, honey," she replied sadly, though in truth she seemed strangely dry-eyed for such an emotional moment. I climbed into the car, pulled the door shut and drove slowly down the street. As I did, I turned round for one last lingering look and that was when I swear I heard her shout, "See you next week, you poor, deluded fool."

Creeslough

The road into Creeslough was as wide as a Parisian boulevard. Not surprisingly, it promised more than it delivered. It was as if the village had rolled over and gone to sleep until summer. It was just before 10 P.M., early March. Fortunately, a shop was still open. I parked in the white glare of the window light. I needed some basic provisions to sustain me until morning: milk, bread, tea, butter, jam.

"Terrible night," I said cheerily to the shop assistant, stepping up to the counter with my arms full. He didn't look up as he counted out my change and put the groceries in a plastic bag. "Disgusting," he said, in a tone that wasn't completely hostile but carried more than a hint that whatever was bothering him—filthy weather, working late for low pay—was my fault. I had heard that old cliché about Ireland being the friendliest nation in the world. He clearly had not. He went back to reading his Danielle Steel novel before I had the chance to say another word.

I got back in the car feeling slightly uneasy. A *Danielle Steel novel*! The cottage was a mile outside the village, back in the direction I had just come from. I took the first right up a narrow lane and drove as far as a gathering of pine trees on the left. The gable end faced on to the road. There was a concreted bay between the garden wall and the front door. I parked the car and lingered in the rain for a few moments.

The house didn't look in any better condition since I was last there. The whitewashed walls were mottled and brown, the sills bore the flaky remnants of an ancient green paint job. The windows were streaked with grime and shrouded in lace curtains the color of a widow's veil. As I pulled open the front door brown sludge washed over the top of my boots. I threw on the light and recoiled at the scene. A water pipe had burst in the attic and emptied its contents down the walls, covering them with a thin layer of blue mold. The fridge and cooker had been coated with something black and alive. A throw rug floated across the miniature lake in the bathroom like the decomposing body of a small furry animal.

I crept through the rest of the house, my depression deepening with every step. The furniture in the living room hadn't changed since I'd last been there—in fact, it hadn't changed since yellow plastic was at the cutting edge of settee coverings and chipboard was the new mahogany. The carpet pattern looked like random vomit stains. The air was damp enough to swim in.

The bedroom, at the far end of the house, had escaped a soaking. It was habitable at least, though I changed my mind on closer inspection. The corner of the mattress—the mattress I was supposed to sleep on—had been chewed. I found tiny piles of black droppings scattered around and guessed it had been eaten by a rat.

Of the many unhappy experiences of my boyhood—French kissing an earwig that had crawled into my harmonica immediately springs to mind—none have stayed with me more vividly than the night I woke up to find I was sharing a pillow with four mice. Even now I sometimes close my eyes and find the scene painted on the inside of my eyelids. The thought of sharing a cottage, never mind a bed, with a rat was my worst fear realized.

I ran out screaming into the night, jumped into the car and frantically tried to insert the house key into the ignition. I was going back home. Of course I was going back. But to what? Ritual humiliation? "Back already, darling? I wasn't expecting you until next week. I'll put the kettle on." My senses started to unscramble. I coaxed myself back indoors. Everything looks better in the fresh light of a new dawn, even rats and 1950s furniture. Of course I was staying.

I had a fitful night and woke early. Thin shafts of sunlight speared through the window grime. I threw some water on my face and stepped outside. The storm of the previous night had abated. An army had been up all night polishing the countryside. The pine trees in the garden were gleaming, the air was freshly laundered and seemed to magnify life itself. Over the crest of the hill by the cottage I could just see the top third of Muckish, a black and smooth table mountain that dominated an otherwise gentle landscape. It looked alien, as if some supernatural force had left it there by mistake. A scattering of clouds so white they could have been boiled floated across the azure sky.

This was more like it.

I set off for the village greatly cheered. It never ceases to amaze me how much a splash of sunshine lifts the spirits and helps buff up the most unpromising of buildings. I passed a tatty, abandoned petrol station, which looked as alluring as an Edward Hopper painting. Not even Hopper could have made much of the farm supplies warehouse across the street but, farther on, the Red Roof Restaurant and Par Three Golf Course had the inviting air of the Old Course at St. Andrews on the first morning of the Open Championship.

The road narrowed and curved left. In the distance I could see the vast expanse of the Atlantic Ocean bathed in godly white light, like *Brigadoon* after global warming. The landscape rolled toward me for miles in a patchwork of greens and browns until finally it came to rest at my feet. I stood there for ten minutes with a single thought in my head: "It's a film set."

The rural Irish landscape often has this effect on visitors, especially from Hollywood. A splash of sea, forty shades of green, the white homestead, the priestly collar, the village pub. Before you know it Tom Cruise and Nicole Kidman are dressed in peasant rags, playing out a torrid love affair in ridiculous accents even the deaf would recognize as Scottish. If you ask me Hollywood's version of Ireland is always ridiculous. If the John Wayne of *The Quiet Man* came back from America tomorrow he'd be selling mobile phones in Dublin for a living and settling his arguments over women with a flick knife.

But, trust me, the view from Creeslough really was like a film set.

I snapped out of my trance. There was work to be done. I needed food, coal, a new mattress, a box of J-cloths, disinfectant and an elephant gun (or failing that, three hundredweight of rat poison).

Creeslough's shopping center stretches for no more than fifty yards. It comprises one hardware store, one small grocery shop, one large grocer's-cum-post office, a petrol station, two pubs and two public telephones. There is a bridge, which affords another stunning view of the Atlantic, and a split-level thoroughfare, one half called Main Street and the other High Street. Fifty years ago, and this seemed hard to believe given its size, the village even had its own railway station.

I discovered this last piece of information in a splendid local history book on sale in one of the grocer's shops, which hinted at a past as epic as the Habsburg Empire. According to my book, there had been a scattering of houses in this part of Donegal for hundreds of years but it wasn't until the mid-nineteenth century that a village began to take shape. A police barracks was built in the 1830s, and a row of farmworkers' cottages.

A thatched-roof cottage that served as a soup kitchen during the potato famine of the mid-nineteenth century is still standing on Main Street. People were poor back then; starving poor, dressed in rags and surviving on potatoes (when the crop didn't fail), seaweed and whatever diseased animal carcass they could get their hands on.

After the famine the village began to develop more rapidly. The local English landowner built a market house where traders and farmers could come to sell their produce. A popular fair day was held on the tenth of every month. Shops began to open: a tailor's, two blacksmiths', three butchers'. The locals ought to have been grateful to the landlord for encouraging the local economy. They killed him instead, and to be honest I couldn't blame them. I hate guns but if I'd been around at the time I think I would have volunteered to hold the assassin's jacket for him.

William Sydney Clements, known to his chums in ermine robes as the third Lord Leitrim, was the kind of English landlord that nineteenth-century Irish republicans would have invented if he hadn't already existed. A former military officer and Member of Parliament, he inherited a huge chunk of Donegal in 1854 from his father and then embarked on a campaign to prove that man's inhumanity to man knew no bounds.

Tenants were arbitrarily evicted for crimes as innocuous as cutting branches off his lordship's trees. One farmer who found a dead horse on the beach and sold the skin was ordered to hand it back by the estate manager then thrown out of his home. He and his family went to stay with his brother for a single night. Leitrim's men found out and the brother was evicted. The rule was that anything cast up by the sea belonged to the landlord— seaweed, driftwood, even dead horses—and Leitrim had a particular fondness for enforcing his own rules.

Another thing he was said to be particularly fond of was

potential housemaids. It was possible to live on the estate as long as you forgave his lordship's little eccentricities, like his penchant for removing the prettiest daughter from each house and, as it was delicately put in those days, "bringing her to shame."

One such incident hastened Leitrim's demise. A young girl who was living on the estate gave in to his demand that she start work for him as a maid or her family would be evicted. She started on Monday and drowned herself on Saturday. Leitrim was accused of "seducing" her.

On the morning of April 2, 1878, three men waited in ambush for the earl. Two of his employees were shot. Leitrim fought for his life but as he tried to strangle one of his assailants, his skull was smashed by a gun butt. One hundred tenants were due to be evicted on the day he was assassinated. They had a party instead. Small wonder, then, that no one was ever convicted of the murder and the five-hundred-pound reward offered for information about the crime is unclaimed to this day. Yet, and this is testament to the lottery that is land ownership in places like Ireland and Scotland, there are people living in the village today still paying ground rent to Lord Leitrim's descendants.

The railway came to northwest Donegal in 1902 and the area blossomed. The population almost doubled. People from across the county flocked to Creeslough for fair day. William Butler Yeats paid a visit, and G. K. Chesterton. Percy French, the local drains inspector and a part-time balladeer, wrote a song that made the place famous:

Och! It's well to be you that is takin' yer tay
Where they're cuttin' the corn in Creeslough today

The village even staged its own horse-race meetings.
But as quickly as they appeared, the horses galloped off over

the horizon. The railway line was dismantled. The economy went the way of many of the local young men: due south, to Dublin and beyond, in search of employment.

And today? I looked around me. Doris Duke had been wrong. The view from a helicopter might have been different but from where I stood modern Creeslough couldn't be described as beautiful or picturesque. It was as much a thoroughfare as it was a village, a place where people stood to admire the view beyond and drove through to get to prettier places on the coast, like Dunfanaghy and Dungloe. The squat white church, built to echo the shape of Muckish, was the only splash of extravagance amid the prosaic dealings of a working community.

The street was lined with cars, no one dressed in rags and the shops were well stocked. The hardware store, however, was fresh out of elephant guns.

I settled for as much rat poison as I could carry. I explained to the shop assistant that an army of rodents had feasted on my bed. He promised that someone would deliver me a new mattress within the hour. I was deeply impressed, as anyone who once signed fourteen forms and waited six weeks before a London department store delivered a venetian blind to his front door would be.

I spent the next few days washing down walls and laying out poison. I hung the carpet out to dry, and transported the fridge and what was left of the mattress to the local dump. After a long search I found the withered body of a rat lying in the corner of the attic. It was long dead, the victim of a diet of horsehair and coiled springs.

I was ecstatic. To celebrate I carried the television set into the garden and put a hammer through the screen. I had wanted to do this for years, or at least I thought I did. I have long been one of those confused people who combine a passionate belief that television turns people into antisocial morons who can barely string a sentence together with a three-year unbroken record of watching *Brookside*. The puritan in me felt a certain satisfaction as the screen crashed and splintered. This was soon replaced with the emptiness that comes from knowing that never again would I set eyes on Susannah Farnham's hair or hear Jacqui Dixon's dulcet Scouse accent as she chastised her errant brother, "Aw-er ar Mi-kill."

To fill the terrible void in my life I thought it best that I find myself a job.

Ain't Gonna Work on
Johnny's Farm No More

There are some words and phrases that can safely be retired from the vocabulary when opting for life in rural Ireland. "Get the best china out, the Queen's coming to tea" is one. "Can you show me the way to the nearest S&M club?" is another. "Tube strike" is redundant, for obvious reasons, along with "Versace" and "Vivienne Westwood." "Smog," "bedsit," "beer garden," "art-house cinema"—all are totally useless in a place like Creeslough.

"Suburbs," to my great surprise, was not. In fact Creeslough had more suburbs than Greater London: Ballyboes, Rooskey, Terlin, Roscad, Grogagh, Kilfad, Creenesmear, Keenaghan, Pol, Umerafad, Cashel, Doe Castle and Doe Point, Duntally, Magherablade, Magheraroarty, Massinass, Kilmacloo, Gortnalake. The list was endless—a legacy, I guessed, of the days when the houses weren't numbered and people had nothing better to do on dark nights than sit around and make up quaint names for the patch of grass outside the front door. (One of the local historians later told me that I didn't live in Creeslough but in Ballyboes, land of the horses, which used to be called Baile No Bó, land of the cows, until a flood of objections by demure local women.)

John Connolly's farm was in Terlin, a short drive through urban Creeslough, across rural Creeslough, past the right fork at Creeslough Beg that takes you to Ballyboes, follow the road signs to Doe Point, past Gortnalake and Umerafad. With a short stop to admire the ancient turrets of Doe Castle the journey took about a minute and a half.

The farmhouse was straight out of central casting, painted pristine white and hidden behind overgrown hedgerows. It was flanked on either side by outbuildings with sagging roofs. There were two cars and a Land Rover parked in the driveway. A mangy brown dog bared its teeth as I walked up the drive. It hurled itself toward me until the chain round its neck gave it a violent yank backward.

It was just before noon. There was no response when I knocked on the farmhouse door so I wandered round to the rear where I saw four men standing around a black and white cow. The animal had been corralled into a rectangular pen, two feet wide by eight feet long, with its head stuck through the bars at one end. One person was holding it by the horns as another gave it a haircut an army barber would have been ashamed of. The third man had the cow's tail in his hand and was pulling it as high as it would go. The fourth, much older than the others, was standing beyond the pen leaning on a fence.

"I'm looking for Johnny," I said, though I might have been speaking in Polish for all the attention anyone paid me.

"Come here. Hold this a minute, would you?" one of the men said. He took my hand and placed it round the tail. As he did, a huge lump of shit the size and color of a Hovis loaf fell out of the cow's rear end. He took off his jacket, laid it on the ground then took the tail out of my hand.

One of two up front pulled what looked like a water pistol from his trouser waistband and jabbed the animal in the head with the nozzle.

He stood back, pulled the belt on his trousers tighter and rolled up his sleeves.

"You're the vet, right?" I said, guessing.

He nodded. "We're takin' the horns off this lot." He slapped the cow's flank.

I hate the sight of blood. The sole blemish on my otherwise saintly childhood came when I ran away from home to avoid having my tonsils out. Even now, I can't go near a hospital. I feel other people's pain even if, happily anesthetized or merely wearing layers of convincing television makeup, they couldn't care less.

Despite my lifelong cowardice, I was overcome with curiosity. The vet reached into his bag and pulled out a red-handled saw. A rope harness was placed round the cow's head. I took a couple of steps back.

The vet nodded round the circle. "Ready?" He grabbed one of the horns and began sawing frantically at the point where it disappeared into the animal's skull.

I have seen Canadian lumberjacks with a lighter touch. On the first stroke, the beast let out a throaty roar summoned from the depths of hell. Imagine the greatest pain you have ever felt— my mind wanders back to the afternoon I spent with my mother at an Andrew Lloyd Webber musical—and it still wouldn't fully capture the expression on the poor animal's face. Its body went as rigid as if it had just had a surprise encounter with six million volts. I turned my head away and my eyes met those of the fourth man.

"Fuckin' cruel this stuff, isn't it?" he said, showing a masterful grasp of the obvious.

I looked back at the cow. The vet was holding one of its horns in his hand. He threw it to the ground. Twenty or so cows in the field across the road had stopped chewing at the grass and wandered over to the fence to get a better view, like rubberneckers at a particularly nasty car crash.

Blood was dripping down the animal's face and into one of its soft brown eyes. The vet wiped it off with his hand and began sawing at the second horn. Thankfully, it came away easier than the first. He had it in his hand within thirty seconds but as it came away a thin stream of blood started spraying from the hole onto his face. Jesus. This was Quentin Tarantino's *All Creatures Great and Small*.

"It's just like cutting your toenails off," the vet's assistant said, wiping his bloody hands on his trousers.

"Not in our house it isn't," I managed to say between gagging.

The vet poked around in the cow's head with a pair of tweezers, caught hold of a membrane and twisted it until the bleeding stopped. His assistant then grabbed an aerosol and sprayed a blue-colored disinfectant over the wounds. That was clearly the sum total of post-operative aftercare in the animal kingdom.

The pen was opened, someone slapped the cow's backside again and it danced off to the farthest corner of the field. A couple of minutes later it was cropping grass, as if nothing had happened. Another five animals were waiting for the same treatment. And here's a thing: they all walked into the pen as if they were about to pose for a family photograph. They were queuing up. Cows are wonderful in many ways but—and as an animal lover it pains me to be so cruel—they have about as much native wit and common sense as Prince Andrew.

By the time he'd finished with the fourth cow, the vet was bathed in sweat. He laid the saw on his bag, leaned on the fence and lit a cigarette.

"Hard going," I said, thinking a friendly conversation might give me the chance to impress with a few phrases learned from schoolboy days spent reading the collected works of James Herriot.

"Not really. You've just got to hang on and go like fuck."

"Jobs can't come much worse than this, can they?"

"You want to try cutting a dead calf out of its mother's belly."

Having left that charming image etched forever on my sub-conscious, he threw away his fag and went back to sawing.

As the last horn came off the last cow his assistant beckoned me over.

"Come and look at this."

What the hell? I had already been sick three times, a fourth helping from the pit of my stomach wasn't going to make much difference. He pointed at the hole in the cow's head where the horn used to be. I looked inside and at the end of a narrow, swirling tunnel of bone, I could see something red and alive.

"Fuck, is that its brain?"

"Good *craic*, innit?"

"You mean to say that inside there . . ." I forced myself to look at the hole again ". . . is that poor animal's brain?"

He grinned. "Good *craic*, innit?"

The vet wiped the blood off his hands with a rag and removed his waterproofs. He threw his bag of equipment in the back of the Land Rover. "Thank Christ, that's over," he said, although his assistant looked more than a little downhearted.

They drove off, leaving the three of us standing in the yard.

"Nice lad, that," said the younger of the two. "One of the best vets we've ever had. Didn't you think so, Pops? He was that kind and gentle. Good with the animals. Mind you, I usually like women vets."

"He was nice enough," said the older man, who'd clearly had a rethink since standing back from the carnage with his fingers covering his eyes. I knew less than nothing about animal hus-bandry but to avoid being left out ventured that, on the whole, female vets were better-looking than their male colleagues.

"Yer right enough," said the younger man, as he pushed open the farmhouse door, saying "Are you coming in for a cup of tea?"

"Don't mind if I do," I replied. I took off my muddy boots and left them on the steps.

As I did, a cartoon lightbulb seemed to switch on above his head. "What did you say your name was?"

His name was John Connolly (Young Johnny). He worked the farm with his father, John Senior, a small, neat man with silver hair so thick and shiny that I wanted to tug it to see if it was real. Young Johnny was healthy and handsome too, with skin beaten ruddy by a lifetime spent outdoors and cheekbones you could hang your coat on. Both were wearing overalls, wellies and shapeless brown woolen caps, which sat on their heads like cow-pats. They spoke quickly, in voices that sounded as if they'd never been raised.

We spent a wonderful hour drinking tea in front of the dancing yellow flames of a coal fire.

Young Johnny couldn't have been more enthusiastic when I mentioned we had a mutual friend who'd suggested I might be able to work on the farm. It was as if they had been expecting me for months, as if I was the answer to their agricultural dreams. I was pretty sure I wasn't (in fact, I know I wasn't) but it never occurred to them to laugh in my face, scribble out the dole-office phone number and send me on my way. There is a streak of anarchy buried somewhere in the Irish psyche that compels people into acts of enormous generosity, regardless of the harsh economic realities. It hardly mattered that Irish farming was going through its worst crisis in history, that prices were so low sheep were changing hands for a pound, or that they could hardly afford to feed their cows, never mind pay me.

"No bother at all. Isn't that right, Pops?" Young Johnny said, reaching into a cupboard and pulling out a set of overalls, which he held against my body. The legs stopped somewhere north of my shins. "Perfect, perfect," he said. John Senior disappeared outdoors and came back after a few minutes with a pair of wellies for me.

The rain was falling in huge gray waves as I drove home but I hardly noticed. I was daydreaming about long summer days under the burning sun and the restful sleep that follows a hard day at the soil. I was thinking of vast fields of swaying yellow corn, of Steinbeck, James Herriot and Catherine Zeta Jones bursting out of her corset in *The Darling Buds of May*. I certainly wasn't thinking that my career as a farmer would be over in three weeks.

I was up early the following morning. The first day of any new job is always a nervous time but there is a particular kind of apprehension that comes with ignorance. You're like a balloonist adrift, a fisherman in a squall, a virgin naked inside Madonna's bedroom. What I knew about farming could be scratched on the point of a blunt pitchfork. Yet I was excited, too: the future stretched out before me like a vast, soft landscape, inviting me to make an imprint.

It took me a while to find a pair of overalls that didn't make me look like Coco the Agricultural Clown. The two Johnnys were fussing around by the barn. They liked to fuss. No job was too small or too inconsequential that it didn't require planning like a military campaign. This morning they were repairing a fence and I could hear them clucking over the selection of wood, nails and, thereafter, the required force to drive one into the other. "Just gi' the thing a fuckin' skelp," I heard one quietly anguished voice say.

I thought it best if I stayed out of their way for a while. I passed a few minutes watching one of the hornless cows trying to empty the remnants of the previous night's rainfall from the hole in its head, thinking, not for the first time, that David Attenborough didn't know the half of it. There was enough water in there to fill a teapot. Eventually, the cow got bored and went back to chewing grass.

I wandered over to the barn. Work on the fence had been abandoned. Young Johnny was inside, cleaning up cowshit, which seemed to be everywhere. It was on the walls, on the floor, on the roof. It looked like the place had been Artexed with the stuff.

"Take this," he said, handing me a brush. It felt like a moment of some significance, as if I'd been handed the keys to the executive toilet. Methodically, and with as much care as the chambermaids at the Dorchester Hotel, we soon had the place gleaming.

When we had finished we went back outside. It started spitting rain. John Senior had disappeared off to the peat bog, leaving the two of us to feed the cows. Young Johnny pulled out his knife and sliced open one of the huge bales of silage lined up along the side of the barn. He threw me a face mask. "Here, put this on otherwise you'll end up with a chest like me," he said, coughing.

I slipped on the mask but not before the acrid smell of silage filled my nostrils and began to sandpaper my lungs. I have only one rule when it comes to food and it is never to eat something if the person serving it has to wear protective clothing. Silage— and I can now speak as an expert on the subject—is the remnants of last year's grass cuttings, wrapped in black plastic sheeting and left to sweat over the winter. It smells as bad as you would imagine yet it is the bovine equivalent of a Michelin three-star meal. Cows just can't get enough of the stuff. By the time we had forked and laid out half a bale in the fodder trays, most of the herd was already tucking in.

Johnny rattled his car keys to attract the stragglers from the far end of the farm. As they lumbered toward us, he gave me a rundown of their breed, family history, outstanding personality traits and ambitions. Picture, if you can bear it, a beauty pageant featuring Monica Lewinsky and her closest friends.

Contestant number one was a large gray-haired cow, weighing in at five hundred and twenty pounds. She didn't have a name but was easily recognizable by her long face and a quiff on loan from the Elvis Presley collection. Born in March 1993, she lost her virginity at the age of eighteen months to two gentlemen from Go-Faster Artificial Insemination (company motto: "No dicking around—we get straight to the job"). She'd had one lovely daughter, the little fawn heifer who was walking up just behind her. Her ambition was to eat so much silage in the next twenty minutes that at least one of her four stomachs would explode.

Most were Charolais, a French breed, like contestant number two. She had adapted perfectly to the Irish lifestyle due to her thick coat of wiry black hair. Alas, she was still waiting to meet the bull of her dreams. This may have been due to her habit of kicking out at any living thing that came within striking distance of her hind legs. On one memorable occasion she leapt over a five-foot-high stone wall and disappeared for three days. She was eventually found holding up the traffic on the main road between Creeslough and Letterkenny.

Leaping over tall fences and an unerring ability to sense a visit from the vet, even before Johnny had made the appointment, featured heavily in the biographies of the others. By the time the whole herd had gathered round the troughs it was clear that I was in the presence of a hugely talented collection of animals. Small wonder they hadn't all left years ago and joined a circus.

They had probably decided to stay because they were treated

so well. Despite his protestations, it was obvious that Young Johnny loved them to bits. And vice versa. They were forever nuzzling into his pocket, looking for sugar lumps. My own offers of sugar lumps were spurned. Whenever I got to within a couple of feet the animals jumped away nervously, as if I was about to produce a cleaver from behind my back.

"Watch this," he said, shooing me into the background. He reached out and rubbed one of the cows on the thick fold of skin under its neck. As he did the enormous beast stretched and sighed with pleasure. "They're pets, just like cats and dogs. And they're tastier too."

When feeding time was over Young Johnny offered to show me round the farm. "It won't take long." He laughed. "It's not so big that I'm like John Wayne every day, riding around the ranch on my horse."

The tour was over in five minutes. He had nine fields, all about half the size of an Olympic swimming-pool and, because they were low-lying, twice as damp. Beyond that were another twenty-six acres of mountainside grazing that didn't appear to be blessed with a single blade of grass. He wasn't born into farming, he explained, he stumbled into it. The place in Creeslough had belonged to his uncle until he became too ill to work. Young Johnny gave up his job as a car mechanic in Glasgow. That had been fifteen years ago.

"There were about six or seven cows back then. I thought about growing crops but that was back-breaking stuff and you needed too much machinery, so I stuck with animals. I had hopes of getting it up to about fifty or sixty head." He looked wistfully across the field to where the herd was now grazing. "I've got twenty now—the most I've ever had."

They were fine-looking cows and, though I knew as much about cattle as did Coco Chanel, I was certain that none of them was a pedigree champion likely to fetch five thousand pounds at market. Looking around, I doubted if the entire business was worth much more than that. Young Johnny was on the dole. He lived in fear of being called up on some compulsory government work scheme that involved cleaning the public toilets in the nearest big town. At least he'd kept going. There were plenty of others who'd thrown in the towel, or the milking stool, or whatever it is a small farmer throws in when destitution comes to call.

Forty years ago more than a third of Ireland's workforce was employed in agriculture. Now it was less than a tenth. Thousands of businesses had gone under in the last few years because of poor animal prices, a succession of rain-drenched summers and other acts of God, like mad cow disease. Most young Irishmen and -women wouldn't dream of following their parents on to the land when they could take better paid jobs in the towns and cities. It wasn't hard to understand why. How would you prefer to spend your working life: up to your knees in cowshit for next to nothing, or building microchips for five-hundred quid a week?

It seemed like an industry in terminal decline. Yet there were still 150,000 people working the land. In rural counties like Donegal, farming was easily the most important sector of the economy—a point that farmers rarely missed making. Barely a month passed without Dublin's O'Connell Street being blockaded with combine harvesters or trucks full of manure being unloaded on the doorstep of the agriculture ministry.

And when they couldn't be bothered making the trip to the capital, the nation's farmers leant on the nearest gate, gazed wistfully across the landscape and contemplated the deplorable state of the world.

That was how I ended my first day, elbows on a gate and chin cupped in my hands, enjoying the last rays of daylight and gently discoursing on the general public's ignorance on the subject of animal feed price—"Do they think it grows on trees?"—and the vexing question of why it cost three pounds fifty for a couple of lamb cutlets in the supermarket when whole lambs were selling at market for two pounds.

Young Johnny said I would find the answer in the big supermarkets' annual profits. I nodded in silent agreement. When he removed his hat and sighed I took it as a signal for me to make a contribution. I regurgitated a headline I'd read that morning in the latest edition of the *Farmers' Journal* (a wonderful publication, incidentally, full of interesting articles about how to treat lambs suffering from dung-stained tail-ends and the soaring cost of milk tanks).

"I see the Libyan beef market has collapsed," I said. Johnny looked at me as if to say, "Listen, son, you've got a future in this farming lark."

I went home exhausted and slightly uneasy. "A dreary wilderness" is how the great agrarian improver Arthur Young dismissed this part of Donegal back in the early nineteenth century. It was an uncharacteristic but understandable bout of pessimism: most of the land was about as fertile as an AstroTurf football field. Yet generations of men and women like Johnny Connolly had proved Arthur Young wrong. Some people, like John J. Silke, Alex Jacob and Jim Thompson, had even gone as far as making a fool of him, setting the world record for potato-growing (thirty-five tons and six hundredweight per hectare of Arran Banner spuds) in 1929 on a reclaimed bog to the east of Creeslough. Their efforts were a remarkable tribute to the tenacity of the human spirit.

Of course I was full of admiration for Johnny and his father and Donegal's proud farming heritage—it was just that it seemed a bit too much like hard work for the likes of me.

• • •

In the end, Young Johnny made the decision for me. It wasn't that he hadn't enjoyed having me around for the last three weeks—God knows, he'd never seen anything as funny as the day I fell into the hole the three of us had dug for a dead cow—it was just lack of money. He'd spent hours doing paperwork and concluded he had to cut costs.

When I hinted earlier that a farmer's lot was little better than that of the average Grafton Street busker, I wasn't being strictly accurate. The fact is the industry is massively subsidized. In 1997, for instance, the European Union handed over £1.5 billion in grants to Irish farmers. The Irish taxpayer chipped in with another £200 million. Johnny had filled in his application forms, done his calculations and come to the conclusion that he wasn't getting enough of it.

"My suckler-cow allowance is going down," he said. "And my headage, not to mention the acreage money and the special beef allowance. There used to be this under-privileged area scheme that I might have got a bit out of but that's finished now."

"What about claiming disability allowance?" I added helpfully. "Do none of the cows walk with a limp?"

It had long been one of Johnny's greatest dreams that Donald Trump would pass through Creeslough one afternoon, catch sight of his farm and decide on the spot it was the perfect location for a fifty-story skyscraper. The newspapers were always full of stories about property developers buying up the unlikeliest corners of the country—only that week an American computer firm had paid £5 million for a peat bog in Limerick, news that finally convinced him Donald Trump wasn't destined to discover this little corner of Donegal.

Something had to give, and that something was me. He wasn't paying me much but he couldn't pay me any longer. He had to buy a new car and needed money to top up the trade-in value of his 1979 Lada.

"You can't sell the whole farm—it's your heritage," I pleaded.

"Ha bloody ha." Quite reasonably, Johnny didn't take kindly to some smart alec making light of his trusty Russian motor car, nor his financial plight. Besides, he wasn't in the mood for laughing. Some of the cows would have to go because he couldn't afford to feed them anymore.

"I've booked six of them into market for next week. You can take them there, if you like," he said softly. "I don't feel like going myself."

Traveling behind Willie Hay's ancient red cattle truck as it wound its way to market, I wasn't optimistic. Wherever farming folk gathered in Creeslough, the talk was not of the Asian economic crisis or Bill Clinton's sex life but of the pig that changed hands at Belfast market for a bar of chocolate and the three mountain sheep in Falcarragh that had fetched the grand total of 50p earlier in the week.

Willie ran a taxi service for market-bound animals. He was a tall, cadaverous man, with a great swirl of hair and the bearing of an undertaker. No one knew the perilous state of the market better than he, and no one was better suited to expressing it. "I wouldn't begin to guess," he replied darkly, when I asked how much he thought we'd get for our animals.

One thing you learn when you hang around the farming community long enough is that people never say what they mean, especially when money is involved. What Willie was really saying was, "Whatever Johnny gets it will hardly cover the price of my petrol."

Young Johnny was equally reticent. "As long as I get a fair price," he said, as he loaded up the last animal. (If my translation skills hadn't deserted me this meant, *I want three times the market value or else.*)

Willie sucked his teeth. "Who knows what's a fair price these days, John?" (*Listen, you fucking idiot, Moses wouldn't get a hundred pounds for the Israelites' golden calf right now.*)

"Ah, we'll see. You never know. I hear prices are picking up again." (*Don't you call me a fucking idiot. I know a good cow when I see one.*)

"Don't worry, Johnny, I'll try my best," I chipped in. (*Christ. This has all the makings of* Jack and the Beanstalk *without the happy ending.*)

Johnny slapped me on the back. "That's the spirit, lad. Can't ask for anything more." (*If you come back with less than five hundred for each of them I'll never forgive you as long as I live.*)

Here is a story that might sprinkle a little happiness around the cynical modern world in which we live. Long, long ago (when Spandau Ballet were the last word in fashion) there was a young lad who had two ambitions in life. The first was to wake up one morning to find Meryl Streep lying beside him in bed. The second was to work for the world-famous *Guardian* newspaper.

The Meryl Streep fixation was a little unrealistic. She lived in a New York apartment, he lived in a third-floor council flat in a Scottish town called Stirling. She was beautiful. He wore specs, had greasy hair and spent his teenage years squeezing blackheads into the bathroom mirror. She was rich, he stole money from his mother's purse to buy sweets. It was never going to happen between our young friend and the millionairess movie star.

Yet in truth he had more chance of a French kiss from Meryl than a job with the *Guardian*.

On the housing estate where he lived "the guardian" was the person appointed by the juvenile court to look after you when you were arrested on shoplifting charges. Requests for a copy of the newspaper were greeted disparagingly by the local newsagent. "Are you taking the piss or what?" Mr. Patel would say from behind his pile of that morning's *Sun*. "And don't think I didn't see you put that Mars Bar in your pocket."

The *Guardian* was on another planet, London, and it was full of clever people who used words like "communitarian" and asked, "Shall we do lunch?"

Yet this young lad refused to let go of his dream. He studied hard at school and went to university where he took a degree in political economy. Somewhere between the students' union bar and a lecture about the role of the Winchester rifle in nineteenth-century Mexican politics he and his friends decided to form a pop group. Just for fun, you understand. They wrote a few songs, which they refused to play in public for fear that people would laugh. One day the guitar player's brother said it was his birthday next week and insisted they perform at his party. They panicked. But after intensive rehearsing, careful selection of stage outfits—black Levi's, black polo necks, desert boots—and some strong cider, they took to the stage.

To their immense surprise it wasn't half as bad as they thought it was going to be. Other people agreed, including the tall man standing at the back of the dingy bar wearing sunglasses. Rick Spangle, chief talent scout for one of London's top record labels, came into the dressing room (it was the bottle store, really) afterward and said he'd like them to "cut a record."

"You mean, like, for sale to the public?" the young lad in our story said. "How much do we need to pay you?"

"No, you don't understand, I'm going to make you pop stars," Rick replied.

Even the dogs on the street know that record-company executives take too many drugs for their own good and generally talk 100 percent bullshit but, believe it or not, Rick kept his word. He helped them "cut a record." A few months later this young lad was at home in his council flat eating a bowl of soup when the phone rang. It was Rick, to tell him that the record ("Perfect Skin") had entered the charts at number twenty-six and that the band (Lloyd Cole and the Commotions) had been invited to appear on *Top of the Pops*.

The next four years were a blur of hit records, chemical stimulants and endless rejection by women who said, "Of course I'm not going to sleep with you. I couldn't care less if you're in

a band—no, you don't remind me of a young Robert Redford."
It was scant consolation in the face of such sexual failure but the
wall of our young lad's toilet was decorated with gold discs,
from Australia to Iceland. Lloyd Cole and the Commotions
went from appearing in backstreet pubs to playing Wembley
Arena in front of ten thousand people.

It was great—or, at least, it was for a while.

In quieter moments the young lad in our story tried to imagine what it would be like being onstage when he was fifty, wearing a long gray ponytail and brushed-denim jeans. He
concluded that a slow, lingering death by immersion in a vat of
rancid whale blubber sounded more appealing.

His thoughts drifted back to his childhood days, and dreams
of Meryl Streep and the *Guardian*. He enjoyed his life in the here
and now but thought it prudent to make plans beyond the week
after next. This was just as well because one day the lead singer
of Lloyd Cole and the Commotions—a charming gentleman
called Lloyd who wrote most of the songs and in truth had most
of the talent—said he wanted to pursue a solo career. The band
split up.

For once the young lad in our story (though he wasn't so
young anymore) got off his backside and did some work. He put
himself through journalism college. He found a job on a local
newspaper in the north of England, where he spent many a long
day in a cramped office with a bald man called Cliff, writing boring stories about car crashes and local councillors who'd been
caught fiddling their expenses. One day he thought, Sod this,
and went to London.

Before long, and he couldn't quite understand why, he
found himself being ushered into the *Guardian*'s newsroom
and told to find a desk. After a morning spent staring at a
blank computer screen and thinking that he was completely

out of his depth, he was approached by a friendly new colleague called Stephen who tapped his shoulder and said, "Shall we do lunch?"

In that instant, the young lad knew that he had arrived at where he'd always wanted to be. He thought he had died and gone to heaven.

I know all of this to be true, my friend, because in the words that Hank Martindale, or Wank Hinkerdale or whoever it was who had a hit with "Deck of Cards," almost sang, "I was that young lad."

I've told this story in the hope that it will convey fully how ridiculous I felt as I took a right turn out of the cattle market and headed back toward Creeslough. I had given up all of that for all of this: the job of my childhood dreams—heck, the *life* of my childhood dreams—for no job, a dank cottage in the Middle of Nowhere, Ireland, and a future which made serving coffee at McDonald's seem like glittering over-achievement. I was alone, except for a wind that swept down the chimney as cheerlessly as Santa with an empty sack.

The cattle market was a disaster. Of course it was: I'd never sold cows before. It wasn't just that I was out of my depth in the choppy, unpredictable sea of animal sales, I was wearing a bloodstained shirt and a sign on my head saying "Sharks, This Way."

Willie and I booked the cows in for sale just before 8 A.M. The auction wasn't due to start until noon. I frittered away the hours, drinking tea in the canteen and hanging around the cattle pens where the farmers had gathered to speculate on the day's proceedings. I felt almost like one of the crowd. I knew my Limousins from my Belgian Blues. I bumped into someone I vaguely knew. He had a farm on the other side of Creeslough and had once brought a sickly ram to Johnny's place one afternoon when the vet was there.

"How's the ram?" I said.

"Grand. Back with the ewes yesterday."

"What was it? Pneumonia?"

"Aye."

"Thought as much." This was fantastic, like riding a bike for the first time without stabilizers.

We chatted for a while and watched as the market hands slapped and shouted at the animals, herding them through for weighing and tagging. The vet's assistant was helping out for the day. He wielded a bigger stick than anyone else, three-foot long and wrapped tightly with red tape.

Our eyes met. I nodded. "Hello."

He grinned—"Good *craic* this, innit?"—then whacked a huge black and white bull on the flank and danced back over the fence as it veered round to face him. There was a sad paragraph in that morning's newspaper about a farmer in Tipperary who'd been mauled to death by a bull. A part of me wished that same bull had been standing beside me sharpening its horns and watching this little cameo with retribution on its mind.

Eventually, our cows came through. They seemed to have shrunk since the morning. Their rib cages were showing big as whalebones, their skins filthy and matted. Watching them go past I gradually felt myself turning into my mother. "Why can't you at least get tidied up when I take you somewhere? And did you have to stay up all night rolling round in manure? You might have brushed your hair. Why can't you be like Lot 114 over there? Look at her glossy coat, just back from the dry cleaner's. Don't you ignore me when I'm talking to you! Just remember who brought you into this world, though God only knows why . . ."

The sales ring was already busy when I went through. Row after row of weathered, wearied grimaces under gray caps greeted me. My eyes fell on a cheap lime baseball cap with the slogan "Divorced and delighted." Underneath it, the vet's assistant pulled a cigarette away from his lips and smiled but not, I'd bet, as much as the woman who'd divorced him.

I sat as far away from him as possible, beside an older man with a face like a punctured accordion.

"Afternoon," I said cheerfully.

He turned his back. "You're the taxman, aren't you?"

I'd only ever been to one auction before in my whole life. It took place in London, not long after Robert Maxwell had fallen over the side of his yacht. His possessions were up for sale. His baseball cap sold for a ridiculous figure—twenty thousand pounds or so. I can still remember the gasps as the auctioneer languidly kept pushing the price upward in thousands and the eruption of noise when he brought his gavel down on the lectern. "GONE! To the gentleman who'll regret this moment for the rest of his life." (I've often wondered what happened to Maxwell's cap. Does the new owner have it locked away with the family jewels in a Swiss bank vault, or does he wear it when he goes out shopping?)

The cattle market was nothing like the Robert Maxwell auction. For a start, no one seemed to want to part with twenty pounds, never mind twenty thousand. Nor, to the best of my recollection, did the auction house in London have sales assistants who appeared to be auditioning for the French riot police. Every minute or so a cow would rush into the ring to escape an indiscriminate beating from two sadists in dungarees. Its lot number and weight were scribbled on a blackboard as the auctioneer started the bidding, usually at a figure plucked from his wildest fantasies.

"How about six hundred?" he said, as a wave of incredulity swept across the room.

Once everyone had stopped sniggering, the price dropped faster than a corpse from the top of the Empire State Building. Finally, someone made an offer, though such was the subtlety of movement that if I was still sitting there today I couldn't begin to guess who it was.

The auctioneer leapt on it with the gratitude of a medieval thief spared a slow, painful death in the stocks. "Iambidone-twennybidabidabidabida-bid-bid-onehundredandtwennybidbid-bid . . ." he cried.

Apathy prevailed. The price climbed to £124 and the machine-gun clip of his voice spluttered to a dejected halt.

That was when the auctioneer turned to a little cubicle off to the side where the seller was seated. If the offer wasn't enough, the seller would give the thumbs down and the auctioneer would shake his head at the ring and say, "No sale." If the seller was happy (though no one was ever "happy" to sell the finest animal to come on the market in the history of Irish agriculture for what they considered a pittance) the cry went up, "On the market," and the bidding would start again.

Our cows had been allocated lot numbers 814 to 819, the last six animals in the sale. I didn't know this until afterward but this was not the place to be. Most people had gone home by that stage, what money there was around had all been spent. The auction ring had a sorry, deserted air as I took my seat next to the auctioneer.

The sparse gathering watched as lot 813 reluctantly made its way into the ring. It was a huge beast, with an angry walk and thighs that would have fed a family of four for a month. In Spain its name would have been El Toro con el Diablo and it would have featured large in the nightmares of the nation's matadors.

In Ireland it couldn't get arrested. The hammer came down at £212. I feared the worst.

Lot 814 ambled into the ring looking more like Bambi than the answer to a butcher's prayers. "Whatamibid-twohundri. Oneeighty. Fifty. Hundred." An embarrassed silence descended.

"Eighty?" This was the lowest figure I'd heard all day and still no one bid.

"Come on, now." And the auctioneer hadn't said that all day either. At last, someone signaled. The bidding crept up to a hundred pounds and the auctioneer turned to me and said, "What do you think?"

I was paralyzed with fear. "I don't know what I think. I've never done this before."

The next cow was already in the ring. The auctioneer was getting impatient. "Come on, then, sale or no sale?"

One hundred pounds, less than half what it was worth, but Willie had taken his cattle truck and gone home. Johnny wanted them sold whatever the price. I had visions of driving home with six cows in the back of my car. Apart from anything else I wouldn't be able to fit them all in for the journey home. And think of the mess. I'd only just vacuumed the seats.

"Go on then," I said, reluctantly.

"On the market," the auctioneer yelped but to no great response from the ring.

He brought the hammer down at £120.

The other five animals sold for between a hundred and two hundred pounds. Frankly, I was glad to get shot of them, although relief turned temporarily to parental indignation as Lot 819—a tiny fawn bull with liver spots round its mouth—entered the ring to general derision.

"You'd be as well with a big dog," a voice said, as it ambled in.

"Come on, now, this could be the bargain of the week," the

auctioneer chided, sympathetically. He knew I was under instructions to sell at any price and forgot to ask me before declaring it on the market. It went for seventy-five pounds, the lowest price of the day—an achievement of a sort, though I wasn't so sure Young Johnny would see it like that.

With a deep sense of dread and a light wallet I drove back to his place. When I arrived he'd laid out the silage and was closing up the barn for the night. He smiled as I walked up the driveway.

"Home already, I see." *(Come on, tell me the worst, then.)*

"I've not counted it up yet, about nine hundred quid the lot." *(£727.50.)*

Johnny shook his head and said nothing. *(I'm speechless.)*

"Honestly Johnny, the prices were as good as I could get." *(No way was I bringing six cows home in the back of my car.)*

"I suppose I could go back to Glasgow and drive taxis for a living." *(I knew I should've taken them to the market myself.)*

"I'm truly, deeply sorry." *(Hey. What'd you do that for? Look, blood. You've burst my lip.)*

The first thing I did when I got home was turn the radio on. I needed cheering up and the local station was guaranteed to do that. It had captured my heart the first day I arrived in Donegal when the newsreader interrupted the twelve o'clock bulletin to announce there was a mouse in the studio. For reasons that could only be connected with staff shortages the afternoon slot was hosted by a man who shared both my grandmother's musical taste and her mastery of advanced compact-disc technology. It was aural carnage, with long silences punctured by bursts of Val Doonican and the sound of CD cases falling in a heap to the ground, and absolutely unmissable.

Alas, the early-evening show, to which I had tuned, was a slick, professional presentation of two hours of the best of country and western. This, to my ears at least, is about as cheerful as a venereal ulcer. Hank Williams singing "Oh, Lonesome Me" drifted out of the tiny radio speaker like a cloud of mustard gas, followed by the news and the weatherman doubling up as the grim reaper to read the obituary notices. Then the job vacancies: a hotel chef in Letterkenny, a lorry driver, an apprentice plumber, a third-year apprentice electrician, a PVC-window glazier, a canteen assistant, a laborer on a mushroom farm.

"Honest, I've always wanted to stack boxes of mushrooms." I wondered for a moment if I could walk into an interview room and say that with a straight face.

I switched the damn thing off. The cottage filled with the sound of rain dancing off the roof, mocking me. It was getting late. I felt hungry. I hadn't eaten anything since breakfast in the market canteen. I didn't feel like anything fancy, which was just as well because I didn't do fancy. An omelet would have been nice, or a bit of fried steak. Come to think of it, I didn't do omelets or fried steak either. All I did was tinned steak and kidney pie and baked beans.

This was another reason for my depression. I had intended metamorphosing into Albert Roux within a month of arriving in Creeslough. In my imagination I'd seen a dining table groaning with exquisite menus culled from a cookbook I'd packed. Like most people I never got past page one. The village shops were all out of a savoiardi, shiitake, trompettes de mort and rocket with those tiny William Morris leaves. Three of the four rings on my cooker didn't work. Anyway, Creeslough didn't seem like the kind of place for informal kitchen suppers for eight over Blakean Fish Pie (because the yellow sauce reminds one of a Blakean sunburst, apparently), especially when I didn't know seven other people.

I jumped in the car and drove to Lafferty's shop. When I got there Danny Lafferty was standing by the cash register with his arms folded, smiling. Danny was the Bill Gates of Creeslough, minus the megalomania and greed. He owned the supermarket, the hardware store, the milk float, the Corncutter's Rest pub, the petrol station and probably a lot more besides that no one knew about because he didn't like to boast.

Thirty years ago, a factory on the western edge of the village was the biggest employer for miles around. It produced handcrafted, hardwood veneer until someone came along and invented Formica. It closed in 1981. The building was still there, collapsing slowly like rotten teeth. Now people like Danny provided the jobs. I felt like I'd met him years before, in John Healy's brilliant book about rural life in Ireland, *Death of an Irish Town*. "We want people who will work," Healy wrote. "We want people who will give leadership. People who because they give leadership will defeat apathy and indifference." That was Danny Lafferty.

I liked him a lot. He was my best friend in Creeslough, although to be honest the competition wasn't fierce. I hardly knew anyone apart from Young Johnny and his father, and I was too embarrassed ever to speak to them again. I was on nodding terms with the bar staff in the pub. The local friars always said, "Hello," but I didn't know if they were being friendly or recruiting. I exchanged pleasantries over loose change with the women at the cash register at Lafferty's. Danny was different. I could have proper conversations with him.

"How's the form, Lawrence?" he said.

I was standing by the door, flicking through the local newspapers. "Desperate, Dan."

The *Tirconaill Tribune* was the last newspaper I picked up from the pile on the bottom shelf.

Donegal seemed to have more newspapers than Fleet Street.

The *Democrat*, the *People's Press*, the *Journal*, the *News*. I flicked through them all, looking for the job adverts. I could have been anywhere in the world. It was all the usual stuff: irate local politicians, planning rows, sporting triumphs, wedding photographs featuring fat brides with big hair and grooms with bad teeth. The jobs didn't signpost a lifetime of adventure: tractor driver wanted; assistant required by Gary's Pet World; Sales! Earn £400 a week.

The *Tribune* was different from the others. It didn't have job adverts or many adverts at all, just stories as rambling and epic as a Dickens novel. Page one declared,

> The Irish Republic has become a nation of entrenched little Catholics because of the absolute stranglehold of the bishops since the foundation of the state and the last twenty-five years have been a disaster reflecting the whole manifestation of corruption in our midst and there are more scandals ahead," said John Cooney, in a speech during which Councillor Fred Coll walked out in protest saying he would rather go to mass than listen to this nonsense.

I was exhausted just reading it.

I turned to the inside pages. Every story read like the public lynching of someone in authority: the Church, the government in Dublin, the phone company, the electricity board. On the back page there was a story about drugs which read like it had been written by a journalist on LSD:

Big Drugs Get-together in Fanad
Gardai were called to a number of drug-related incidents on Monday following a major weekend of acid

parties, raves and fun activities on beaches. Concerns were first aroused on Sunday after several bouts of erratic behavior and couples (believed to be of the opposite sex) were seen to be acting strangely and passionately along public roads. In a different townland another youth was found trying to make a phone call from a local bush and it was presumed that he was frustrated because the entire Telecom Eireann network had gone down again but on closer observation this man was having a spiritual experience with God.

There was another thing I liked about Danny: he didn't care if you read his newspapers and didn't pay for them. I stood there for fifteen minutes flicking through the *Tribune*. It wasn't like any local newspaper I'd ever read before, not least because it had a medical column headlined SOLVING FLATULENCE!, which began with the eye-catching sentence, "Everyone has wind; if you don't you're not alive."

Looking back it was obvious. Sure, it was a step down from the *Guardian*—let's be honest, it was a drop through a trapdoor from the *Guardian*—and it meant going back on all those promises I made to myself about seeking new challenges. So what? I never did have much time for all that New Age gibberish anyway.

"Do you know this paper, Danny?" I said, as he walked past. He nodded. "Think they'd give a job to a trained journalist like me?"

"Good lads at the *Tribune*, you know." He smiled and walked toward the door, carrying a pensioner's shopping bag. "Game for just about anything. You should go and see them."

• • •

Milford was three villages south of Creeslough, a fourteen-mile journey. The main street marched straight up a ten-degree hill. The *Tirconaill Tribune*'s office was halfway up, on the ground floor of a white terraced house, opposite a hairdresser's.

When I arrived a white-haired man was sitting on the front steps. He was smoking a Sherlock Holmes pipe. A small fawn dog was lying at his feet. The newspaper's name was painted in brown above the door in a script that went out of fashion with Gannex raincoats and Terry Thomas. The *T* of *Tirconaill* and the *b* of *Tribune* had flaked off.

"I'm looking for the editor, John McAteer."

He took the pipe from his mouth. "Who wants him?"

I explained I was looking for a job. He stood up. "You'd better come in," he said, the beginning of a smile in place. "I'm John."

We went inside, turned sharp left through a glass door and into the office big enough for two desks. The walls were bare white plaster but for the scuff marks near the skirting and a foil pennant hanging from a nail at eye-level, a present from the Murmansk Trawler Fleet. I sat behind one desk, facing a computer, a Macintosh Classic, *circa* 1985. I noticed it had a German keyboard.

A red-haired man, around thirty with chalk white skin, was sitting behind the other desk. "This is Francis," John said, nodding toward him.

I'd never been interviewed for a job before by a man stroking a dog on his lap, like one of the bad guys in a James Bond movie. He said nothing while I told the story of my life. I left out Meryl Streep but didn't spare him the rest. School, university, rock bands, journalism college, the north of England. Childhood dreams. Cliff. The *Guardian*. The cattle market. Young Johnny's cows. Danny Lafferty. I can do shorthand. I can do typing (a lie).

I can sell adverts (ridiculous). I would gladly sit through any boring meeting he cared send me to (negotiable).

I told them their newspaper was fantastic, its spirit, its obvious pride in the community, the humor. I lied about Charles Dickens and said that all newspaper articles should have at least 234 words in the opening paragraph. Really, I couldn't have felt more at his mercy if I was naked and he had a branding iron in his hand.

"Sorry, but we don't have any jobs," John said.

"I'm cheap," I said.

"We still couldn't afford you."

In the end, I had to beg. "Listen, John. I really need a job. I'm desperate," I said, and as I did he stood up, smiled and said, "Funny that. So are we." He shook my hand. "Okay, let's see how it goes but do me one favor, will you?"

"Anything."

"Stop groveling. If you work for the *Tribune* you don't grovel to anyone."

Stinky

The North Atlantic looked hungry three hundred feet below as it crashed on the rocks, sending the seagulls scattering. The white rush subsided to reveal the gray-pink flesh of a beached whale. Even from this height I could see splodges of bird droppings splattered along the length of its massive back. The stench of rotting flesh wafted upward on the breeze, like nothing I'd smelt before except an egg mayonnaise sandwich wedged down the back of a radiator for a week.

John McAteer was standing behind me, gagging. One hand clasped a hanky over his nose. The other gripped tightly to the barbed-wire fence separating the safety of solid green turf from crumbling cliff-face. His dog, Bouncer, was panting excitedly by his side in the expectation that gravity would soon throw me to the rocks. Theoretically, it might have been possible to pick out a route down the grassy crevice to sea-level but only with crampons and Sherpa Tenzing for company. I was wearing tennis shoes and John appeared deeply reluctant to loosen his grip on the barbed wire.

"I don't think this is safe," he said. "Let's go home."

"Hang on. One more try."

I took a few more steps along the ledge, mentally composing my last will and testament. If I had been wearing a blindfold and stilettos I couldn't have been in more danger. Whale dentistry wasn't exactly what I had in mind when I signed on for the *Tribune* but it was my first assignment. I was with the editor. I was trying to impress. But not that much.

"Actually, you're probably right." I dropped to my knees and crawled back to safety.

The *Tribune*'s "Win a Whale's Tooth" competition had been John's idea. He wanted to provoke the local council into removing a forty-eight-foot sperm whale that had washed up onshore weeks before and been left to decompose. Its arrival coincided with the launch of Make Donegal Glitter, an anti-litter campaign for which his contempt was boundless. "The whale has obviously not heeded the council's warning not to litter the place, particularly our beautiful seaside areas," he'd written in the last edition of the *Tribune*. "It is proving impossible to reach the mammal with the council's new mobile litter unit and we understand that it may be necessary for the council officials to undertake a rock-climbing course in the Austrian Alps."

The competition, the first in the *Tribune*'s eight-year history, had spent a lengthy gestation period in the tiny kitchen at the rear of the office. It was there, underneath the shade of damp wallpaper strips that hung from the wall like dying palms, that John would sit most days with the dog at his feet and ponder on how to fill the *Tribune*'s thirty-two pages every fortnight.

It wasn't a solo effort, of course. Other staff would chip in with suggestions—Francis, of course, and Noel, who occasionally dropped in to answer the phones and type up great piles of handwritten stories, from village correspondents, which spewed from the fax machine. Kathleen McGrory, a neighbor of John's, came in twice a week to help Noel with the typing. She worked full-time at a fish farm, appeared to be on first-name terms with everyone in Donegal and was always up on the latest news.

This core cast was supplemented by Declan Kerr, a day-care nurse who wrote football reports in his spare time. Patrick collected rent for the council and used the *Tribune*'s office as a dropping-off point for his mail. Every once in a while he'd join us for a mug of tea after his day's work, sit and read the paper, wincing: "Jesus, John, I can't believe you wrote that about the council. I know what they're like in there. They'll go crazy."

A bewildering number of other people dropped in just to pass the time of day: the local undertaker, the woman who worked in the butcher's up the hill, John's relatives, Francis's relatives, assorted friends of Noel who came in to discuss the previous night's Manchester United match, people buying copies of pictures of themselves that had appeared in previous editions. Some gave us stories, others were stories themselves.

Example: John and I, fresh from canceling the whale competition due to a lack of teeth, were alone in the office when Hugh Devlin arrived. He was tall, and spoke with a quiet, measured intelligence. He was a community health visitor at the same hospital as Declan. "And he plays draughts," John said, as Hugh and I shook hands.

So? Everybody plays draughts, but to be polite I said, "You do?"

"A bit."

"A bit, my cock," John said. "He's excellent."

"You are? Come on, how good?"

"Twelfth best in the world."

Three hours later I was sitting in a semi-detached house on an estate in Letterkenny with the twelfth best draughts player in the world telling me his life story as he jumped five of my pieces at once.

That's how the *Tribune* filled some of its pages. After a few days, I began to wonder how it filled the rest. Only Francis seemed to be aware of the startling fact that we were actually supposed to be producing a newspaper. He was forever dashing out to take pictures of golden wedding celebrations and school plays.

Noel whiled away the hours in a room upstairs making picture frames (I never got round to asking why). John spent a lot of time taking long walks on the beach with Bouncer. He arrived in the office around 4 P.M. most days, spent an hour whispering into the phone, held court in the kitchen then went home to make his mother her dinner. It was only later I discovered that, like Dracula, he did most of his work at night.

I sat around doing virtually nothing and feeling guilty—for a couple of days at least.

"Don't panic," John said, whenever I asked if there was something that needed to be done. Even when he caught me with my feet on the desk reading an Elmore Leonard book the most censorious thing he could find to say was, "Elmore who?"

One afternoon I was feeling especially guilty (actually, I had just finished *Freaky Deaky* and was bored) and tagged along with Francis for something to do. The policeman in the neighboring village was retiring after thirty years' service. Francis took some pictures of him pretending to lock the door to the station while I lobbed him some searching questions about law and order in Ireland.

"How many crimes do you get in a place like this in a year?"

"Six."

"He's lying," Francis whispered, as we walked back to the car. "Three a year—if he's lucky."

Our next stop was at a meal to celebrate the gathering of the four chieftains of the Sweeney Clan. They were together again for the first time since 1567 when they faced the mighty O'Neills and the O'Donnells on the battlefield of Farsetmoor, according to the press release Francis handed me as we drove to the hotel.

We were ushered through to the dining room. The meal hadn't started yet. Francis organized the clan chieftains and assorted dignitaries into the standard *Tribune* pose, a close approximation to a football-team photograph. I stood to the side and read the menu: . . . *warm crostini of buffalo-cheese mozzarella with caponata of vegetables, followed by grilled fillet of red snapper with creamed oyster mushrooms, spring onions and dill sauce, a selection of homemade ice-cream* . . . It was all I could do to stop myself sticking a napkin into my shirtfront and clamping a knife and fork in my fists.

I galloped through an interview with Captain Mingo Sweeney, chieftain of the Banagh branch of the Sweeneys. He was a Canadian soldier, a dignified and charming man, which was why I allowed him the courtesy of finishing a fascinating story of how his family came to inherit the clan leadership before asking if we could stay for dinner.

"Of course, dear boy," he said. "I forgot to mention . . ."

I shouted across the room, ecstatic, "Francis, he says we can stay for dinner." The Captain pressed on with his story. "My great-great-great-uncle fought against the English . . ."

"Look, Francis, rich chocolate gateau with raspberry sauce."

". . . it was 1607. Have you written that date down?"

Francis looked harassed. "We can't stay. We've got to go and photograph the Fanad Community Band."

"Have you seen this?" I held up the menu. "What's so important about photographing the Fanad Community Band? Are they posing in the nude?"

"Let's go, Lawrence. Please." He looked pained. "If we don't photograph the Fanad Community Band, we don't have a newspaper."

He was right, of course. The front page of the *Gammy Bird*, the fictional newspaper in E. Annie Proulx's wonderful novel *The Shipping News*, carried a picture of a car crash every week. It filled the white space. The Fanad Community Band photo did the same job in the *Tribune*. If it wasn't the band it was the Rainbow

Theatre Group or the Milford Boys' Brigade, the Sweeney clan chieftains or the Donegal branch of the Manchester United Supporters Club. They were all posed the same way, in two rows, the rear standing, the front sitting, someone holding the trophy or the check. Like a football team. At least it was more orderly than a car crash.

Francis Diver didn't seem the type to own a newspaper. His voice never wavered from calm, his manner was as serene as that of an elderly doctor. He was the type grandmothers and mothers liked. He was thirty-one and always looked as if he'd spent the night on the sofa. His eyes were permanently rimmed red, his face lined with responsibility. His clothes—chosen for comfort and proximity to hand when he woke—were always crumpled. Fashion had passed him by, not because he wasn't interested but because there was always work to do. The *Tribune* was his life. He didn't drink, didn't go out much—at least, not without a camera round his neck. He hadn't had a holiday for eight years. "Christ," he confessed, "I haven't even got a passport."

Only when deadlines started to loom was it possible to detect the steeliness hidden inside the shy young man who, eight years ago, had thought he could do something as outrageous as start his own newspaper.

In another life John McAteer had been Gore Vidal with stronger opinions, Henry Ford with ambition. An agitator, a troublemaker, an entrepreneur. Somehow, in this life, he ended up as a day nurse in the "Mental" in Letterkenny. "They used to call it the Derry and District Lunatic Asylum," he told me. "It's called St. Conal's now. Makes the people in there feel better, even if they're not."

We were sitting in the office kitchen, the day after the

Sweeney Clan dinner. Francis was out again taking more photos. I was trying to imagine that the rock bun I was chewing
was really warm crostini of buffalo-cheese mozzarella with
caponata of vegetables. John was sitting opposite, spreading
waves of soft butter across a slab of soda bread and giving me
his life story.

"My father was a postman, my mother brought up the family. Six of us, five boys and a girl. I left school at thirteen. The
thing to do then was to take the boat from Derry to Glasgow,
find work there. Couldn't blame them. There was nothing for
them here. Still isn't. I didn't want to go. I learnt a bit about fixing electricity and worked at that for a few years. I knew a few
people who worked at the Mental. They put my name down for
a job. Eventually something came up. I wasn't fussy either way,
didn't dislike it, didn't like it, but the money was good. And it
meant I could stay here."

He placed half of his bread on the floor. The dog sniffed it,
picked it up and carried it over to the corner by the fridge. The
conversation stopped while we watched it eat. "Good boy," he
said. "I love animals. Wish I'd been a vet." He lit his pipe.
"Where was I?"

"The Mental."

"That would've been about nineteen sixty-six. The training
took three years. There were a lot of new treatments, new drugs
back then. You had to learn a lot. The job was hard going. You
saw the worst of human behavior, human beings only in name.
There was a lot of sitting around. It's like being a brain surgeon,
the most boring job in the world. Nothing changes. The human
brain hasn't changed in ten million years.

"I started writing, let me see . . . about nineteen seventy. For
the *Derry People*—that's one of our rivals."

"I know."

"It was a terrific paper back in those days, with a good editor. I was trying to get some publicity for Fanad, up where I live. We were in dire straits, the usual—no jobs, no investment. I went to see him and he said, 'Sure, you know what's happening up there, write it down and send it in.' I went to the hospital that night and wrote six hundred words about the local festival. Next week the words appeared exactly as I'd written them.

"I never stopped writing after that. About everything. Farming, fishing, the fact that we had no fuckin' jobs, I wrote stories about those things I didn't think were getting covered in the papers. And the paper kept printing them. I had a platform. I found it hard to believe it could be so easy."

He stopped talking, relit his pipe and cut another slice of bread. Patrick came in, his rent-collecting over for the day. He poured a mug of tea and spent five minutes fretting about the business involving the whale and the rock-climbing course.

"You can't print that stuff, John." He snorted, cigarette smoke coming out of his mouth in spurts as he tried to stop himself laughing. "Is it true?"

"Course I can print it. It's my paper."

John and Francis met in the early 1980s. Francis was a wedding photographer who'd branched out into journalism. He worked as a freelance for the biggest paper in the county, the *Democrat*. John was nursing less and writing more. He took a sabbatical from the hospital and became a full-time journalist, writing stories for the *Derry People* and press releases for whoever needed the publicity. He knew he'd never go back.

The two of them met on a few jobs, became nodding acquaintances. Nothing more.

One week John wrote a story about housing and the council, the details of which he could no longer recall but he was sure they were an affront to democracy in Ireland. He'd put a lot of work into the article. It didn't appear and when he called the *People* he was told there had been pressure of space. This was a new phenomenon for a Donegal newspaper, where the only difficulty with space was how to fill it.

When he telephoned the editor the following week he was told there was still no space. He put the phone down and thought, Wouldn't it be fucking great if there was a paper in Donegal that would print a story, regardless of who it offended? Or that took adverts? Wouldn't it be great if that paper always took the side of the people, regardless of whether the people were right or wrong?

Four years later, February 1991, John McAteer and Francis Diver drove back from a printing house in Sligo, the back axle groaning with the weight of two thousand copies of the *Tirconaill Tribune*.

They had typed out every word on a second-hand Macintosh —the German model that was sitting in the front office—bought from a teacher for seven hundred pounds (with computer lessons thrown in). They had pasted the stories by hand onto A3 sheets. It was crude, but recognizably a newspaper. The name took an age. A thousand alliterations later they settled on *Tirconaill* because it was the old name for Donegal, and *Tribune* because there wasn't one already. When they arrived in Sligo the print-shop manager acted shocked, saying, "I thought you weren't coming until next week," then winked.

Posters had been up in every shop window in northwest Donegal for weeks. It was ten o'clock at night when they got back. About a hundred people were waiting in the main street in Milford. They applauded as the two men held up copies of issue number one, with its front-page story about the proposed amalgamation of two local schools: "Milford Community College—A.S.T.I. says NO WAY!"

Francis could remember the headline better than any of the W. B. Yeats poems the nuns had taught him at school, that, and the reaction of the man standing beside him on the street that night as freshly minted copies of the newspaper were passed like samizdat from hand to hand. "It was the one and only time I ever saw John McAteer looking really happy."

I spent a couple of afternoons leafing through back issues of the *Tribune*. There were piles of unsold copies in a wall cupboard at the back of the office. The masthead had changed about a dozen times since issue one, from a small white-on-black Times typeface through a dozen variants of Celtic font to the current prosaic square black lettering.

Like everything else about the paper, the present was better than the past. John volunteered that the spelling was so bad for the first half-dozen issues that English teachers from the local school called in to offer help. Typing mistakes were another feature: *"Roads Closed as Gaels Sweep across Donegal," "Save the Corncrackers," "Quick as a Flatch."* They were bad, but I'd read worse, like the story I once wrote about a youth who'd been charged with possession of a fireman. (This would have been fine for the *Gay Times* but on the front page of a daily newspaper it cost me two months of filthy looks from the editor and, thank God, the position of industrial correspondent.)

It was hard back then, with just two people doing the work, but once Kathleen and Noel volunteered to help, the mistakes started to thin out. Francis concentrated on taking pictures and collecting adverts, John had more time to dig out stories and write them up. Confidence rolled in like a slow tide. The *Tribune* found a quiet voice.

Nowadays it screamed. The comment page sprayed streams of vitriol across the local scene like a fire hose. Whatever was going on was an affront to democracy/natural justice/the people of Donegal. The news pages never knowingly missed the chance to pass comment either. "The Council has canceled its award for journalism, one of the reasons given was that councillors were not fit to pass judgment on journalism. No reporter in Donegal would disagree with that." I could hear John saying every word as my eyes skipped across the columns.

There isn't a reporter in the world who didn't dream about being this insolent. In London, John McAteer would have had a permanent parking space outside the Press Complaints Commission to save him the trouble of going home between hearings. He would have been on first-name terms with the clerks of the libel courts. Not that he would have lost a case. He was careful. He knew his ground in Donegal, knew every story. The fact is, there weren't many stories to know. You could tell that by the way the same half-dozen each took turns at filling the front page every couple of months. Whales getting stranded on the beach were a welcome diversion.

Flicking through the back issues, I could see the future stretching out in front of me: a steady procession of priestly retirals, Boys' Brigade anniversaries and somnambulant council meetings. Woodward and Bernstein would have been pushed to find some excitement in that lot. My heart sank and my brain began to compose a begging letter to the editor of the *Guardian*: "Dear Sir, You may not remember me but I was once . . ."

I got as far as the part where moving to Ireland had been a massive success but now that phase of my life was over I was prepared to do my old job for a tenth of the money he used to pay me when my eyes fell on page five of a *Tribune* from 1996. It was dominated by a picture of farmland lost beneath floodwater. Below the photograph there was a paragraph that read:

Death

Bernard Lafferty, formerly of Creeslough, died of a heart attack last week in Los Angeles, California. As many people will know Bernard was the butler to the American heiress Doris Duke, who made him executor of her will after she passed away in 1993. Outrageous claims that Bernard murdered Doris Duke were never proved. The funeral was held in Los Angeles last week. Sympathies are extended to his relations and friends in the Donegal area.

John was late back from a council meeting. He was carrying a green hardcover notebook and a sheaf of long-winded press releases from councillors.

"How was it?" I said.

"The usual nonsense. As for this lot, there's only one place they're going," he said, crunching the press releases into a ball and dropping them into the wastepaper basket. He'd been up most of the previous night and looked exhausted. The *Tribune* was due on the streets in two days. Noel and Kathleen were typing. Francis was out collecting adverts.

John put his notebook on the desk, sat down and rubbed his face in his hands, as if trying to wash away the painful memory of the last few hours. Eventually he spoke. "The council has gone and spent twenty thousand pounds on a superloo. They've closed the old one in town. Apparently it was overrun with homosexuals. Who would have thought that a God-fearing, Catholic country like Ireland would have such a thing as homosexuals?" He took his pipe out of his pocket and lit it. "They've invited George Michael to perform at the opening ceremony, you know."

"John, have you seen this?" I showed him the page with the picture of the flood and the paragraph about Lafferty.

"Lennon floods. Happens every winter. And?"

"No, not the floods, Bernard Lafferty."

He looked again, smiled. "I remember that. Ber-*naaard* Lafferty. Now I'm not a gambling man but I'd bet my life he'd have been down at the old toilets the odd night."

"Did he murder Doris Duke?"

"I don't know. That's what it said in some of the papers at the time. Does it matter?"

"But what if he did? What if the boy from Creeslough murdered the richest woman in the world and the *Tribune* got the story? That would make them sit up at the *Guardian*, wouldn't it? It might even make a paragraph or two in the *New York Times*. Can I do the story?"

"You can, if you like." He shook his head. "But not now. Creeslough Hall has been demolished. Speak to a couple of people in the village and write a thousand words, will you? I'd do it myself but I don't have the time."

Sarah McCaffrey lived with her brother Michael in the cottage next door to the Edward Hopper garage. It was painted white with sky blue trimmings and a mahogany front door that opened to reveal a small woman wearing a large pair of glasses. I explained that I was a new reporter on the *Tirconaill Tribune*. "Come on in," she said.

It was the first house in Creeslough I had been inside apart from my own. I felt as if I had walked into the Ritz after spending a month in the grottiest B-and-B in Blackpool. This was indisputably a home, with central heating, pictures on the wall, fitted carpets, and Michael watching TV.

My own efforts at home building were beginning to resemble *A Year in Provence* in reverse. The longer I stayed, the more derelict the cottage was becoming. I would have started on the repairs but there was so much to be done I couldn't decide where to start: the leaking roof or the brown mulch that slid out of the cold-water tap? The wet rot or the electrical wiring that fizzed and sparked like the aftermath of a train crash? All of this would cost money, which was in short supply.

Anyone who has read Peter Mayle's harrowing, gritty account of life on the French Riviera will recall the steady stream of craftsmen who transformed the impoverished author's old stone farmhouse into the palace of Versailles in twelve short months. They were all called Gustave or Ramón, sweated Gallic charm and were happy to accept a bowl of Pete's freshly picked wild strawberries as payment.

It was early days yet but I got the impression life didn't operate quite like that in Ireland. The only Irish craftsman I'd had contact with was a telephone engineer called Mick. I was sure he had never sweated in his life and he charged me a fortune for installing a phone socket that I had to repair myself after a week. He was the last person I would have given my wild strawberries to.

The smell of good cooking drifted through from the kitchen. Sarah saw my nose twitching. "Would you like something to eat?" she said. I could have hugged her.

Sarah McCaffrey was one of the people John had told me to interview for my article about Creeslough Hall. She was in her seventies, had lived in the village all her life and taught for years at the local school. According to John, she was the world's greatest living expert on Creeslough.

"It's about the Hall," I said sitting down.

"The Hall?" She smiled and disappeared immediately into another room. I could hear her fretting and rummaging through drawers. Five minutes later she came back carrying a dark blue ledger. It was the Creeslough Hall cash book, meticulously maintained in black ink from the day the first sheet of corrugated iron for the roof was bought on March 9, 1929 until December 1938.

"Right," she said determinedly. "What do you want to know about the Hall?"

When I was living in the city I complained about life all the time but barely considered what had shaped the environment around me, or what it used to be like, how it had become the way it was, who was responsible for changing it, or how I could make it better. These were big, important questions and I must have given them thirty seconds of thought. This was the time it took me to decide to start cycling to work—my total contribution to tackling urban blight in ten years. I feel guilty about that now but at the time I was usually too knackered to care, or there was golf on the TV.

Another thing I never did in the city was hang out with pensioners. What would we have talked about? Hip operations? The new Harmony Korine movie? Sarah was different. I could have been locked in a prison cell with her for years and never got bored. She could have talked for days about the things that had shaped her environment and I would have sat there enthralled.

A small for-instance: the name Creeslough, Craos Loch in Irish, meaning Throat Lake or Gullet Lake. Why? Because there was a tiny lake at the top of the village that gathered a lot of rainwater from the surrounding hills and leaked only a little away through a tiny stream. Where did all the water go? It had been swallowed by the hungry lake, obviously. Why not call the village Hungry Lake? It wasn't poetic enough. Throat Lake, Craos Loch, Creeslough. I didn't need to know this tiny piece of local history. I didn't think that I wanted to know it but once I did it made me feel strangely good.

Being a soggy liberal type who likes the idea of communities pulling together, the story of Creeslough Hall made me feel even better. In the mid-1920s the villagers decided that the community needed a focal point, a place where people could socialize together. The local tradesmen built the hall in their spare time, using cost-price materials bought at the local co-op. Six months later the doors opened on forty years of dancing, theater, arts festivals and—lest we get too misty-eyed—a regular Friday night punch-up.

The ledger deserved a place in the national museum in Dublin. It was a perfectly preserved record of an age when it cost seven shillings and sixpence to transport borrowed stage scenery back to Carndonagh, eight gallons of oil would set you back eleven shillings, and the Orphelian Dance Band wouldn't unpack their gear for less than five pounds ten shillings. The first dance was held on November 27, 1929, and was described in the book as a "long-dress occasion"—evidence, surely, of the villagers' pride in their new hall. Most people at that time had so little spare money they were delighted to own a dress of any description.

Sadly, the first flush of enthusiasm waned. Whoever had maintained the ledger stopped abruptly on New Year's Eve 1938. The hall began to lose money. Sarah's father bought it at the end of the Second World War. He kept it going for another thirty years, long enough for Creeslough Hall to earn an unwanted reputation as one of the area's roughest dance venues. It played a small part in launching the career of the Irish singer Enya.

"Here she is," Sarah said gleefully. She had retrieved a scrap-book from one of the cupboards in the bedroom. She showed me a picture of a black-haired girl dressed in a simple white dress. "She sang at the Creeslough Feis. Her name then was Eithne Brennan."

On the page opposite there was a photograph of a young boy standing in front of a white marble statue of the Virgin Mary. He'd just taken his first communion and was wearing his best clothes: dark double-breasted blazer with white hanky in the top pocket, black short trousers and gray socks pulled up to the knee. His hands were pressed together as if in prayer. The smile caught my eye.

"Who's that?" I asked.

She touched the photo. "That," she said, "is poor Bernard Lafferty."

"The Doris Duke Bernard Lafferty?"

"A lovely, lovely boy." She stood up, started closing the various books. I had more than enough material for my article. "What they wrote about Bernard and all the things he was supposed to have done—it was terrible," she said.

Her friend taught him at school. He was one of the quietest boys in the class, was always interested in lessons. He'd had a tragic family life: his father dead from cancer, his mother killed climbing off the back of a bus in Glasgow. An only child. There was nothing left for him in Creeslough so he went to America. Next thing anyone knew he was all over the newspapers.

Michael McCaffrey had barely looked away from the television since I'd arrived but mention of Bernard Lafferty's name diverted his attention from the horse-racing. "I was the president of the Legion of Mary back then and Bernard was one of our young members." The three o'clock from Lingfield was coming to a climax but Michael talked over the commentator. "As the stars are above me, he was a model boy."

Wednesday was the *Tribune*'s publication day. Tuesday night was spent writing last-minute stories and pasting up pages in the attic of John McAteer's house in Fanad.

The drive from Creeslough took forty minutes, through a conifer forest and out along Mulroy Bay toward the Atlantic. I took a couple of wrong turnings. Eventually I found the bungalow on its own by the side of a freshwater loch too small to feature on my map but big enough to have a name, Shannagh Lake.

I pushed open the back door into the kitchen. John was by the sink peeling spuds, the dog at his feet barking. "Lawrence," he said. "Welcome."

The door through to the living room was partially open. I could see a woman sitting on a straight-backed armchair reading a newspaper. She was wearing a heavy tweed skirt, a thick gray woolen cardigan and fur-lined felt slippers that covered her ankles. She must have been well over eighty. Her hair was a color somewhere between sky blue and violet.

"Come through here, Donegan," a female voice shouted from the room. "Let's have a look at ye."

I went next door. A young woman of about twenty, with shoulder-length dark hair, was stretched out along a two-seater sofa. She was smoking. A blonde of about the same age was sitting at a table over by the window.

"He's not that bad, considering he's old," said the blonde.

"His arse is a bit big," said the other, blowing a jet of smoke. I wondered if it was my lack of a social life (I hadn't spoken to a member of the opposite sex under the age of fifty for at least a month) or if she really was sexier than Lauren Bacall.

John came through from the kitchen. "You've met my charming nieces, I see," he said, then pointed at the old woman. "And this is my mother, Annie."

Annie looked up from her newspaper, only half interested. "Huh. You're here at last, Donegan." She went back to reading.

"Come on upstairs," John said. "I think you'll find it's a bit different from the *Guardian*."

I followed him out into the hallway and up a set of home-made ladders through the loft door. The attic was hotter than hell and twice as uncomfortable. Francis was sitting in front of a screen, stripped to the waist. He was typing, though he looked like a man into his second hour on an exercise bike.

"Open the window, let some air in," John said.

"Can't." Francis kept typing but nodded toward the window. "Look at the insects."

Through the glass it was just possible to see a mess of flies and moths driven crazy by the only bright light for half a mile. The room itself was about as spacious as the inside of a Russian space capsule. The hardware scattered along the work-top was hardly more advanced: a couple of old computers, a photo-graphic scanner and an ancient paper-waxing machine. The room smelt like a cross between a church and a jockstrap. The ceiling had been decorated—I use the word loosely with brown carpet tiles, the floor with old newspapers. Most of the furniture had a fine coating of fawn dog hair.

"You're right, John," I said. "It's not like the *Guardian*."

We spent the next six hours finishing off the paper. I wrote my story about Creeslough Hall and an obituary of a priest who was famous locally for telling young couples that marriage was a daft idea and giving his sermon in Arabic then repeating it in Latin for those at the back of the church who didn't understand what he had been saying. "Don't put that stuff in, for Christ's sake," Francis said, handing me a faxed copy of the Bishop's oration at the funeral earlier that day. "Just copy some of this out."

Over the previous couple of days John had written a dozen stories. He finished off his council report in longhand and gave it to Francis to type up: "No one at the council would comment on the rumors that George Michael is to perform at the opening ceremony . . ."

"Fuck, John, we can't print this in the newspaper."

"Oh, Francis, will you just cop on to yourself and keep typing."

We went downstairs around midnight for something to eat. The living room was packed now. Another of Annie's sons had turned up, along with her daughter Peggy, some friends of the family and a scattering of grandsons. The number of nieces had risen to five, each more vivacious and outspoken than the last.

I ate my dinner on the floor with the plate balanced on my knees while they discussed whether or not they'd climb over me in bed to get to David Beckham. From what I could gather my arse wasn't that big, after all, but I was definitely beginning to lose my hair and they had all seen better dressed scarecrows. If push came to shove they'd all slit my throat to get to David Beckham.

Francis, John and I went back upstairs. Sometime after 1 A.M. I fell asleep. The rest of the night was lost in a dreamy haze of hot wax and cursing. At one point someone I didn't recognize came up the stairs with an embarrassing picture of his friend. John gave an evil laugh and decided that it was sufficiently cruel to be published, which I suppose is how things must operate on Rupert Murdoch's newspapers.

Francis woke me just before dawn. I lifted my head, wiped the dribble from my sleeve and the sleep from my eyes. John was holding the pasted-up front page between his fingertips. "What d'you think?" he said, smirking.

Francis was trying hard not to laugh. The main story was about a group of villagers who were campaigning to stop a mobile-phone mast being erected near the local school on the not unreasonable grounds that the radiation it produced might give them cancer. Next to it, above the fold, was a picture of me typing at the computer and beneath it a few paragraphs about my arrival at the paper:

Guardian Journalist Joins *Tribune*

The *Tribune* has a new reporter. Lawrence Donegan was formerly a correspondent with the *Guardian* newspaper in London. In his more fashionable days, he was a pop star and once appeared on *Top of the Pops*.

Tribune editor John McAteer welcomed the new member of staff on his first day. He said: "It's a bit different from the *Guardian* here on the *Tribune* but Lawrence seems to be keen enough. It will take us a few weeks to see if he's good enough for the *Tribune*."

"That'll get everybody talking," John couldn't contain his mirth any longer. "*Guardian* journalist not good enough for the *Tribune*." He laughed. "Holy fuck."

He handed the page to Francis, who placed it with the others in a shallow cardboard box and slipped on a lid. "Here, you can take this downstairs." Francis handed me the precious cargo. "Your first paper. How does it feel?"

"It feels good," I said, smiling. The funny thing was, I meant it.

Francis went for a shower, delighted that he'd managed to fit 536 faces (not including crowd scenes) into thirty-two pages. John cleared up the debris left by the previous night's visitors. I could tell he was high on adrenaline and the certain knowledge that later in the day someone somewhere, probably in the council offices, would pick up the latest issue of the *Tribune*, turn to his colleague and say, "Have you seen what that bastard McAteer has written this week?"

We had breakfast by the window overlooking Shannagh Lake, complimenting God on the sunrise and ourselves on producing an excellent newspaper.

"Something in it to keep everybody happy," John said—except the medical column, headlined "Diarrhea—Nobody Escapes It," I wanted to say but didn't. It would have spoiled the moment.

Francis and I set off about nine o'clock for the print works in Derry. John stayed behind to help his mother out of bed and give her breakfast. We arranged to meet up at noon in the car park of the Letterkenny shopping center where, according to John, the *Tribune*'s extensive fleet of distribution agents would be waiting with their engines revving, ready to dispatch the paper to shops across the northwest of Donegal.

• • •

The return trip to Derry took three hours. The print works were on an industrial estate on the city outskirts. The papers would be ready in an hour. Francis announced he would give me a tour of Derry. "War-torn Derry," he said, like he was wearing a fright mask.

War-torn Derry. I recognized a lot of the names from the news bulletins down the years: the Bogside, the Creggan (home of the mighty Undertones, of course), Waterside, the Diamond, the famous walls.

Actually I'd been to the city once before, years ago. I thought at the time a more appropriate description would have been Impoverished Derry. Back then, the city center was deserted but for a handful of women shoppers trying to escape the attentions of intrepid French television reporters. If anything the shops were even more forlorn than the streets, with empty window displays and the smallest, shabbiest, most ragged-arsed selection of food and clothes this side of a Bulgarian supermarket. Now I knew why the Undertones dressed so badly. There was nothing else for them to buy.

The outlying areas were equally depressing. Admittedly I didn't conduct an extensive survey of the housing but most of it looked barely habitable—not because it had been ravaged by the bombing campaign, but because it had been designed in the sixties by an imbecilic architect, who thought that rows of windowless cells without any amenities was the cutting edge of municipal accommodation.

It was impossible to miss the evidence of what Kate Adie would breathlessly describe from underneath the shelter of her tin hat as the Troubles. But most of what passed for religious hatred seemed pathetic and futile, like kerbstones painted to signify whether a street was Catholic or Protestant. To think that someone had roused themselves in the dead of night rather than stay in the warm embrace of his wife to spend the hours until dawn painting the road green, white and gold for the cause. Every third lamppost had been converted to a flagpole. Again, to think that someone had actually risked their life shinning up a pole on a windy night so that a Union Jack could flutter unnoticed on a busy thoroughfare. The Queen must have been delighted.

The ordinary people, on the other hand, just looked pissed off. No wonder. Flagmakers, Kate Adie and the bloke who invented Semtex might have done well out of the last twenty years but it sure hadn't been much fun for Derry.

Well, what a difference a decade had made.

To this day-tripper at least, modern Derry seemed perfectly normal. I mean that as a compliment. People were walking around with carrier-bags from newly opened branches of chain stores you would expect to find in any prosperous community—Dixons, Boots, Marks & Spencer, Virgin Records. Francis spotted an RUC officer walking down the street alone and unarmed: this sight had been unthinkable at any point in the last twenty years. You couldn't walk five yards without someone trying to sell you a copy of the *Big Issue*. Buskers were murdering the Oasis songbook. Derry was slowly becoming just another city like Reading or Milton Keynes, which must feel wonderful after two decades of being like Beirut.

We went into a café on the Diamond, site of the war memorial and scene of some terrible confrontations between Nationalists and Loyalists over the years, and had cappuccinos and some gluttonous cream cakes (now *that* is what I call progress) then drove back to the print works.

When we got there the presses were just about to roll. Despite working in the business for nigh on ten years, I'd never actually seen a newspaper being printed. It was just like it is in the movies. Gradually, like a steam engine leaving a station, every inch of air was filled by the clatter of machinery and the whir of newsprint rolls. I half expected Edward G. Robinson to burst through one of the doors, take a cigar out of his mouth and tell me to hold the front page. I stood there hypnotized by the sight of my own picture, again and again and again, like Narcissus's bedroom wall, until it was time to put the papers into bundles. There were so many I didn't think they would all fit in the car.

The *Tribune*'s circulation was something of a trade secret. "It depends who is asking," Francis said, as we loaded them into the car trunk. "If I'm talking to advertisers and journalists from the other papers I usually try to be vague, mutter something around the three thousand mark. But since it's you, the issue before last sold 2,745 copies. That was up twenty-three on the issue before that."

We drove back to Letterkenny. The cool dawn had turned into one of those great-to-be-alive mornings when the air seemed clean enough to bottle. I felt smug watching the landscape scroll past, thinking that I could make my fortune selling those bottles of air on the corner of Oxford Circus. I looked across at Francis. If anything, he looked even happier than I felt. I got him to retell the story about driving home with the first ever edition of the *Tribune*—I could listen to the part about the cheering crowd a thousand times—and when he finished he took a deep, satisfied breath and said, "I love the smell of newsprint in the morning."

"Tommy's not coming," John said.

He was resting against the trunk of his car reading the latest edition of one of the other Donegal papers. "Would you look at this?" He held up the front page to show me the headline: FEED

CRISIS FOR DONEGAL PIG FARMERS. "Quick, phone Gay Byrne, broadcast the news to the nation." He shook his head.

It was one of the self-evident truths of John's world that the *Tribune*'s rivals were so bad it was hardly worth anyone's time writing for them, printing them or buying them.

"What's wrong with Tommy?" Francis asked, opening the trunk of the car. He lifted out a handful of loose papers and handed them round. Everyone flicked through their copy and made general murmurs of approval.

"He's singing at a funeral," John said eventually, then turned to me. "Tommy's got a lovely tenor voice. Lawrence, you can do his round with Bridie."

Bridie was sitting in the back of John's car. She saw me looking over and waved. She and Tommy, Declan, John, Francis, Noel and now me—the *Tribune*'s extensive team of distribution agents was complete.

I struck lucky. Tommy and Bridie had the best delivery run of the lot. It took them out west of the county, past Creeslough and along the Atlantic coast through picturesque villages with names plucked from the Gazetteer of Ridiculously Quaint Irish Place-names: Portnablagh, Dunfanaghy, Falcarragh and Gortahork.

When we stopped in Creeslough Danny Lafferty was standing by his shop door. "Gimme a look," he said, taking one of the papers from the top of the pile. "What's this then? 'Guardian journalist joins the *Tribune*'? My God. Have you got an extra thousand copies?"

We pressed on. Dunfanaghy looked far too beautiful in the sunshine not to stop and take in the view. I pulled over at a car-park by the sea and went for an ice-cream. Bridie dug into her shopping bag and pulled out a sandwich box and a flask of tea. We sat in the car for half an hour with the windows wound down, exchanging life histories and congratulating ourselves on our good fortune in not being stuck in a traffic jam on the M25.

She and Tommy had emigrated to London in the early 1960s to look for work. They had brought up a family in England. Their grandchildren had Cockney accents. They came home for good five years ago. "I wanted to go back to London again on the first plane." She laughed at the memory. "It was so lonely I couldn't stand it. The family was back in London, I missed the shops and the excitement. It took me three years to get used to Donegal and its ways again."

"What d'you mean, its ways?"

"The way nobody acts as if they've got a clock in this place. People here have just got two gears, dead slow and stop. I love it now, can't understand why we stayed away in London for so long."

She rolled her eyes, put the flask back in her bag and brushed the crumbs off the seat. I turned the ignition key, reversed out on to the road and headed west toward Gortahork. "Bridie," I said, "I know what you mean."

The Bridge

This, I confess, was everything I knew about Gaelic football . . .

(1) It is Ireland's national game and is played on a much bigger field than soccer. The ball is round, the goals look like the ugly offspring of a marriage between soccer and rugby. Each team has fifteen players who can use feet and hands to pass and shoot. There are three points for a goal and, strangely enough, one point for a point. A player can't carry the ball unless they *solo* it. I didn't know what soloing was: I'd heard the commentator use the word when I saw a game as a kid on the BBC in the mid-1970s but I don't think the commentator knew what it meant either. It was Gaelic football's only ever appearance on the BBC. I think the horse racing from Chester had been snowed off.

(2) The umpires wear knee-length white coats, like butchers. They wave big white flags, like Italian army generals.

(3) Playing the game was the only way I was going to make another friend in Creeslough besides Danny Lafferty.

I knew this because Francis and John told me as much. "Gaelic football is the very lifeblood of Irish community life," Francis said, in a rare poetic outburst while we were sitting in the kitchen one afternoon. "Take the GAA to your heart and the people will take you to their heart."

John nodded and removed the pipe from his mouth. "Plus it is a scientifically proven fact that there isn't a woman in the whole of Ireland who can resist a man who plays Gaelic football."

I knew it was time to make friends in Creeslough because the cat had given birth to three kittens a couple of nights before.

Normally this would have been cause for celebration, except I didn't have a cat.

I'd been out covering a council meeting. The cottage was in darkness by the time I got home. Squalor is my confirmation name—I won prizes for untidiness at school—but even I couldn't quite believe the mess that greeted me when I unlocked the door and went inside. The white Venetian blinds I'd bought to replace the net curtains had been ripped off their bindings. Newspapers were strewn everywhere. Most of the household ornaments had been knocked over and smashed.

At first I thought I'd been burgled. I grabbed an ornamental brass cow bell and tiptoed through the rooms. The place appeared to be empty. Nothing was missing except some bread from the kitchen. Naturally I was relieved, though slightly offended that someone had gone to all the trouble of breaking in only to find nothing worth stealing.

Wounded pride quickly gave way to fear when I heard a faint yelping. At first I thought it was coming from outside. It got louder and more persistent. Whatever was making the noise was still in the house. My pulse galloped off over the horizon, taking with it whatever manly courage I'd been born with. The noise was coming from the bedroom. I pushed open the door. I could see something moving underneath the sheets, anonymous yet sinister. (What was it about my bed that wild animals found so irresistible? And might the attraction, like mad cow disease, cross the species barrier and infect female humans?)

The details are messy and best kept for the script of the horror movie I plan to write one day entitled *Revenge of the Killer Placenta*, except to say there were three lovely newly born kittens underneath the sheet, one pure black, one pure white and another with tigerish orange and black markings. Their mother had ripped the cottage apart in her frantic efforts to get back outside to find food, then squeezed through the window, left open a crack, and hadn't been able to get back in.

I drove down to one of the village pubs, the Corncutter's Rest.

Looking back, I must have been in a state of shock. For some reason that can only be explained by total brain malfunction I thought my plight required a vet. Bernadette, the barmaid at the Corncutter's Rest and one of a handful of people in Creeslough who knew me by name, said, "Half of Guinness, Lawrence?" as I burst through the door hyperventilating.

"Kittens." I tried desperately to form sentences. "In the house. My bed. The vet's telephone number. Does anyone have it? Jesus, you should see the mess."

There were six people in the bar. Three were drunk and ignored me, the others listened with expressions that varied from pity to amusement. "Isn't a vet you need for the kittens, it's a pail of water," someone said, after I'd finished babbling. Everyone went back to talking about something far more interesting and important, like the rocketing price of tractor tires.

"There's your Guinness," Bernadette said, kindly, ushering me over to a table in the corner.

I sat there for a while, alone with my story of coming home to find kittens in the bed. My brain started to unscramble. (How could a vet have helped, except to tell me the kittens were fine but my bedspread needed a spell of recuperation at the launderette?)

I'd made a fool of myself. It was embarrassing, I suppose, but I could have lived with the shame if I'd had someone to share it with. I sat there for a while, trying hard to look as if I really wanted to be on my own. My eyes drifted across the bar and stopped on a picture of the County Donegal team, which won the 1992 All-Ireland Gaelic Football Championship. I took this as a sign.

It wasn't a sign that I was ever going to play Gaelic football for Donegal, of course. I knew that anyway and if I didn't I certainly knew it after watching five minutes of my first live game. The Bridge, home ground of St. Michael's GAA club, was at the other end of the parish. I couldn't miss it, according to Danny Lafferty—just follow the sound of cheering.

When I got there the match had already started. "Two pounds to get in," said the man at the gate. He handed me back my change. "You're the Donegan fella, aren't you? The one who lives in the place down Ballyboes? Wrote the article about Creeslough Hall."

This was a promising start; a friendly conversation. As we chatted he let slip that he was a member of the club committee. I explained that I wanted to take up Gaelic football, that unfortunately I'd never played the game before but I was famed throughout the world of sport for my enthusiasm.

"You don't have a wooden leg, do you?" He stuck his head through the car window and checked me out. "You'll do." He laughed. "I don't think you'll be ready yet for the first team if you've never played before. Speak to the reserve team manager, Liam Ferry."

The ground itself was far . . . grander would be the wrong word because that implies pretentiousness. It was far more ambitious than I imagined it would be.

By any measure St. Michael's was one of Donegal's smaller clubs. Like every other club in Ireland it was a parish team. Only people who lived or worked in the villages of Creeslough or Dunfanaghy were eligible to play—a catchment population of, say, six hundred. Excluding the obese, the infirm and the downright lazy, the number of potential players was probably around thirty. Applying Donegan's law of sporting dyslexia, which says that anyone who can't kick a ball with their instep shouldn't be allowed within five hundred yards of a playing field, this left a squad of twenty-five. Some of the teams St. Michael's played against every week had hundreds of players to choose from.

The club didn't have a huge potential support either. Fans were not being bussed in from all over the county to watch St. Michael's. Part of Gaelic football's appeal is its fierce parochialism. No one in Creeslough, or any village in Ireland for that matter, would ever dream of dashing off on a Sunday to support the local equivalent of Manchester United. It's the parish team or nothing.

Despite its disadvantages St. Michael's was a thriving club, with an impressive little ground. It even had a grandstand, a modest breeze-block and corrugated-iron construction that had recently been painted white with red trimmings. As I took my spot near the front a hundred people were sheltering from the rain. Most were in a state of high excitement. They'd heard the news that I wanted to play for the club, right? Actually, no.

The players had all gathered in the goal-mouth off to the left. Through the forest of bodies it was just possible to see two people rolling around on the ground fighting.

At this point, the president of the Gaelic Athletic Association (or GAA, the august body that runs the sport) is, no doubt, dictating a letter accusing me of perpetuating the caricature of this magnificent game as an outlet for the most violent impulses of the Irish psyche. I plead not guilty. The problem, I was later told by people who know, is that the rules of Gaelic football don't define what constitutes a tackle. This oversight has allowed some players to adopt a more expansive interpretation of the word than, say, the *Oxford English Dictionary* has. As a result there have been some terrible battles on Gaelic football fields down the years.

Aficionados recall a match in 1996 between Meath and Mayo that descended into a brawl involving sixteen of the thirty players on the field. Fifteen were later suspended. The 1983 match between Galway and Dublin was probably the game's nadir, with four players sent off and another unable to continue after tripping over his laces in the players' tunnel at halftime.

What made it all the more upsetting for the purists was that both of these games were All-Ireland finals, traditionally the climax of the football season. It is difficult adequately to convey to anyone who isn't Irish the cultural and sporting significance of the occasion but a friend—admittedly he was drunk at the time—told me that the All-Ireland final was like the FA Cup final multiplied by the state opening of Parliament. To have the occasion disrupted by brawling was an affront to Ireland's national pride. "Imagine the uproar if the Queen was sent off for a late tackle on Vinnie Jones," my friend helpfully explained.

The postmortems after the '83 and '96 games were long and bitter. Mercifully, but only just, they didn't involve dead bodies. Since then the GAA has made strenuous efforts to rid the game of its violent reputation. Hence, it would have come as a terrible shock if they ever found out that the two people involved in the unseemly brawl I was watching were the match umpires.

"An argument about a square ball," the woman standing next to me said, when I asked what it was all about. "When a player already inside the square touches a ball as it enters the square," she added, when I asked what *that* was all about. I was just about to open my mouth. "Think of it like the six-yard box in soccer," she said. On and on our conversation went, as if we were peeling an onion.

The umpires were finally pulled apart and the game restarted.

The St. Michael's team was in red. It developed into an exciting match, decided in the last minute by a superb long kick for a point by one of the visiting players. As both teams traipsed off the field, the woman standing next to me agreed to answer one more question: yes, the man with the pained expression was St. Michael's reserve team manager.

I introduced myself. "Training's here on Tuesday night, seven o'clock. Ask for Michael Kelly," Liam Ferry said, his voice hoarse with shouting.

There were already a few cars parked outside the dressing rooms when I arrived for training. I went inside, as apprehensive as a first-day schoolboy. Half a dozen people were already getting changed. I recognized some of them from the pub. One had been there on the night of the kitten incident. "I'm looking for Michael Kelly. Someone told me he's in charge of training," I said meekly.

"That's me." A black-haired man, who'd been tying his bootlaces, lifted his head. He had a cigarette in his mouth but still managed a smile. "How's the form?"

I gave a brief account of why I was there, leaving out the part about being desperately short of friends, emphasizing my enthusiasm for the game but admitting that I'd never actually played Gaelic football before (because that much would become apparent within five seconds of me stepping on the field).

Michael Kelly smiled. "You'll do for us, then." Everybody laughed, which made me feel good.

The training, however, made me feel ill.

By 7 P.M. around twenty people had turned up. Most of them were younger than me and had physiques that hinted at day jobs which involved lifting heavy objects and carrying them over long distances. A couple of people even had washboard stomachs like those you see on the covers of magazines that smell of aftershave and have men with chiseled jaws on the cover.

I had always thought of myself as quite fit—at least I didn't have to bend over to see my toes—but as everyone got changed there was an air of seriousness that made me feel uneasy. The absence of one truly fat slob, someone with whom I could hang out at the back of the pack and compare heart fibrillation stories, was another worry.

The session lasted ninety minutes. I spent half of it in the home team dugout wheezing and trying to hide the fact that I'd been sick. The rest of the time, I trotted along fifty yards behind everyone else. We had a bounce game of Gaelic football at the end, during which I successfully managed to avoid touching the ball.

When it was all over, everyone sat drinking hot tea at the back of the grandstand. Light spilled out of the changing rooms, casting shadows across the grass. In the darkness it was just possible to pick out the sheep grazing on the hill across the other side of the field. If I was looking for rural tranquillity I had come to the right place.

Michael Kelly came out of the kitchen and sat beside me. "The training takes a bit of getting used to." He laughed.

"No, no. It was fine. I feel great," I lied.

We had a long chat about nothing much: Sunday's game, training, the GAA, the *Tribune*, the Corncutter's Rest. He asked me if I was staying in Creeslough and when I said, "Yes," he said he'd see me in the pub on Saturday for a pint.

"We'll be in about ten o'clock," he said.

It took all of my self-control not to hug him there and then. John and Francis were right. I'd found myself a friend. I got up to leave. "Here, Moses wants to speak to you before you go," Michael said.

Moses Alcorn was the club secretary, one of a little knot of people who had been standing at the side of the field during the training session. "Lawrence, right?" he said, when I introduced myself. "Yeah, we'd better get you a game."

Play in a game. I was too stunned to say anything. A mixture of pride (he must think I've got what it takes to play Gaelic football) and fear (what if someone tackles me?) coursed through my veins as I stood watching him rummage through a folder.

"Can you fill this in some time this week?" He handed me a form. "It's for the insurance, like."

Sales of the *Tribune* had gone up since I joined the staff, not on a scale likely to provoke crisis meetings at the *New York Times*, or even the *Donegal People's Press*, but enough to make Francis smile and me feel a little smug as he told me the news.

"About fifty copies," he said. This wasn't quite the scale of increase I'd hoped. He went on, "We sold eight more copies than usual in Creeslough. And we had an E-mail about the Hall story. All the Irish words in it had the wrong spelling, apparently."

This was not unexpected. A lot of the plays and events staged at the Hall down the years had Irish language titles. Sarah McCaffrey had spelled them out for me but I couldn't have been listening properly. Hence, *Mise Éire* (I Am Ireland) became Miss Eire (a qualifying round for Miss World) and *Seachtar Fear, Seacht Lá* (Seven Men, Seven Days) became *Sachet Fear, Sachet Lar* (total gibberish).

The *Tribune*'s website was our principal claim to a place in the information revolution. It was a masterpiece, actually, designed for free by a French computer expert who had a holiday home near John's place. Francis updated it every week. It was extremely popular, mostly with Donegal exiles living in America who dispatched a constant stream of E-mails to Francis. Their appreciation of his efforts on the website was really quite gratifying, even if they were a bunch of pedantic bastards.

"Have these people got nothing better to do than send whinging E-mails," was the only defense I could come up with. But, to be honest, I could hardly have cared less about Patrick from Philadelphia and his hang-ups on Irish grammar. I was more caught up with life in Donegal which, touch wood, was beginning at last to feel as if it fitted me.

Working for the *Tribune* had got me noticed and not just because I couldn't spell in Irish. A couple of people introduced themselves in the queue at Lafferty's shop and congratulated me on the article about the village hall. It brought back fond memories, was the general view among the over-fifties. Someone else asked me if it was true that George Michael was coming to open the new public toilets in Letterkenny.

On the Saturday night I met Michael Kelly in the pub as arranged. And the following weekend too, when he was with his wife, Patricia. It turned out she had been serving me in Lafferty's shop every day. It was a relief to get beyond "That'll be two pounds forty-two please," and "Thanks."

There were Gaelic football matches every Sunday. I couldn't play, of course. Registration problems. The forms were going to take weeks to process and, anyway, I was having difficulty in finding out how to spell my name in Irish—a requirement for GAA team-sheets, according to Moses. I'd have been straight in the team otherwise. Honestly. Or, at least, I would have been, had every able-bodied man under the age of forty in the parish succumbed to bubonic plague.

Training was becoming easier but not so much so that I could get to the end of the session without wanting to vomit. On the plus side, I now knew what *soloing* was—drop-kicking the ball back into your hand while still running. I just had to work out how to do it. "You've got a good pair of hands," Michael said, by way of consolation. This would have been encouraging news if I was modeling gloves or engagement rings for women but I was trying to make it in the rough, tough world of Gaelic football.

Life on the newspaper was beginning to settle down, too, after a couple of Jesus-what-am-I-doing-here? wobbles. Once when I went into a newsagent's in Letterkenny and saw a copy of the *Guardian* the front-page story had been written by an old friend. It was headlined M15 PLOT TO KILL GADDAFI, and was an interesting story under any circumstances, but I'd just spent an hour trying to persuade a charming but stone deaf 102-year-old to reveal the secret of her longevity. I felt like crying with envy.

More serious was an argument John and I had over an article that appeared in the *Tribune*. The first line asked, "Are pro-abortionists psychopathic or are they only immoral?" What followed was a model of intolerance and bigotry. I felt as if I'd woken up to find I was sharing a bed with Saddam Hussein. I told John he should never have printed such rubbish.

He was probably right to be taken aback. It was his newspaper, after all. "I'm not here to censor anyone," he said, with admirable restraint. "If someone has taken the trouble to write an article about abortion I think it deserves to be published, even if the editor doesn't agree with what it says."

"Even if Adolf Hitler wrote a thousand words for the *Tribune* about why everyone in Donegal should wear jack-boots?"

"And please tell me, Lawrence, what are the chances of that happening?"

What might have been an interesting, thought-provoking debate on newspaper ethics descended into a schoolyard squabble. In the end, I stormed off home. John must have been really worried about the *Tribune* losing my journalistic talents, so upset, in fact, that we had no contact until I telephoned him three days later to apologize and ask if I was still invited to his mother's birthday party the following night.

"Of course," he said, as if nothing had happened.

The house was full when I arrived. Annie was sitting in her usual seat, surrounded by her oldest friends. She was dressed in her Sunday best. Her hair had been dyed for the third time in a month. (One sacrifice of old age was that Annie was a captive model for her two granddaughters who were training to be hairdressers. For her eighty-fifth birthday she had gone from sunrise blue to an early-Madonna blonde.)

I'd bought her a birthday present, a Maeve Binchy novel she flicked through and dismissed with a snort as a load of filth and pornography.

It was easy to forget, in an age of promiscuity and unfettered materialism, that there are still people around who live according to traditional values. Annie was truly a product of a more innocent age. In eighty-five years she had never traveled any farther than Derry. What was the point? Everything she needed was here in Donegal. She had a huge, loving family, a roof over her head and a faith that would have the Pope blushing with Catholic guilt.

"What d'you want to go to the cinema for? You were there last week," she chided me one night. She'd been to the pictures once, in 1952, to see *The Song of Bernadette* (a film about a nun that—judging by Annie's tone of approval—was not a daring examination of the sexual mores of convent life).

Annie was skeptical about things she decided were modern, like cinema and me. I suspected she viewed me as the earthly representative of metropolitan life and to her that was something little different from extraterrestrial life.

I wouldn't have minded her throwing the Maeve Binchy book in the bucket but it had cost me £16.99. John told me not to worry, he would give me a refund. He insisted that his mother liked me a lot. I wasn't convinced. Later, when she responded to my party rendition of "I Belong to Glasgow" with the offer of the bus fare back to Scotland I wasn't convinced at all.

Newt's Roots

For some unknown reason the man who turned up at the *Tribune*'s office one Wednesday afternoon to deliver stationery thought my surname was funnier than the collected works of Flann O'Brien. "Donegan?" he said, almost wetting his pants. "It's not, is it? You're kidding, aren't you?"

A lifetime spent sharing a surname with the man who sang "Does Your Chewing Gum Lose Its Flavor on the Bedpost Overnight?" had left me immune to any form of mockery. No doubt when this book wins the Nobel Prize for Literature the chairman of the judging panel will shake my hand, then lean over and ask, with a cheeky smile, "Any relation to Lonnie?" I won't mind if he does. I never do. But this was different. This guy was irritating.

It didn't help that he hated anyone who was English or Scottish. As soon as he'd heard my accent he started haranguing me about centuries of misery visited upon Ireland by the "bloody Brits." My grasp of Irish history is slight but judging from his tone he was under the mistaken impression that I was personally responsible for what had happened four hundred years ago. I was just about to tell him it was nothing to do with me, I was only a twinkle in William Wallace's eye at the time, when Francis jumped in as peacemaker.

"Don't mind, Lawrence, he's only joking," he said.

The hairs on the back of my neck were bristling like a bog brush but I let this gross misrepresentation pass. Civility was restored. The three of us exchanged banalities about weather and the price of staples. It was then that Ireland's most objectionable stationery supplier discovered my surname really was Donegan and lapsed into a convulsive fit.

"That's right, Donegan," I said, menacingly.

I could see Francis in the corner of my eye making frantic hand gestures. I ignored him. "Has been for a few years now. Ever since I was born in fact. D-O-N-E-G-A-N. You have a problem with that?"

"No, no." He laughed, clearly under the impression that he was getting revenge for the plantation of Ulster.

This wasn't the first time I'd been the subject of mirth in my adopted country. Ever since my name started appearing in the *Tribune* a steady trickle of people had come into the office for no other reason than to check that Donegan wasn't a pseudonym. I was beginning to feel paranoid. What was wrong with Donegan? Was it the Irish word for small penis? Or the Donegal vernacular for dog breath? Perhaps the Donegans were a notorious family of sheep seducers from Dungannon. Surely not. My grandfather came from Dungannon but he'd had thirteen children, a drink problem and a cousin who'd been in the IRA back in the 1950s. No doubt he would have been a hero to our Neanderthal stationery supplier.

I pondered these questions as I drove to Letterkenny to interview the owner of a bicycle shop. He'd telephoned that morning to say he'd found a green insect inside a box of Taiwanese mountain bikes. I was about to say, "Well, hold the front page, would you?" when I remembered that the *Tribune* couldn't afford to be—how can I put this?—as fussy as the likes of the *Guardian*.

When I got there the insect was on display in a jam jar by the till. The trip from Taiwan had clearly been too much. It was dead but still impressive, Day-Glo green and the size of a 10p coin.

A couple of customers came in. We stood around for five

minutes speculating what it might be. The shop-owner was clearly enjoying all the attention and retold his story in all its fascinating detail. When he finished I explained that the *Tribune* might be interested in carrying a short article but to stop the readers falling asleep mid-paragraph it might need jazzing up a little. Perhaps I could throw in a life-or-death struggle between man and insect when it jumped out of the Taiwanese box?

"No bother, Lawrence. Write whatever you want," he said. "Anything to sell a few bikes."

When I got back to the office I could hear laughter from the kitchen. John, Francis, Declan and Patrick were lost in a fug of pipe smoke. Phonsie, the Milford undertaker, was recounting in his mirthless voice the story of a local traveler family who had refused all offers of help in digging their patriarch's grave.

"It took them less than half an hour. The hole was only a couple of feet deep. The idea was that when Judgment Day came their man would be able to get out of his grave quicker than anyone else and be first in the queue to get to heaven."

The burial customs of Ireland's indigenous traveling community was a subject about which I knew little but the story carried the whiff of rural mythology. I said the story sounded like Donegal's equivalent of the vast underground caverns at Trafalgar Square stacked floor to ceiling with captured spaceships.

"I'm surprised to hear you say that, Mr. Donegan." Patrick laughed. "You're one of them yourself."

"What do you mean?"

"A traveler. A Donegan."

I looked at John, who slowly took his pipe from his mouth. "Oh, aye," he said, giving Phonsie a lesson in funereal solemnity. "I've been meaning to tell you this, Lawrence, but I've never found the right moment. You are a Donegan."

Everyone in the room started laughing. I was a Donegan—so?

John continued, "And, as anyone around here will tell you, the Donegans are the worst family in Donegal. They are drunks, gyppos, tramps, thieves. They are the ones responsible for every bit of trouble that happens in the county."

This was news to me. "Are they?"

"Of course not." He looked at me as if I was retarded. "But they're travelers so everybody just says, 'What the fuck?' and blames them for it anyway. We're like that in Ireland—*Céad míle fáilte*, unless you're a gyppo."

John had a point. Ireland had been consumed with the fate of some Romanian refugees who'd recently turned up in Wexford, a town described in one of my guidebooks as one of the friendliest in the country. Clearly, no one had told the *Wexford Leader*. The local paper had accused the Romanians of living in luxury at the taxpayers' expense, frightening old ladies and trying to get young Irishwomen pregnant to secure passports. Maybe Bucharest was buzzing with the news that pensioners in Wexford scared easily and the women took lessons in chastity from Heidi Fleiss. But I had my doubts.

So did a lot of people. The *Leader*'s thoughtful intervention had caused a national uproar. The *Irish Times* led the way, quoting a poem by W. B. Yeats that, for once, I could actually make sense of:

> *Hurrah for revolution and more cannon shot;*
> *A beggar upon horseback lashes a beggar upon foot;*
> *Hurrah for revolution and cannon come again,*
> *The beggars have changed places but the lash goes on.*

and pointing out that it was a bit rich for anyone in Ireland to be snotty toward immigrants when so many of their own were dotted around the world. It wasn't so long ago that Ireland was the "beggar."

More often than not, when there were no Romanian immigrants around to pick on, Ireland's traveling community caught the flak for living in luxury at taxpayers' expense. But—and this is the absolutely vital point—such was the travelers' animal cunning that they hid this opulent lifestyle behind life expectancy statistics ten years below the national average and infant mortality three times worse than the rest of Ireland. What's more, some traveler families endured living conditions that would have earned a sharp rebuke from the RSPCA if animals had been subjected to the same.

This isn't to say that all travelers were saints. They weren't. Some of them had an unhealthy appetite for family feuds. No one really knew why the Wards hated the McDonaghs but it was a generally accepted tenet of Irish life that if both clans were in town on the same night it was best to stay indoors and watch *Coronation Street*.

The litter allegedly left by "transients"—am I being too sensitive or does that word have a curl on its lip?—when they abandoned a site was another perennial whinge, as if no one in Ireland had ever rolled down the car window on a summer's afternoon and thrown away an ice-cream wrapper. Only that morning there had been a story on the radio about the Catholic Church taking legal action against families who'd parked their caravans next to the holy shrine at Knock.

"No doubt the priest would have called the cops if Joseph and Mary had turned up on Christmas Eve with their donkey," John said, then relit his pipe. When the smoke cleared he was grinning and I knew he'd just had an idea.

• • •

It took me two days to find the Donegans. The idea was that I'd write a story about trying to find my long-lost relatives. All John wanted was a folksy modern parable about how we are all the same underneath the skin. If I could be rude about that shower of so-called Christians in Knock, he said, I might get a bonus.

I visited every travelers' caravan in Letterkenny.

A couple of things occurred to me as I was making my rounds. First, no one was living in luxury. Admittedly, one woman had a pay phone and another family had a satellite television dish, but I figured that must have been God's way of compensating them for the rats I saw cavorting around in the uncollected rubbish lying outside their caravan. Almost without exception the adults I spoke to had the listless air of the permanently unhealthy. The children all had stalactites of snot hanging from their noses. It was all depressingly Dickensian.

Second, the people couldn't have been friendlier or more helpful. Too helpful in one case. "The Donegans? They're all in Derry," the woman with the phone said. "I'll give them a call. Get them to come over and collect you." I had a vision of being conscripted just in time for the mother of all family feuds between the Donegans and the McDonaghs.

"No, no. Please no," I said, grabbing the receiver from her. I explained I wanted to find the Donegan brothers from Letterkenny.

She looked puzzled. "They're all dead, except one, John Donegan."

"That's him. I want to interview him for the *Tribune*."

She laughed. "What would anyone want to interview John Donegan for? He's probably fighting up the town center or lying drunk somewhere." I made a mental note to write her out of my story. I don't think she'd read the W. B. Yeats poem.

She said John Donegan's caravan was parked outside the cathedral. It wasn't but there were four others, cream-colored and propped up on bricks amid the bedlam of kids, dogs and a cold-water fountain spraying from a hole in the ground where the council standpipe used to be. Soaked and down to the last dregs of journalistic curiosity, I got talking to a middle-aged man, the worse for sherry, who directed me to a battered little caravan parked by the side of one of the town's busiest roads.

John Donegan was at home, staring blankly through an open door. He looked a picture of ill-health, with translucent skin and a cough that sounded like a shovel on gravel. His caravan was hardly bigger than a dog's kennel. Its roof leaked. The cracked windows were held together by insulation tape. In a battle of nauseous smells, the malfunctioning fridge narrowly beat off the fumes from the petrol station next door. It fitted no one's definition of luxury, not even the *Wexford Leader*'s.

We spent an hour chatting though mostly at cross-purposes. He was partially deaf and I struggled to fathom his uncompromising Donegal brogue. His story was one of itinerant hardship: he never went to school, emigrated to Scotland at the age of thirteen to look for work, came back to Ireland when he was forty. His life was a procession of shitty second-hand caravans and bad health.

John wasn't my long-lost cousin, or my long-lost anything. All we had in common was our mothers' birthday—20 July— and an uncanny sense of the folksy sentiment that would appeal to the editor of the *Tirconaill Tribune*. "There's no one above me, Lawrence," he said, as I was leaving. "Not you, not the priests, not God. We're all the same as each other."

I told him I couldn't agree more.

However, on reflection I am prepared to make an exception for the gentleman at the natural-history museum in Dublin who picked up the phone when I called to ask about the Taiwanese bike insect. He was lower than pond life.

"We only deal in Irish insects," he said, unhelpfully.

I explained that an insect had been bugging me for two weeks and that my editor believed it was the biggest story to hit Ireland since Charles Parnell took up with Kitty O'Shea. I told him if I didn't find out what it was I could end up as a laborer on a mushroom farm.

His apathy was unshakeable. "There are three million insects in the world. How am I to know what they all are? The good Lord didn't print the names on the backside of every one."

I was about to point out that it was just as well Alexander Graham Bell hadn't shared his lack of scientific curiosity otherwise we'd have been conducting our conversation using two paper cups and a 110-mile length of string when John came into the office. He looked as excited as I'd ever seen him, which is to say rather than wearing a half-smile he was positively beaming.

"Forget the insect," he said, when I put down the phone. "Do you know someone called Newt Gingrich?"

"Not personally."

"Well, smart-arse, he's coming to Donegal tomorrow to trace his Irish roots."

"Gingrich is an Irish name?"

"No, but Doherty is. He claims he's a Doherty."

The Doherty Clan Centre was on Inch Island, on the Inishowen peninsula. Gingrich was scheduled to turn up at 9:30 A.M. This was a big story. It wasn't every day that the Speaker of the United States House of Representatives turned up on the *Tribune*'s doorstep. I assumed John, as the editor, would want to be there for such an occasion. But he insisted that I go, saying, "After all, you're the genealogy correspondent."

John had garlanded me with this title after the article about John Donegan. He was delighted with it and spent a lavish amount of time dreaming up a headline, THE DONEGANS: TWO OF A KIND, then a sub-headline, *A Heart-warming Tale of Two Soul Brothers*. The readers responded with equal enthusiasm. A subscriber from California even took the trouble to write a short history of the Donegans and sent it in.

Apparently, we are a noble and warlike clan. Scholars had traced fifty variants of the name Donegan. My most famous kinsman was Thomas Donegan, framer of the celebrated New York Donegan Charter of 1686. I was grateful for the interest but reading page after tedious page of this stuff I couldn't help but think, Who cares?

The answer is that a scarily large number of people do care. A whole industry has been built around people tracing their "Irish roots." There are Irish genealogy clubs all over the world. Believe it or not, there are more websites devoted to Irish family trees than there are to photographs of Cameron Diaz naked (I've checked). Enthusiasts even have their own magazine, *Irish Roots*, which is full of fascinating articles about the surnames of Irish Brigade officers who took part in the American Revolution, and doubles up as a handy cure for insomnia. According to Board Fáilte, seventy thousand tourists visited Ireland in 1997 to look up their ancestors. More importantly, they spent £30 million while they were at it. The numbers are expected to double within five years.

The tourist board's target audience is the United States, where forty-five million people of voting age were said to be of Irish descent. I couldn't quite believe this figure but driving through the horizontal rain toward Inch Island the following morning it occurred to me that if Newt Gingrich, prospective candidate for the American presidency, was prepared to travel to Donegal on a day like this in a feeble attempt to suck up to the Irish-American community then it just might be true.

Inch Island was connected to the mainland by a mile-long causeway. I had been told that it was an exceptionally pretty place but this was hard to judge through the thick gray murk. I dismissed the idea of sightseeing and drove directly to the Doherty Clan Centre. Or, at least, I intended to. Like most places of any significance in Donegal, the Centre wasn't signposted. (Francis assured me that 75 percent of Ireland's road signs have been stolen and now adorn the walls of Irish-themed pubs in California.)

I drove aimlessly around the island for a while. There was no sign of life, no house lights flickering in the gloom, no cars, no children on their way to school, just an inhospitable wind howling across open fields.

Eventually I came across the sub–post office. I hammered on the door for five minutes without any response and was just about to leave when a post van arrived.

"Where is everyone?" I said, as cheerily as I could.

"Haven't you heard who's coming today? Newt Gingrich," the postman replied in that are-you-thick? manner public servants across the world adopt when they're faced with polite inquiries from the general public.

"Yes I know, to the Clan Centre. Can you tell me where it is?"

He shook his head in disbelief and pointed to a large white house on the other side of the road. "There."

I'd driven past it four times. I just hadn't noticed the huge American flag flapping in the gale or the huddle of people sheltering under multi-colored golf umbrellas on the front lawn. From the outside the Clan Centre was an impressive Georgian mansion. I began to suspect that something had gone terribly wrong when I saw the two plastic battleaxes nailed to the wall on either side of the front door. I stepped inside and knew straight away that I was right. It was a citadel of tack, a festival in blue woodchip wallpaper. The furniture was dark and heavy, the carpets threadbare. The walls were decorated with ancient portraits—Spanish admirals, women with Barbara Stanwyck hairdos and Fred MacMurray features, Evita—and clan regalia so amateurish it looked like something I'd made in school woodwork class. The room smelt of decay, as if it had been empty for a generation.

A few people were milling around. A middle-aged man was issuing instructions. He was wearing a dark blue suit and floral tie but looked uncomfortable, as if he was dressed formally for the first time since his wedding.

I assumed he was the man in charge. I introduced myself. He told me he was the clan chieftain and asked if I would help carry a table through to the Ohio Room.

The Ohio Room was much like the entrance hall, except darker and mustier. The table was laid out with mismatched crockery and plates of cream cakes that rotted your teeth just looking at them. The kitchen was next door. I could hear someone being scolded for forgetting to put the kettle on.

My antennae can sense acute embarrassment at five hundred paces. They were twitching frantically at the thought of one of the world's most powerful politicians trying to refuse a cup of lukewarm tea and a lethal chocolate éclair without offending his hosts and forty-five million Irish-American voters. I'll be honest. My heart sang with joy at this prospect. Not because I had anything against the Doherty clan but because Newt Gingrich happened to be one of my least favorite politicians in the world; one of my least favorite people, in fact.

Don't get me wrong. I admired Newt for building a career on "family values" while conveniently forgetting that he once visited his cancer-stricken wife in hospital to tell her he was having an affair and wanted a divorce. How could anyone fail to be impressed by the first House Speaker in history to be fined for breaking congressional ethics rules who still had the chutzpah to lecture Bill Clinton about morality? If a hypocrite could persuade the Irish-American community to vote him president just because his great-grandad once owned a croft in Donegal, then you just have to shake your head and say, "That's politics." I was just delighted that he would have to squirm a little in the process.

Newt was delayed by the weather, which by now was pleasingly foul. With any luck he'd catch a cold as well.

As we waited I found myself trapped by the clan historian and forced to listen to his interminable stories about great Dohertys down the ages. They were an undistinguished bunch, actually, enlivened only by the tendentious inclusion of Eva Perón on the grounds that her Spanish maiden name (de Duarte) sounds like Doherty as pronounced by a drunk. Thankfully John Hume—yes, the Nobel Peace Prize winner—arrived and the Doherty clan's answer to A. J. P. Taylor dashed off to shake his hand.

The reception area was packed by now. In the crush I found myself next to an attractive blonde New Yorker called Barbara. She'd arrived at the Clan Centre the day before on the off chance someone could help trace her great-grandmother. She stayed for the night and woke up to discover she would be having breakfast with her worst nightmare. "Newt Gingrich." She sighed, clearly still in shock. "I can't stand the guy. He's a creep."

The two of us got along famously.

John Hume must have had enough clan history for one day because before too long he'd joined in our conversation. I was deeply impressed. It was hard to imagine a more down-to-earth and thoughtful politician. I was just about to explain to Mr.

Hume, because I'm sure he was itching to know, my ideas for bringing the Irish Peace Process to a successful conclusion when the cry went up from outside, "He's here."

There was a smoothing of dresses and straightening of ties. Through the crush I could see the familiar helmet of gray hair in the doorway. It really was Newt Gingrich, the third most powerful politician in the U.S.A. I'd never been in the same room with someone so powerful. When he walked into the room I could have sworn, and Barbara agreed, the air temperature dropped by ten degrees.

Behind Newt trailed a steely-faced female, who I later discovered was his press officer, carrying a briefcase. She was followed by a photographer, Mrs. Gingrich and two secret servicemen with bulges under their jackets (presumably it would be their job to shoot whoever had baked the cream cakes).

"Wonderful," Newt cried, as he surveyed the room. He was either a fantastic actor or had never been to a house-clearance sale before. "Just wonderful. Oh, look, a photograph of a Spanish admiral. Look, darling, a photograph of a Spanish admiral. Wonderful. Evita. Is that Evita? It is. Wonderful. Fantastic."

Once Newt had calmed down, the clan chieftain made a short speech welcoming him to Donegal. John Hume then told the story of how he met the Speaker at a White House dinner on St. Patrick's Day and discovered that both their mothers were called Doherty. The clan historian then gave a lecture about great Dohertys down the ages.

A procession of local dignitaries then shuffled forward to present Newt with a variety of Doherty clan certificates. He received them graciously, promised to hang them on the wall of his Washington office and handed them to his press secretary who rolled her eyes.

The clan chieftain stepped forward once the presentations were over. "And now the bad news," he began, sheepishly.

My ears pricked up. Barbara started giggling. People started murmuring. The clan chieftain stumbled on: "The thing is, Mr. Gingrich, we can't find any record of your family tree on our database of two million names. Perhaps if you could provide us with more information . . ."

A politician friend of mine once told me that there were two golden rules in politics: never get caught in bed with anyone younger than your daughter (or your daughter), and never ask a question if you don't know the answer.

Newt had broken one of the golden rules.

Some politicians have the ability to retain a semblance of composure in the most stressful of circumstances. This is a talent that separates world statesmen from mere mortals who hang around on the fringes of politics, like press officers and journalists. This probably explains why Newt kept smiling and his press officer looked as if she wanted to wrestle the clan chieftain to the floor before he said another word. But it was too late. Forty-five million Irish Americans now knew that Newt Gingrich wasn't one of them. Oh, deep joy. Barbara and I hugged like two lovers at the end of a long war.

The honored guest disappeared into a side room to be filmed by the BBC. The party dispersed. I sidled over to his press secretary to ask if Newt would mind being interviewed for the *Tirconaill Tribune*.

"One question," she barked, with a look that said, "Any more than one question, I'll rip your head off and stuff these clan certificates in the hole."

I toyed with the idea of asking him about his first wife ("How did you break the news of the divorce, Mr. Gingrich? 'How's the cancer, darling? By the way, have you met my next wife?' "), or the story in *Vanity Fair* magazine about his 1979 visit to a Washington hotel with a professor's wife ("You didn't, you old Republican rascal, did you?").

In the end I went for something topical: "Now that you've lost the Irish-American vote, Mr. Gingrich, does this mean you have now got less chance than me of becoming American president?"

After fifteen minutes Newt emerged from the side room, shook hands with the clan chieftain and thanked him for all his help. He declined the offer of tea and cake, saying he had an urgent appointment elsewhere, and strode purposefully out of the Doherty Clan Centre—never to be seen again, if I'm not mistaken.

He didn't hear my shouted question, or pretended not to, until he reached the car. He opened the door then spun round and glared at me. "What did you say?"

I asked him again, more meekly this time, "Now that you're officially not an Irishman, Mr. Speaker, would you agree that you've got no chance of becoming president?"

The words "Not at all, son" squeezed out through his thin-lipped smile but his eyes said, "Go fuck yourself."

Five Sorrowful Mysteries

Life in Creeslough wasn't always an exciting whirl of visits from foreign dignitaries. Quite often it was nothing other than sitting at home watching cockroaches formation-dancing across the kitchen floor while the ceaseless rain that passed for springtime weather in Donegal drummed on the windows.

I'll be honest. The novelty of rural life was beginning to wear off. I was spending a lot of time on my own in the cottage—an experience that inspired existential crises and passing fads. I tried teaching myself French. I did sit-ups and press-ups. I grew a selection of beards. I was Lenin for a week, Tom Waits for an hour, and late-period George Michael for thirty seconds. Just before bedtime I often closed my eyes and imagined that when I opened them again Christina Ricci would be lying on the fire-side rug wearing only a glistening coat of body lotion. I was so bored that I even got out of bed one Sunday morning and went to church.

Catholicism and I had been estranged for many years. I blamed my grandmother for imposing a strict dress code on my childhood attendances at mass. This was the 1970s, when pre-pubescent boys weren't allowed to say, "Push off, Grandma." I suffered in silence every week while she dressed me in purple Crimplene trousers, checked jackets with lapels as wide as a whale's fins, white socks and spats. I looked like a trainee pimp.

As I was saying, I was bored. I figured that going to church dressed in clothes selected by myself might be a way of exorcizing the painful sartorial memories. Mass was at 11 A.M. I got up at 10:45, slipped on my jeans and a *Wayne's World* T-shirt, made my hair as untidy as I could and set off in the car.

One depressing feature of the rural Irish landscape is that the local church is invariably the grandest building for miles. I'd lost count of the times I'd driven through pretty little villages that had been despoiled by a grandiose chapel and house that looked far too big for one man who, we were given to understand, did very little entertaining. More often than not there was a fancy car in the driveway. Small wonder that respect for the church in Ireland was at an all-time low when parishioners saw their hard-earned donations being spent on Volvos and buildings that appeared to have been modeled on Liberace's mansion.

Creeslough's chapel was a more modest affair, although St. Michael the Archangel—to give it its full name—wasn't exactly a shack. Uniquely, however, it was restrained, designed in the shape of Muckish Mountain and built with obvious care by the local tradesmen whose names were etched round the doorway. The interior was spacious and filled with natural light, the pews were laid out in a semi-circle in front of the altar. Not that I'm Frank Lloyd Wright or anything, but to my eyes it was tasteful.

By the time I arrived there was hardly a seat to spare. I squeezed into the back row beside a harassed young mother who was battling to stop her baby ripping the hat off the woman in front. I read the parish newsletter while we waited for the service to start and was gratified to see the editor had plagiarized my article about Creeslough Hall. Eventually the church band struck up. The priest appeared as if by magic. It wasn't exactly Las Vegas but it was definitely a flashier show than I recall. When I was last at church the music was provided by an organist who appeared to have had a terrible accident in a sawmill. Now there were guitars and recorders and tambourines. If memory serves me right, guitars were only one step up from condoms in the Devil's armory in the old days.

The service itself hadn't changed much in the intervening years. It was still the same old threats of eternal damnation and the sermon was so boring that even the priest looked as if he couldn't be bothered to pay attention—no one did. Three-quarters of the way through he asked us to show a sign of friendship to our neighbors, just like Diana Ross does in the middle of her concerts. It *was* Las Vegas. I shook hands with the young mother and got a palmful of baby dribble for my trouble.

Thankfully, it was all over in forty minutes. The congregation spilled out on to the street, filling the air with excited chatter. I bumped into Michael Kelly and Johnny Connolly. I hadn't spoken to Young Johnny since the cattle market. I was delighted to discover that I hadn't put him out of business. Michael gave me a row for missing Gaelic football training. "If you don't train you won't get a game."

My heart leapt. "You mean I might get a game?"

He smiled knowingly. "Stranger things have happened."

On the way home I stopped off at the supermarket. I bought an Amazonian forest's worth of Sunday newspapers and enough food to feed an army of Christian soldiers. I was planning to have a four-hour breakfast.

"Don't tell me you've been to mass," Danny Lafferty said.

"That's right. I've signed up. I'm going to be a lance corporal in the army of the Lord."

I hate to admit this but I felt strangely euphoric. I'd actually enjoyed the experience of going to mass—not the religious part but the act of attending. I think the reason was this: the occasion had a sense of a whole community coming together. This is something you experience only at New Year in cities like London and Glasgow and only then if you're prepared to wade through pools of vomit and pay a twenty-pound surcharge on the taxi ride home. Mass seemed to be as much a social event as it was a spiritual one. People were pleased to see each other and their happiness was infectious. I felt as if I belonged.

I must have had a reasonable time because I went back the following week and the week after that. I can't say I was converted but I started to wear an ironed shirt and polished shoes on Sunday mornings. And when John asked if I'd mind doing a few religious stories rather than saying, "You must be joking," as I would have done a couple of months before, I found myself nodding enthusiastically.

The *Tribune*'s relationship with the Catholic Church was best described as sunny with occasional thunderstorms. There had been a long-running feud with some local nuns, who tried to sell a house bought with public donations and keep the profits. It cumulated with a phone call that started with one of the sisters telling John he couldn't speak to the Mother Superior because she had gone to the bank and ended with him replying, "Well, it must be the sperm bank she's gone to because it's eight o'clock at night."

Every issue carried at least three photographs of different priests, two of the local bishop, an interview with a returning missionary and one snide comment in the editorial about the latest Church scandal involving fornicating bishops. (Which reminds me: why does every edition of the *Irish Times* ever published carry a story that starts, "A 67-year-old priest was yesterday charged with seventeen offenses relating to incidents in a vestry at . . ."?)

We were spiritually agnostic but commercially devout. One afternoon I suggested we change our name to the *Tirconaill Tablet*.

"In case you haven't noticed, Lawrence, Ireland is a religious country. There's a market for this kind of thing," John said, with one of his I'll-get-you-back looks. Which he did.

For a while life was a seamless conversation with gray-haired men in black suits and clerical collars telling dull stories about how they had spent their lives doing starving Africans a favor by introducing them to the Word of the Lord. As if that would fill their bellies.

But there was one priest I liked. He was over sixty, wore an Eddie Cochran quiff and swore a lot. He'd just come back from an island in the South Pacific. "It's famous for its women," he informed me, with what looked remarkably like a wink. As far as I could judge, this priest had single-handedly saved the island community from extinction by teaching the locals agricultural techniques he had picked up as a young man in Donegal. He was a great man. I thought that was worth more than a quarter of a page in the *Tirconaill Tribune*.

"You're turning into a religious maniac," Francis said, when I demanded he set aside two pages for the story. "Of course, it'll never last."

"Of course it will last," I insisted.

It didn't last.

The turning point was an interview with a particularly unpleasant priest that ended with him calling me unChristian and me accidentally-on-purpose spilling tea into the sanctimonious old git's lap. I told John to find another ambassador to God. He didn't say a word. The following night we were sitting in the office when he announced that the two of us should go for a drive. "Just for the fun of it," he said.

I should have known then that something was up. John never did much just for the fun of it. In fact, he never did anything apart from take the dog for walks and work. I knew it wasn't always that way. Francis told me that years ago John was the sound and lighting technician for the local theater in his spare time. Nowadays he didn't go near a theater, or the cinema, or even into a bar for a drink.

The idea of him going for a recreational drive in the country was odd but I was happy to tag along. A couple of hours together would give me a chance to straighten out something that had been niggling me.

I'd been on the *Tribune* for two months now. Like everyone else in the county I got along famously with Francis. But it was different with John. He and I weren't exactly best buddies. At least, not in the way I understood the description. I didn't know that much about him, except that he owned a newspaper, had sexy nieces and a mother with the comic timing of George Burns. I was sure he suspected I was some kind of down-shifting dilettante who would be off home at the end of the week. I wanted to let him know that I was grateful for the job and that as long as I didn't have to interview any more priests I wanted to stay at the *Tribune* for good. Donegal was my home.

We drove to a beautiful wilderness called the Glenveagh estate, parked the car and went for a walk across the heathland. I gave him my spiel about wanting to work for the *Tribune* for the rest of my life and how I'd like us to be proper friends. He looked embarrassed, then changed the subject and told me a story I'd never heard before. It sent a chill down my spine.

In November 1997 a Derry-born housewife based in Alabama, U.S.A., ran for election as president of Ireland. You may have heard of her in another context. Her name was Dana, winner of the 1970 Eurovision Song Contest with "All Kinds of Everything"—a song so saccharine that scientists once believed repeated listenings could be the cure for diabetes. Alas, the side effects were awful: nausea, vomiting, an irritating skin rash . . .

Dana's politics had pretty much the same effect on me. Her campaigning mostly consisted of singing a cappella versions of her biggest hit. This made it difficult to judge where she stood on the issues of the day but it seemed she wanted a return to good old Christian family values and strong discipline—Billy Graham meets George Graham, you could say.

The history books show that Dana finished a respectable third out of five candidates in the election, with 18 percent of the ballot. But in one remote Irish village the former Eurovision songbird won 90 percent of all the votes cast. African despots spend most of their lives arranging that kind of support in elections. Dana did it legitimately. Needless to say it was by some distance the greatest proportion of the vote she secured in any single community in Ireland. When the election was over Dana returned to the village in question for an encore. She hosted a celebration party in the function room of the local pub to thank the people for showing the world that at least some parts of her homeland were still good Christian places.

The village's name? Creeslough. Now I understood why there were never any empty seats in church.

Darkness began to blur the shadowless brown landscape. The sky faded rapidly from cream to violet to inky blue. We drove home the long way, through Termon and Church Hill. John did his impersonation of a tour guide. "And now we see Wilkins Pub where Yehudi Menuhin once volunteered to play and the landlord asked everyone in the bar for 'a bit of hush please 'cause Hughie McMenamin here is goin' to give us a tune on his fiddle,'" and so—less excitingly—on.

We came to a crossroads. Instead of heading back toward the main road we turned right along a pot-holed road. It got narrower and narrower until we were driving through a tunnel of trees. Suddenly the forest opened up. We were in a clearing so lush and calm and infested with midges that it felt like summer the first time.

"Where are we?" I'd had enough bonding for one night and

was desperate to get home to find out if Christina Ricci had materialized yet.

"Calm yourself," John said. "You're about to have a religious experience."

Two people circling the bush in the center of the clearing in their bare feet gave away the mystery. He'd brought me to the Doon Well, Donegal's answer to Lourdes. I had heard about this place. It was famous, in as much as anything in Donegal was famous. People came from all over Ireland to pray barefoot for the sick. They filled containers full of "healing" water drawn from the well to take home.

The remnants of illnesses past were scattered under the bush, mostly asthma inhalers and broken crutches triumphantly speared into the ground. We speculated for a few minutes on what had been wrong with the woman who'd left her knickers tied to the highest branch.

John knew the couple who owned the house at the well. The front door was open. He gave it the slightest of knocks and marched in without waiting for a reply. People were always walking unannounced into houses in Donegal. It was one of the things I liked most about the place. I guessed they felt comfortable doing it because there was never any danger of embarrassment; no walking in on orgies, or crack dens or Mormon prayer meetings.

When we went into the living room it was as if we'd been expected all day. We'd hardly sat down in front of the fire when the woman of the house, Mary, bustled in from the kitchen with a tray of tea and biscuits.

John explained that I was just some atheist cynic up from the city who didn't believe all this religious mumbo-jumbo about healing waters. Mary tut-tutted and told me it was a simple fact that the water at Doon Well had healing powers.

We stayed for an hour. Mary gave me a book about the well's history and showed us old photographs of crowds gathering to hear mass. She told us countless stories of people who'd been cured over the years. She was clever, funny and so obviously honest that I wanted to believe every word she said.

"Isn't religious faith a wonderful thing that it can give people so much hope?" John said, as we walked back out to the car. I said I couldn't agree more. How was I to know he was softening me up?

The pilgrims' bus left Creeslough at 8:13 A.M. At 8:13 A.M. and twenty-five seconds the saddest voice in Ireland droned out across the intercom, "Okay now, folks. Let's start with the five sorrowful mysteries."

The journey to Knock took four hours. Or two hundred decades of the rosary. Whatever the measurement it was torture, a slow death by a thousand Hail Marys. I didn't even have the luxury of a seat to myself. The annual pilgrimage to Ireland's holiest shrine was the diocesan FA Cup final. The sold-out signs went up weeks ago but John had contacts, unfortunately.

"Come on, one more religious story. I've got you a ticket for the bus," he said.

"Fuck off," I replied, irreligiously.

"Remember Doon Well, all that stuff you were saying about religious faith and hope?"

The alternatives were a youth-club sponsored walk or a Samaritans' jumble sale.

"No more priests after this—promise?"

"As God is my witness."

The only seat left was next to a heater with only two settings, hot and hair-sizzling. The ergonomic genius who'd designed the bus had forgotten to install windows that opened. By the end of the five Glorious mysteries the atmosphere was sub-tropical. General murmurings of discomfort began to circulate. Everyone was over the age of sixty, except a handful of children press-ganged into keeping their grandparents company, and me.

There was an air-vent in the roof that Arnold Schwarzenegger in his prime might have been able to force open. I was volunteered for the job. It took twenty minutes and the lever broke off in my hand, but I did open it in the end. A rush of cool air flooded in and I sat down to a burst of applause.

This was exactly what I didn't want. I had hoped to sleep for the whole journey—anything to avoid religious participation—but my cover had been blown. I was a hero. The woman I was sitting next to offered me one of her evil-smelling tuna sandwiches. A trawl of the bus produced a spare set of rosary beads.

"Remind me, how do these work again?" I asked my new best friend, as we embarked on the five Glorious mysteries for the fourth time of the day. I must have been doing something right because we hadn't even got to the end of mystery number two when the bus pulled into the car park at Knock. This was glorious indeed.

There is no kind way of saying this. Knock was a dump, a depressing compilation of greasy-spoon cafés and stalls selling every kind of religious tat imaginable, from Virgin Mary cuckoo clocks at twenty-five pounds to "I prayed for you at Knock" plastic water holders (priced at an extortionate £1). All of it was displayed in untidy heaps or stuffed willy-nilly into packing cases. It was as if burglars had ransacked the entire town and departed empty-handed in disgust.

In the midst of the disarray stood a huge church with a spire that stretched into the sky like Fireball XL5. The best that could be said of the building was that it was an innocent victim of the 1970s fashion for prefabricated concrete blocks. Its saving grace was the gardens, advertised in one brochure as "a tranquil haven where the pilgrim can spend some time thinking about all that Knock stands for." They were and I did.

Cynics insist the story of Knock is the nineteenth-century version of the "I saw Elvis in my local supermarket" stories that turn up once a year in reputable newspapers like the *Daily Sport*.

On August 21, 1879, Knock was just another village in the west of Ireland, with a post office, a church and a handful of cottages. That night the Virgin Mary, accompanied by a few friends and a pet lamb, appeared near the gable end of the parish church and floated around for a couple of hours. Now, this must be true. Two Church inquiries decided it was. Presumably, they were in no way influenced by the possible embarrassment for the Church if it was found that generations of pilgrims had been duped by a handful of imaginative villagers trying to drum up business for the tat stalls.

Within days of the apparition pilgrims flocked from all over the country. The local churchman, Archdeacon Cavanagh, kept a record of those who had recovered after visiting the shrine. It was on display in the Knock folk museum and was nothing if not sensational. People were supposed to have been cured of all sorts of diseases in those first few months, from cancer to epilepsy and something called "a rolling of the eyes." But my favorite entry featured a parishioner from Kilmovee: "**EVIL**. John Flynn, of Cloonmanagh. Cured of an evil. Medical remedies had all been tried in vain."

Even allowing for the Archdeacon's lack of medical expertise this was a little bit on the vague side. The truth is that all of his entries were heavy on wild assertion and light on hard fact. But no one seemed to mind. Cavanagh's diaries became famous the world over and people just kept flooding into Knock. They've never stopped coming—one million a year at the last count.

Judging by the crowds as I walked from the folk museum back to the Our Lady Queen of Ireland basilica, most of them had turned up that day. There were queues to take confession, at the candle stall and the holy-water taps. The service wasn't due to start for another hour but already the church was filling up. I'd made a solemn vow never to attend mass again and headed off in another direction in a taxi to the airport.

Less spiritual observers will tell you that the real miracle of Knock is that a tiny Irish village with a permanent population of less than three hundred somehow managed to acquire its very own international airport. Figuring out exactly how this happened is Ireland's national sport after Gaelic football and hurling. Some people are content to believe that it was the Good Lord's work. Others claimed that the CIA stumped up cash so that U.S. planes could use Knock in the event of the Third World War breaking out. The latter version inspired the great Christy Moore to write a song.

My own personal theory, gleaned from a book I bought at the shrine bookshop called *The Memoirs of Monsignor James Horan*, is that it happened because of one man: Monsignor James Horan.

Not even Monsignor Horan's friends—and he had plenty of them, especially in high places—would describe him as a modest man or lacking in grand ambition. In a parallel universe he is probably building casinos in Las Vegas right now. Somehow he ended up as the parish priest at Knock. That was in 1963. Within twenty-five years he had turned a ramshackle religious shrine in the back of beyond into a ramshackle religious shrine in the back of beyond with a gargantuan church and a landing strip capable of handling everything from tourist charters to Stealth bombers.

How did he manage it? Energy, public donations and—according to Father Horan—a refusal to go away when people laughed in his face and said that spending £13 million on converting a County Mayo bog into an airport would be like tossing the money onto a bonfire.

Horan's persistence paid off in the end. Knock Airport was formally opened in May 1986. Within three years it was turning a profit and was heralded as Europe's fastest growing airport. Today, the priest's airport is used not only by pilgrims but by tourists, émigrés and businessmen who can't bear the tortuous drive home at the weekend. It is generally accepted as a masterpiece of regional economic development, a crucial factor in the financial well-being of the west coast of Ireland. If I couldn't admire Horan's church then I was more than happy to admire his airport.

I sat in the observation lounge for a couple of hours engrossed in his memoirs, until it was safe to go back to the village. Mass was over. There was just enough time before the bus left to grab a pint in Knock's only pub and buy an apparition snowstorm and musical Our Lady statue that played "Ave Maria" as presents for John.

The day had clearly sated everyone's appetite for saying the rosary. Mercifully, the first half of the journey passed off quietly. We stopped briefly just beyond Sligo, at Drumcliffe, where W. B. Yeats is buried in the churchyard beneath the flat-topped Benbulben Mountain.

The poet's great-grandfather was rector at Drumcliffe. Yeats was taken there on holiday as a child. The church itself clearly hadn't had a lick of paint ever since. It was sad to see that the poet's grave was scruffier than you'd expect for a literary colossus. Thankfully, neglect and the passage of time hadn't damaged the inscription on the gravestone, written by Yeats himself:

Cast a cold eye
On life, on death.
Horseman, pass by!

Now that's what I call an epitaph.

Unfortunately the sight of a church set the religious impulses racing again. The bus had barely pulled out of the car park when the voice of doom boomed over the intercom and we embarked on yet more rosaries. I surrendered and joined in.

I've obviously got a talent for praying because we stopped after just twenty minutes and had a singsong instead. The woman sitting next to me dashed up to the microphone and sang a hymn called "Lady of Knock" that was catchier than anything by the Spice Girls. Trust me, I still can't get the tune out of my head.

Someone else sang a Gaelic song. A couple of kids had a go at Aqua's "Barbie Girl." The journey home turned into a bit of a party. The voice of doom even told a couple of jokes, which were bad but a lot funnier than the five sorrowful mysteries.

By the time we reached Creeslough the party was in full swing. I was one of only three people who got off the bus. Everyone else was going home to villages out in the west of the county. I stood by the roadside and watched a row of smiling faces slowly scroll past as the bus drew away. I smiled back. The pilgrimage was clearly a highlight of the year for these people. They'd prayed a lot, filled their bottles full of holy water and reaffirmed their faith. I could respect that. I was happy that Knock had made them happy. But I was happier still that I'd never see the godforsaken place again.

Father Tierney Park Blues

In my dream it happened at Croke Park on All-Ireland Sunday. Sixty thousand fans. The green and gold shirts of an historic Donegal team: Langan, Carr, Sheridan, Sheridan, McClafferty, McGarvey, McGinley, Gallagher, Baird, Gallagher, McNulty, McFadden, McLaughlin, McGinley and the rookie sensation, Donegan, the first county ever to reach the All-Ireland with fifteen players from a single club. The club's name? St. Michael's (Reserves). The players gathered centerfield. "Play up for the county lads," said Donegal's legendary football manager Liam Ferry, a man who combined tactical genius with the saintly vocabulary of Mother Teresa. "And, remember, no rough stuff. Keep your elbows to yourself."

Then I woke from a gentle sleep . . .

For weeks I'd been hearing stories that Danny Lafferty planned to stand for the local council. When I mentioned in the shop one morning that an electoral register application form had arrived in the post I knew straight away that the rumors were true.

I didn't think I would be eligible to vote in Ireland.

"You never know. You should fill it in anyway. It's important that people like you should have a voice," Danny said.

What was the point in me having a voice? I wouldn't have known what to say. I knew the names of the Republic's two main political parties were Fianna Fáil and Fine Gael but I had absolutely no idea what they stood for. I'd been to a couple of council meetings and they'd left me bewildered. What were they talking about? Why were they arguing? Frankly, if there had been an election in Creeslough that morning I wouldn't have known who to vote for—unless, of course, there was a candidate I could support out of blind personal loyalty.

"You are thinking about running, Danny, aren't you?"

He smiled. "It's like this, Lawrence. There have been so many people who have been asking me to give it a go. The town hasn't had anything for years. How many industries do you see around here?"

"None."

"That's right, none. I'm not saying we want a factory employing a thousand people but we need at least one decent-sized business—something that would bring jobs to stop the young people moving out of the town to Letterkenny and Dublin and London just to get work. A lot of people are putting pressure on me. I don't want to let them down."

I thought about Danny a couple of days later at the official opening of the GAA football field at Downings. It was a cold and miserable day. I shouldn't even have been there but John called off at the last minute, saying he had a "big story" to chase. "I'm doing you a favor," he insisted. "There's a Gaelic football match between County Donegal and County Laois afterward— you'll be able to see how the game is really played."

The field opening was exactly the kind of ceremonial occasion that featured large in Donegal life: disorganized, windswept and lengthier than the annual sitting of the Libyan People's Revolutionary Congress. The national president of the GAA—the Colonel Gaddafi of the occasion, so to speak—was standing on the back of a beer lorry. He was making a speech in Irish. I was making random guesses at what he might be saying and writing it down in my notebook.

Members of Donegal's political elite—councillors, TDs (the Irish equivalent of an MP) and even a government minister— were sitting behind him, waiting their turn at the microphone.

They were all trying hard to rearrange their features to say, "I'm glad that I'm here," but something was being lost in translation. Most of them still had "What the fuck am I doing here?" stamped across their blue-tinged faces.

The only reason they were there in the first place was that their absence might be noticed and remembered come election day. If Danny became a councillor he would spend the rest of his life sitting on the back of beer lorries, freezing cold and listening to boring speeches. I was making a mental note to warn him when someone tapped me on the shoulder. "Donegan. Why haven't you been at training?" a voice said.

I turned round. I didn't know his name but I recognized the face. He was one of the St. Michael's committee members who stood in the middle of the field on training nights and watched while the players did their exercises.

"Yeah, I'm sorry, but it's been so busy at the *Tribune* I haven't had the time," I lied.

"You should get yourself down some nights."

I tried to act casual but my brain was racing. *My absences at training have been noticed.* Why? *Because the committee has been taking a close look at how I've been performing.* And? *I'm being considered for the team.* Which means? *The committee thinks I'm quite good at Gaelic football.* Or? *They're desperate . . .*

"I'll definitely be there tomorrow night."

The truth was I'd stopped going to training because I thought I was never going to get a game for St. Michael's. I was realistic enough to know that I wasn't much of a player. But the club had a reserve team and I knew they were always looking for people to make up the numbers. How bad a player did you have to be before the team manager would rather play a man short than give you a game? Was I that bad?

I had no idea, and I didn't like to ask. In my limited experience, people in this part of the world had a bluntness that was mostly refreshing but occasionally soul-destroying. I didn't even like to ask when the games were because someone might have asked me what I wanted to know for and I would have said, "Well, I thought I might get a game," and everyone would have collapsed laughing.

The closest I ever got to match day was the vicarious thrill of listening as others relived the previous weekend's game while getting changed for training sessions.

"Jesus, that tackle of yours was wild."

"He was the bastard that cleaned me the last time we played that lot in 'ninety-four."

"You got him in the end, though. Brilliant."

"A badly bruised foot. He'll not be doing his Michael Flatley impression for a while."

Pause.

"What was the score again?"

"Can't remember exactly. But we got beat, though."

They were always getting beat. Which, I suppose, was some consolation for not getting picked.

If anyone at the club had been waiting anxiously for me to come out of my sulk they hid it well.

"How's the form, Lawrence?" Michael Kelly said quietly, as I walked through the dressing-room door, threw my bag on the floor and sat down. A couple of the others nodded. It was the usual crowd, smoking, catching up on the weekend game.

As I started to get changed, Brian McLaughlin walked in. I recognized him from the previous day at Downings. He had played for County Donegal in the challenge match against County Laois. To my untutored eye the game had been fast and skillful but the press-box sages were dismissive. Donegal won by twenty points. Brian scored four of the Donegal points and had stood out as one of the best players on the field. He was the star of the St. Michael's team.

Sitting next to him in the dressing room I began to understand why. Some people just look like athletes. I remember seeing the Manchester United player Ryan Giggs in a hotel lobby once and he seemed to float across the carpet rather than walk. He sparkled, as if coated in high-gloss varnish. Brian had exactly the same sheen.

We started getting changed. My kit had been lying in a plastic bag on the backseat of the car for two weeks and smelt like an animal carcass. Brian's kit bag was brand-new. The words DUN-na-nGALL (Donegal) were printed on the side in big gold letters. His kit was clean, ironed and folded. He changed slowly and deliberately, then stood up and stretched leg muscles that performed the remarkable feat of appearing both lean and enormous. He looked at me and smiled.

I shook his proffered hand. "I'm Lawrence," I gushed. "I saw you playing yesterday, you were great." I felt like a schoolboy ushered into the dressing room at Old Trafford until I remembered he and I were supposed to be teammates.

There is much that I love about Gaelic football but if pressed I'd say the sport's biggest attraction is its evangelical devotion to amateurism. If a player like Brian McLaughlin was lucky enough or good enough to play in front of sixty thousand on All-Ireland Sunday the most he could expect for his efforts was a five-pound meal voucher and, possibly, the bus fare home.

It gets better. When he had finished thrilling the nation he would be back training alongside the likes of me with the parish team the following week. I don't know how Brian felt about that but it made me feel as if I'd walked into the Corncutter's Rest, found REM playing an acoustic set and they'd asked me to join in.

Brian took charge of the training. It may have been the stardust in my eyes but the session seemed more organized, more scientific than any I'd been at before. I managed to keep my dinner down for a change. At the end we played a bastardized form of Gaelic football. We could only pass the ball by hand. It was a bit like netball with big goals, which might have explained why I didn't disgrace myself.

"Jesus, Lawrence, you were moving well in that last game," Michael Kelly said, as we trooped back to the dressing room. He looked at Brian. "Not bad, was he?" I held my breath.

"Not bad," Brian said. "Not bad at all—for someone who's hardly ever played."

The last half of the sentence I could have done without. Otherwise I was happy. "Not bad at all" was better than "I shouldn't be sharing a field with this guy."

I was one of the last to get showered and changed. I was walking back to the car with Michael Kelly when Moses Alcorn, the club secretary, shouted after us, "Remember, lads, there's a game on Sunday." Lads. Plural. Not just Michael but Michael and me. I was happier still.

When I got home from the office the following afternoon and discovered the postman had left a letter behind the door, I was—well, I was delirious. The spidery handwriting on the envelope belonged to Moses. He wrote stories for the *Tribune*, always in longhand, and there was a fight every issue to see who would have to decipher his writing and type it into the computer. I ripped open the envelope. It took me ten minutes to work out what the letter said:

St. Michael's GAA Club
This Sunday there are two games against Naomh Bríd in Ballyshannon with the reserve team game kicking off at

2:15 P.M. The senior game is at 3:30 P.M. The bus will leave Dunfanaghy at 12:15 P.M. and Creeslough at 12:30 P.M. Anyone unable to play please contact me or any member of the committee.

Yours sincerely,

Moses Alcorn, secretary

Michael Kelly and his family lived in a small but pretty cottage by the side of the main road through the village. He knew I was living on my own and was always on at me to drop in anytime. I never did. I'd assumed he meant what people in London meant when they asked you to drop in anytime—don't drop in anytime. But it was a beautiful day and I wanted to tell someone about Moses's letter and I was passing Michael's front door on the way back from Lafferty's shop.

"Oh," he said, when he opened the front door. He smiled broadly. I could tell he meant "oh, good" and not "oh, no." "It's you, Lawrence. Come on in."

He showed me through to the kitchen. The room was small, with an old-fashioned range in one corner, a couple of chairs and a television in another. The walls were covered in religious pictures, mass cards and crucifixes. A three-foot-high statue of the Virgin Mary sat on one of the sideboards. Michael caught me staring.

"It's my grandmother's old house. She turned it into a shrine. We're just living here while our new house is getting built."

"Thank Christ for that. I thought I was back in Knock for a minute."

"You were in Knock?" He started laughing.

"Not voluntarily," I said.

I sat down while he made tea. There was a Gaelic football game on the television. Occasionally Michael explained a rule or pointed out a particular player, otherwise we watched in comfortable silence, as if I'd been visiting the house for years. I waited until halftime to tell him my news.

"There's a game tomorrow," I said casually.

"Aye, Naomh Bríd."

"Yeah. I got a letter from Moses. The bus leaves Creeslough at half twelve."

"I'm driving down, why don't you come with me? I'm leaving . . ." He stopped himself. "No, you can't. You'll be in the reserve team, they kick off earlier."

"It'll be my first game."

"Your first game." He shook his head. "I remember my first game."

Some conversations are so magical, so emotional, so redolent of a place and time and a feeling of well-being that they remain burned into your subconscious forever. This was one of those times. I sat back in my chair and wept (metaphorically, of course, because real GAA men don't cry) as Kelly took me through his first game.

"It was ten years ago. There was about ten of us, all sixteen to eighteen years old. We all lived within a couple of hundred yards of each other. We weren't getting a game for St. Michael's because all the older men were being picked, even though they never went to training. We decided to leave the club in protest. One night the manager phoned begging us young ones to play because he didn't have enough players. We couldn't let the parish down.

"It was a lovely Saturday night. I played full back. We beat Fanad. None of us could believe it. I never knew any sport could be so exciting. The whole lot of us went out that night and got drunk together. It was one of the best days of my life. The best part was the feeling that I had, knowing that we were all in it together.

"I've never been that interested in soccer. With soccer you play with guys from other parishes, with Gaelic you're playing alongside boys you see every day of your life. There's no way soccer has the same bite. Say one of your boys gets a bad tackle. You're in there, aren't you?"

Gulp. "Are you?"

"Of course you are. It's all about pride. The parish. If you don't think so, look at the faces of the older guys who come to watch the games. It breaks their hearts when they've got to stop playing."

Listening to Michael Kelly speak about Gaelic football and St. Michael's was like swallowing a library of motivation manuals. By the time I left his house I was prepared to lay down my life for the parish. I woke up early the following morning and ironed my kit. I phoned Francis to tell him I wanted to write an article about my debut for St. Michael's and asked if he would come to the game to take some photographs.

The bus was late coming from Dunfanaghy to Creeslough. Most of the seats were already taken. I squeezed in beside Moses at the front. Ballyshannon was in the south of the county, an hour's drive away. I don't exactly know when I started to feel uneasy but when Moses said, "Jesus, there's a lot of guys here today," I got an uneasy feeling that I should phone Francis to tell him not to bother coming, I might not be playing.

He was standing at the gates of Father Tierney Park when we arrived, looking like someone about to photograph a royal wedding. I never knew the *Tribune* owned so many cameras. And he'd brought Declan.

"God, what's Declan doing here?" I hissed.

"John thought he could write a match report. You know, give you marks out of ten for style," Francis said, looking hurt. Declan said nothing but looked hurt too.

There were twenty players in the dressing room when Liam Ferry, the reserve team manager, came in. I didn't really know Liam. I'd only spoken to him once, when I went to my first game at the Bridge. He'd never been at training. He told everyone to get changed, disappeared outside and came back a couple of minutes later. He had a scrap of paper in his hand.

"For better or for worse, this is the team," he began, then read out fifteen names—none of them mine—followed by six substitutes until, finally, he waved his hand in my direction and said, "And this fella here—the one with his personal photographer."

The Naomh Bríd reserve team was terrible. It was as if someone had sent out a search party half an hour before the game and rounded up anyone who happened to be walking through the village: beer-bellied forty-year-olds, kids who hadn't even started shaving, pensioners. One of their midfield players looked like Seamus Heaney's older brother. They were unfit, disorganized and leading by eight points after ten minutes.

Liam made three substitutions at halftime, put his head in his hands a lot then walked off to the far end of the field. For a moment it seemed as if he was heading for the exit gate.

"It looks as if you're not going to get a game," Declan said.

"Oh, really," I replied, acidly.

In a sporting career littered with embarrassments it never occurred to me that my greatest embarrassment would be played out on the touchline. Admittedly there was a small crowd but not so many that Francis would go unnoticed. Despite my protestations he spent the second half taking photographs of me in my red St. Michael's shirt as I casually leant against the dugout wall, trying to squeeze an oh-God-I'll-be-the-laughing-stock-of-the-village feeling into an oh-well-not-to-worry demeanor.

Michael Kelly appeared by the touchline with the other first team players. There was five minutes of the reserve match left to play. "Don't tell me you didn't get a game, Lawrence."

"I'm not bothered," I said, a little too quickly.

Declan saw I was in distress. "I don't believe you're that bad a player that you can't get into this team, Lawrence," he said. But I was inconsolable, even when Naomh Bríd won by twelve points.

I lost myself in work for the next week.

It turned out that John's "big story" was a medium story, about an alleged planning scandal. He spent hours in the office poring over piles of documents, and disappeared at least once a day for secret meetings. Whenever I asked for specific details, all he would say was that he'd been getting threatening phone calls at three o'clock in the morning and that all would be revealed in the next issue of the *Tribune*.

Francis and I got on with more mundane matters. I wrote up my report of the Donegal versus Laois match—my first ever Gaelic football match report. Declan helpfully corrected all the mistakes. I was going to write a piece about Danny running for the council but it was too late: he wasn't. He didn't get selected as a candidate.

I'd met him in the Corncutter's the night before the selection conference and he had grown increasingly pessimistic about his chances. Rightly so, as things turned out. "To be honest, I don't know where I would have found the time to do it in the first place," he said, when I sympathized. "That's politics. Don't worry about me, I'll get over it. I'm not proud."

Neither, it should be said, am I. I swallowed whatever dignity I had left in the Gaelic football world and went to training. No one said a word about Ballyshannon, although if I was paranoid

I might have thought the jokes about people having their own personal photographers were directed at me.

I'd finally convinced myself I was never going to get a game—an unshakeable belief that lasted until the end of the session when Michael McColgan, manager of the first team, said that I was unrecognizable as the "headless chicken who turned up to training on that first night." A couple of mornings later another letter from Moses arrived, this time telling me that the St. Michael's reserves would be playing Naomh Ultan in the County Donegal GAA Intermediate (Reserves) Championship quarter-final tie at Killygordon at 2:15 P.M. My football kit was spotless already but I washed and ironed it anyway.

I hid my kit bag underneath a pile of Sunday newspapers on the backseat and drove to the game disguised as a spectator. Killygordon is a pretty village nestling in the lush arable farmland in the southeast corner of Donegal. I got lost on the way there and was late arriving. I left my kit bag in the car and wandered over to the St. Michael's dressing room. If anything it was even more crowded than the previous week.

Liam and Michael McColgan were chatting conspiratorially in one corner. I was about to go back outside when Liam grabbed my sleeve. "Have you got your togs?" he said.

"I think they might be in my car," I said timorously.

"For fuck's sake, go and get them."

I only just managed to stop myself kissing him.

I should explain. In Gaelic football the championship is just what it says, the championship. The pinnacle. The FA Cup, the Premiership and the European Cup rolled into one. Throw in the World Cup final and it might just be possible to imagine the cocktail of nerves and excitement swirling around my guts as Liam started to read out the team: Don Langan, Hughie Carr, John Sheridan, Josie Gallagher . . . names began to blur. I was only waiting for one . . . P. J. McLaughlin, Eamonn McFadden and Neil McGinley.

"The subs are Owenie and Denis . . ." he looked around the room ". . . and Keiran there."

I wasn't playing. Again. My first thought was how to stop the droplet of salty water rapidly gathering in the corner of my eye from rolling down my cheek. Second, I needed to get dressed again and leave the changing room without anyone noticing I'd ever been there in the first place. I was about to give up on both when Liam thrust the number fourteen jersey into my hand. "Moses says your registration hasn't been confirmed yet," he said, *sotto voce*. "If anyone asks, you're P. J. McLaughlin. Play full forward."

The pre-match talk passed in a blur, although the phrases "play for the jersey" and "get fuckin' into them" were repeated so often they lodged in my mind. The air was thick with testosterone and the clatter of metal studs on cold stone tile. It didn't seem like the appropriate time to ask what a full forward did in a Gaelic football team. I waited until we were walking out on to the field before asking one of my teammates.

"Think of it like center forward at soccer." Josie Gallagher laughed. "Except you get kicked a lot more."

I felt sick with nerves. The first sighting of my marker didn't help. He looked as if he'd spent a lifetime pulling tractors out of ditches with his bare hands. He was wearing surgical white gloves and the kind of dark grimace I imagined bears use to paralyze lunch.

"Afternoon," I said, taking up my position.

"Is it?" he replied darkly.

We were five points down after three minutes, double that at halftime and when the referee blew for full-time five minutes early we'd lost by twenty-one points. The best that could be said about my contribution was that I wasn't worse than anyone else wearing a red St. Michael's jersey. I didn't touch the ball more than half a dozen times. Thankfully, I wasn't called upon to attempt anything difficult—like try to score a point, or solo the ball.

The good news was that my marker was friendlier than he looked. He only elbowed me in the face once. Eventually, it dawned on him that wanton violence would not be required to get the better of me. As the match progressed we almost became friends. His name was Seamus and he drove a forklift truck for a living. We spent most of the second half standing on the halfway line admiring the skillful efforts of Naomh Ultan forwards to score and the doomed attempts of the St. Michael's defense to stop them.

Afterward our dressing room had the shocked atmosphere of a field army hospital. One of Gaelic football's great rituals is that the winning captain congratulates the losers on a gallant performance and suggests that, despite the scoreline, the game was a titanic struggle that could have gone either way. "Hard lines, lads, I'm sure the rest of the season will go better," was the best the Naomh Ultan captain could manage.

When he left a dark silence descended. Everyone was mortified. Yet I was struggling to stop myself smiling. My mind wandered back to a point in the match when I heard a voice in the crowd shout, "Come on, Donegan, you useless bastard, get the ball up the field." I knew then that I'd been accepted, that the friendly restraint that greets tourists and visitors to the parish was gone forever. I knew then I was a St. Michael's man for good.

Liam tried his best to gee everyone up. "Never mind, lads," he said, clapping his hands together. "We can still win the league."

Just then I caught a glance from Hughie Carr, who had spent a heroic but futile afternoon at the heart of our defense. He just about had enough energy left to shake his head.

"Where are we in the league?" I asked him, once Liam had disappeared outside.

"Bottom."

The Rise and Rise of Bernie Bubbles

The light on the telephone answer-machine flashed six times. Six messages. I hadn't had that many in total since moving to Creeslough. I assumed something terrible had happened: Newt Gingrich's henchmen had read my piece in the *Tribune* about their boss and wanted a word in my ear, or perhaps the *Tribune* had been taken over by Rupert Murdoch.

"Lawrence," said a voice I took a moment to recognize, "it's Sarah here. I'm in Belfast with Jane. We fancied a night out in Donegal. We'll be there in a couple of hours."

My heart sang with joy. Despite a hundred firm promises from so-called friends before I left, I hadn't had a single visitor since moving to Creeslough. This hadn't been for the want of trying. I'd sent dozens of postcards and hundreds of E-mails. In the end I was reduced to making begging phone calls.

"But you've got to come," I would respond after the initial, swiftly delivered excuse about pressures of work, moving house or shortage of baby-sitters. "A kid. When did you have the kid?" Christ, I thought, this is how much people don't want to come to Creeslough: they invent children.

What was wrong with these strange people I used to call my friends? It wasn't so long ago that I'd had a decent part in the Nora Ephron–scripted film of their lives. Now I was just the forgotten character who introduced Harry to Sally, written out in scene one. "Of course I love it over here. You would love it too," I'd say. "The cottage? A few problems, nothing some rat poison and a lick of paint didn't solve. The weather? Well, it's been pretty good. There was one day a few weeks ago when it didn't rain. What could you do when you got here? Plenty. You could come and watch me play Gaelic football."

"Sounds great," they would lie. "Tell you what, we'll think about it."

I have never been much of a salesman. Sometimes, when I replayed these conversations in my head, I had to admit that even I wouldn't want to visit me in Creeslough. Rats, leaking roof, sleeping on the floor, no telly, a desperate-sounding host. It hardly sounded like the holiday of a lifetime.

The next four messages on the machine were from Sarah and Jane, charting their course out of Belfast and west toward Letterkenny. The closer they got the more hysterical they became. "Where are you, you stupid pseudo-Irish bastard? Phone us, please. We don't want to book into a fucking hotel."

Message number six heralded a distinct mellowing of mood. "Lawrence, it's us. We're in a pub called the Harbour Bar. It's overlooking the sea, we're drinking Guinness. We've died and gone to heaven. There's no rush. See you sometime."

The Harbour Bar was in Downings. It was a decent enough pub but I hardly ever drank there. It was always packed with tourists and the barman had an irritating habit of drawing a shamrock on the head of your pint with the last drips from the tap (a capital offense in my book). I was firmly a Corncutter's Rest man. For Sarah and Jane's company, however, I was more than delighted to suspend my prejudices for one evening.

The light was fading rapidly when I arrived. My two visitors were sitting at one of the tables outside, wearing the happy smiles of people who had recently been reacquainted with alcohol after a long and stressful day. We exchanged greetings, me saying how well they looked, both of them saying how badly dressed I was and asking where did I get the Kurt Cobain hairstyle and the Norm from *Cheers* chins?

"Isn't this place fantastic?" Jane said, spreading her hands toward the sky like an evangelical preacher.

"You are a lucky bastard, Donegan," Sarah echoed. She pointed out toward the sea. "Look at that."

A royal blue fishing boat skipped across the wash on Sheephaven Bay like a happy child on its way home from school. A big red sun was making its lazy way toward the horizon. I took a deep breath. The air tasted better than ice-cream. She was right. I'd stood in this spot a dozen times and never noticed before that it was beautiful, like a painting by a great master. We watched the boat make steady progress, reflecting on man's piddling insignificance in God's greater scheme of things and other big issues of the moment.

"Whose round is it?"

"Not mine."

"Bloody is."

"Isn't."

"Is."

"For God's sake, ladies, handbags away. Let me buy the beers."

I was so pleased to see Jane and Sarah, and not just because it gave me the chance to sample their sparkling intellectual jousting. It was all the things that they inadvertently revealed to me about my new life, although "revealed" is probably the wrong word. I knew most of what Jane and Sarah revealed to me, I just didn't *know* it.

For instance, it hadn't dawned on me that I was now employed by the world's most laid-back newspaper editor until Jane asked me what John McAteer was like. "I suppose he's a bit eccentric but he's a decent enough boss," I heard myself saying. "He doesn't bother when you go into the office, or how much work you do, or if you do any work at all. He never panics, never shouts, never does much of anything really apart from work, smoke his pipe and take his dog for walks."

Nor did I know that the *Tribune* "sounded like the *Washington Post* without the manpower," until Sarah asked me what the paper stood for and I started spouting about exposing corruption in the highest offices in the land (I was extemporizing), fighting for truth and—John's favorite—standing up for the common people, "who were always right, even when they were wrong."

There were other things that I genuinely didn't know and, frankly, didn't care about. But Jane and Sarah insisted on telling me anyway. I didn't know that the Bristol trip-hop scene was, like, so *passé* it wasn't real, or that Tony Blair's first cabinet reshuffle was imminent, the Liberal Democrats were badly split over closer links with the New Labour government and that combat pants were out of fashion.

As the night wore on I felt as if I was slowly being reintroduced to my previous life. I loved every minute of it, not because I desperately longed to return to a world where combat pants and cabinet reshuffles mattered but because it helped me remember a few things I used to hate about my past life and recognize what was good about my new life: Creeslough, the *Tribune*, John, his foxy nieces, Francis, Bouncer, Gaelic football; the fact that I lived a simple, uncluttered existence where nothing was too important that it couldn't be put off for another day.

We got home very late and very drunk. I had warned Jane and Sarah that the cottage was like Steptoe and Son's backyard. They had turned up at such short notice I hadn't had time to wash the dishes or change the bedsheets, the furniture, the ornaments, the wallpaper and the carpets. Or rent another house for the weekend and pretend it was mine.

As it turned out, they couldn't have been more diplomatic.

For at least twenty seconds they made a decent impersonation of two people arriving at Blenheim Palace for a shooting week-end.

"It's absolutely fantastic," Jane said, as I showed them round.

Sarah smiled, a little too broadly. "It's quaint."

"It's a dump," I confessed. "But I've got plans to do it up, you know, like that bloke who wrote *A Year in Provence*. I'll probably start next week."

Jane: "Honestly, Lawrence, it's not that bad."

Me: "Come on, admit it—I can take it."

Sarah: "*Well . . .*"

As a consolation prize I gave them the mattress. I slept on the floor. I woke the next morning just after nine and, because Jane and Sarah were now officially my best, most loyal friends, I decided to cook breakfast for them. Feeling terrible, I walked down to the village to buy papers and Andrews' Liver Salts.

It was a glorious morning. The cottage looked pretty under the big blue sky. Little bell-shaped red buds had appeared on the hedges, bringing some much-needed color to the place. Even the waist-high garden grass swayed seductively in the light morning breeze.

Everyone was up by the time I got back. We had breakfast outside in the sunshine with the sound of *the* Sunday-morning record (Smokey Robinson and the Miracles' *Anthology*) wafting through the open windows. Jane and Sarah read. I lay back and tried to will away my hangover.

"This is brilliant," Sarah said after a while, leaning back to get some sun on her face. "Is the weather always this good?"

"Sure it is," I lied.

"You're so lucky to live here, Lawrence." Jane sighed, then said, as an afterthought, "What shall we do this afternoon?"

It seemed as good a moment as any to break the bad news.

"We're going to have to go to the Creeslough sports day. I'm covering it for the *Tribune*."

Did I say bad news? It was as if they had been waiting all their lives to go to the Creeslough sports day. They loved it. So did I. Most of the village turned up and it seemed as if everyone knew I had visitors to impress. I couldn't walk ten yards without someone stopping for a friendly chat about (a) my impending call-up for the County Donegal Gaelic football team as a reward for my stunning performance as full forward for St. Michael's reserves and (b) the *Tribune*'s impending visit from the CIA for describing Newt Gingrich as "a no-good opportunist, adulterous, phoney Irishman in a suit."

Francis turned up to take a few photographs. I patrolled the finishing line, collecting the names of the race winners. Jane and Sarah disappeared off to the welly-throwing ring, then entered the female (adult) three-legged race. Exhausted and demoralized at coming last, they departed for the Corncutter's Rest with a promise to "get the beers in."

The pub was packed when I finally got there. Jane and Sarah were in the corner being chatted up by a couple of drunk young farmers.

There was a band playing at the far end of the bar. Actually, it was a one-man band but modern technology helped him sound as full as the Berlin Philharmonic. A hand-painted sign propped up against the bank of keyboards announced his name as Ohio. It occurred to me that most of the bands I'd heard playing at the Corncutter's were named after American states—Ohio, Montana, Dakota, Georgia, Colorado. I mentioned this fascinating fact to Danny Lafferty, who was chatting to someone at the bar as I waited to be served.

"No, they're not," he said, a little irritated that his honest efforts to provide some entertainment for the locals provoked only snide remarks from know-alls like me. "Stout. I've got Stout playing tomorrow night."

I quickly agreed there was no such place as Stout, U.S.A., and changed the subject. "I never saw you at the sports. You missed a brilliant day."

"Some of us have to work for a living, Lawrence," Danny said. He nodded at the man he'd been talking to. "Have you met Bernard?"

Bernard smiled. I liked the look of him immediately. He was exactly how you'd want to look if you were heading toward fifty: cropped hair, flat stomach, soft crows' feet at the corner of the eyes and a cool, calm demeanor hinting at maturity. He was wearing a pair of Levi's and a leather jacket like Paul Newman's in *The Hustler*.

We shook hands. "Bernard Lafferty," he said, or at least I think he did. I could hardly hear him above Ohio's version of Olivia Newton-John's "Country Roads."

"Lafferty?"

He nodded.

"Any relation to *the* Bernard Lafferty?"

"First cousin," he replied, matter-of-fact.

My heart leapt. I'm ashamed to admit it but the first flush of enthusiasm about the Bernard Lafferty/Doris Duke story had faded. The problem was that no one other than Sarah McCaffrey seemed to know much about him apart from what they had read in the newspapers. Even Danny Lafferty, my prime source of local information, was uncharacteristically vague. "He was quite a boyo, so I'm led to believe," was the best he could come up with, which hardly counted as a staggering insight. Gradually, against all my journalistic instincts, I lost interest.

I couldn't believe my good fortune. Here was the story on a plate.

Ohio launched into "I lotd California. Christ, what a racket." I had to shout to make myself heard. "What was he like?"

Bernard shook his head. "This is too noisy for me. I'm off home. Phone me tomorrow." He gave me his telephone number and left.

I carried the drinks back to the table. Sarah and Jane had been abandoned by the young farmers but managed to disguise their broken hearts by singing along with Ohio at the top of their voices.

The song ended, mercifully. The band took a break. This gave the three of us a chance to have a normal conversation, the gist of which was that they'd both had a great weekend: my company had been just about acceptable; the cottage was perfectable. Most of all, they loved Creeslough.

"You'll never come back, will you?" Jane said, a little sadly. "Why would anyone in their right mind want to leave a place like this?"

I could have said all sorts of things in reply. I could have said she had seen the village at its absolute best. I could have told her that people left Creeslough all the time because there were hardly any jobs, that the weather was mostly terrible and the pub always had bands that were named after American states and played Olivia Newton-John songs. But why spoil the illusion for her? Why spoil it for me?

"I don't know why anyone in their right mind would leave Creeslough," I said. "But I'm meeting someone tomorrow who might tell me."

The only entrepreneurial idea I have ever had in my entire life is the Bernard Lafferty "How a Star Was Born" bus tour. Who knows? One day I might get round to doing something about it. If I did, it would start at a small, gray-stone cottage off the main road about a mile outside of Creeslough. Until 1965 this was the home of the Lafferty family, Eddie, Angela and their only son, Bernard.

Eddie ran a smallholding—five acres of good arable land, a few cows and a horse. I'd read somewhere that the Laffertys were "poverty-stricken." They weren't. They were poor, like most of their neighbors. In fact, they must have been better off than some because they could afford the luxury of a television set.

One of the most striking features of the Bernard Lafferty story is how much of it consisted of half-truths and fantasy. The idea that the family was poverty-stricken came from the same dark recess of journalistic imagination as "Lafferty grew up in a tiny lakeside cottage in the mists of County Donegal," "Lafferty was an evil, cunning Irishman" and "Lafferty was an Irish tinker."

I suspect the myths were a consequence of villagers' reluctance to talk about Bernard out of loyalty. Most journalists who came to Creeslough looking for salacious gossip left empty-handed. Undeterred, they went back to their office where—and this insight into journalistic ethics might come as a shock to some people—they made it all up.

For instance, it was always said that Lafferty was illiterate. Admittedly, the few surviving examples of his handwriting—"My drinkig is not the proplmem" is one example—suggested that his spelling abilities ruled out a career as a sign-writer. But he wasn't illiterate. In fact he went to Massinass National School. Sarah McCaffrey remembered him as a bright and attentive pupil. Bernie Bubbles was his nickname. He didn't show much aptitude for Gaelic football but he could definitely read and write.

He left school at fourteen, like most people at that time, then worked as a porter in two local hotels, the Shandon and the Carrigart. Eventually, he got a job at the veneer factory on the village outskirts.

Seamus Harkin, Creeslough's undertaker, poet and premier

fiddle player, had lived in the beautiful two story house oppo-site the factory long enough to remember it as a thriving busi-ness. "I knew Bernard from just being around the place," Seamus told me many months later. "There was a shop on this side of the road and all the workers came across to it at lunchtime. They played football out there in the field. Bernard was just one of the group. He was very ordinary as a fellow, you wouldn't have picked him out from the others. Maybe he wasn't so rough and tumble as some. He was a bit more reserved, a bit finer-featured, I suppose. He got that from his mother. She was a real lady, from Scotland, terribly reserved.

"But what I remember most about Bernard was this: when all the other lads were talking about their future they spoke about becoming bus drivers, or farmers or whatever. Not Bernard. He used to say he would never stay in Creeslough, he was heading for Hollywood. I can hear him now, 'One day you'll be reading about me in the papers, lads.'"

The final stop of the Bernard Lafferty bus tour would have to be Doe graveyard, where his parents are buried. (Perhaps this isn't such a whizz-bang business idea after all.) Anyway, my own first visit to the graveyard was for a story I was writing about Bernard's biggest rival for the title of Creeslough's most famous son. Neil McBride achieved national fame in the early 1900s when he was charged with having his name printed in Irish on the back of his horse-cart. Believe it or not this was a crime in Ireland back in those days.

Niall Macgiolla Bhrighde, to give him his "criminal" name, was hauled up before the court in Dublin, found guilty and fined five shillings. His celebrity was magnified because one of his defense barristers was Patrick Pearse, a prominent Irish republican of the day who later played a leading role in the 1916 Easter Uprising against British rule.

McBride's was an interesting story, which might have explained why it appeared in the *Tribune* at least once a year. John was clearly fed up writing it and dispatched me on the anniversary of the poet's death. "I want a fresh angle," he said. I took that to be one of his hilarious jokes.

A huge amount of restoration work had been carried out on Doe graveyard in recent years but there was no escaping that it was still a pretty depressing place. Oddly, given McBride's proclivity for having his name on things, someone forgot to put his name on his gravestone.

Fortunately, Seamus Harkin was able to direct me to a tiny heart-shaped stone just inside the entrance gate. It looked out of place among the huge modern gravestones that bore testimony not just to the dead but to Ireland's burgeoning wealth. Where once people were content with a tiny heart or wooden cross, they now insisted on using more marble than you'd find in a sheikh's bathroom.

The Lafferty family plot was in what might unkindly be described (though I don't suppose the occupants will be particularly offended) as the less salubrious end of the graveyard. It was marked by a modest white marble stone, battered and worn by three decades of wind and rain. It was just about possible to read the inscription:

ANGELA LAFFERTY

DIED 18TH AUG. 1965

HUSBAND EDWARD

DIED 3RD SEPT. 1964

Erected by their son Bernard

R.I.P.

A few months after Angela Lafferty died, her son sold the family cottage and left Creeslough for good.

Jane and Sarah left early the next morning. I called Bernard Lafferty as soon as they left and invited myself to his place for a cup of tea. I would have been there in half the time if I'd remembered to ask for directions. Fortunately, everyone in Creeslough knows where everyone else lives. After a spot of aimless driving in the hills of Donegal I eventually found someone who pointed me in the right direction.

Bernard's house was in the most perfect spot I'd ever seen, tucked underneath Muckish Mountain. "You found me in the end," he said, in a voice so low and becalmed that I had to strain to hear him speak.

There was a quiet dignity about Bernard that made me warm to him straight away. We sat in the front room for the entire afternoon, admiring the uninterrupted view across the village and talking about his cousin.

"Bernard's mother was originally from Glasgow. When Eddie died, Angela and Bernard went back to Scotland. The house in Creeslough was left empty. She was killed as she was getting off a bus. He came back a few months later to sell up. He came down to see us the day he was leaving Creeslough for good. He seemed happy enough.

"He went back to Scotland but not for long. I think he spent most of the time working in a hotel in Aviemore. After that he went to work for the same hotel chain at their place in Bermuda, then to Philadelphia where he had a lot of cousins.

"The first Christmas he was away, he sent parcels to Ireland of selection boxes and games for us kids. After that we never heard another word from him or about him."

Until . . .

Bernard shook his head. "About fifteen years later I got a newspaper cutting in the post from America. It was a picture of Bernard and Elizabeth Taylor." He laughed gently and repeated himself, as if he still couldn't believe it. "Elizabeth Taylor. I think he was escorting her to a fund-raising dinner for the Statue of Liberty in New York."

That was in the late 1970s, when Elizabeth Taylor was one of the most famous women in the world and not just a has-been actress who got married a lot. I tried hard to imagine what the reaction in Creeslough must have been to the news that she was hanging around with little Bernie Bubbles from the veneer factory. Incredulity, I guessed, then jealousy, then immense pride. Many years ago, when I was still at school, I became something of a local celebrity after I found an old cannonball by the river. I even made the local newspaper. God knows what would have happened if I'd done something really good like pairing off with Liz Taylor. They would probably have named the town after me.

Nothing was heard of Creeslough's most famous son for another thirteen years, until he and Doris Duke flew over the village.

Bernard said he remembered that day as if it were yesterday. He was out in the garden cutting the grass. "At first I thought it was a coastguard helicopter. It did a few circuits around the area before heading back in the direction it came from," he recalled.

He only found out later it was his cousin and, though he didn't say as much, I could tell he was disappointed that the helicopter hadn't landed. We speculated for a while about why it hadn't. Maybe he felt guilty about not getting in touch for so long. Perhaps he didn't want Doris Duke to experience Creeslough close up. After all, when you've spent the 1970s hanging out with cokeheads and the beautiful people at Studio 54 the Corncutter's Rest might come as a bit of a culture shock.

Doris and her butler spent a few more days in County Mayo before flying back to Los Angeles, where the heiress had one of her five homes. Two years later, on October 28, 1993, the Richest Girl in the World died. Copies of her will were released within hours. "That's when all the lawyers and the press started phoning." Bernard sighed.

He disappeared off into another room. I could hear him rummaging through a drawer. He reappeared and handed me three newspaper cuttings. "Have a good look at these. They pretty much tell the story."

The first cutting, headlined ACCORD CLEARS THE LAST WILL OF DORIS DUKE FOR PROBATE, was from the *New York Times*. It gave a long, detailed and boring account of what was a long, detailed and exciting courtroom squabble. In her will, Duke had left $1.2 billion in charitable trust. She named Bernard Lafferty as executor, a position that gave him immense powers of patronage.

There followed, according to the *NYT*, "a thirty-month legal drama of sensational charges ranging from misspent millions to murder."

A paragraph near the bottom of the story had been highlighted with yellow marker pen: "In exchange for a flat-rate payment of $4.5 million and a $500,000 annual payment for the rest of his life, Mr. Lafferty agreed . . . to relinquish the enormous power bequeathed to him in Miss Duke's will."

The *Daily Mirror*, source of the second cutting, was scant on legalese but more than made up for that with candor. "WHAT THE GAY BUTLER WORE—HE'S SPORTING M'LADY'S GOWNS AND GEMS," screamed the headline. "I got that cutting from this old woman in the village who I used to drive to the shops," Bernard said. "I turned up one day to pick her up. She showed me that story and asked if it was true. She looked horrified. That was the only time anyone in Creeslough ever mentioned the subject to me.

"People around here thought that they might embarrass me if they talked about Bernard so they never brought the subject up. I wouldn't have cared if they did. Bernard had been away for years, there was nothing I knew or could do about him.

"After that story, there was a whole lot of others. Most of them were about him drinking two-thousand-dollar bottles of champagne, or spending fortunes on clothes and visiting gay clubs—the usual rubbish. A lot of them were funny. Some of them weren't. The worst one of the lot appeared in the Irish edition of the *News of the World*. A couple of reporters spent a few days digging around Creeslough but couldn't find anything at all—no one would talk to them. In the end they made up this really offensive rubbish about Christmas presents. The headline was 'Millionaire Butler Gives Relations Nothing for Xmas.' "

As if cross-dressing and alleged festive parsimony weren't bad enough, Lafferty was then accused of killing his boss. "DEVOTED BUTLER 'GOADED DOCTOR TO MURDER HEIRESS,' " screamed the *Sunday Times* above an improbable tale of last-minute alterations to Duke's will, a whistle-blowing nurse and a morphine overdose.

The alteration, dated six months before the heiress died, made the butler co-executor of her estate. The whistle-blowing nurse was Tammy Payette, who tended Duke on her deathbed and claimed, in an affidavit to a New York court, "Miss Duke did not die of natural causes." The morphine overdose was the alleged murder weapon.

After the first morphine injection, Payette alleged, "Duke clung to life. Bernard Lafferty became very excited and impatient because Miss Duke was lingering and called the doctor, explaining that she had not expired. The doctor returned and

inserted a needle in the IV tube and began to push in the morphine."

I'd been around newspapers long enough to know that the
furniture—the details—of some stories is such that journalists
can't resist the urge to dredge up every pathetic cliché and pun
imaginable. The Bernard Lafferty/Doris Duke story was one
of those stories. "The Princess and the Pauper," "The Irish Jeeves,"
"Upstairs Downstairs," "Rags to Riches" and, my favorite,
"Wad the Butler Saw"—they all made an appearance.

I often wonder why highly trained, professional journalists
lower themselves in this way. It's so infantile. I handed Bernard
back his newspaper cuttings, shaking my head. "So tell me," I
said, "the butler did it—right?"

By the Rivers of Babylon

I turned on the local radio station expecting to find the mid-morning DJ talking someone down from a window ledge or, even more depressing, playing the new single by Cher. Happily he was doing neither. He was interviewing a local councillor about plans to revive Donegal's economy with a £20 million railway modeled on Japan's bullet-train network.

I had recently acquired a copy of Edward M. Patterson's indispensable (particularly for anyone who wants to know the color of rail tickets in the nineteenth century) *The County Donegal Railways* in which the author charts the demise of the local railway system. "Deferred permanent-way maintenance had resulted in the imposition of speed restrictions and a stage was reached when the complete relaying of much of the track had become a necessity . . . Throughout 1959 the railway functioned as vigorously as ever and then, greatly to the regret of the countryside which it served, it ceased operating at the end of that year," Mr. Patterson wrote, in what passes for tear-stained prose in trainspotting circles.

The reasons for the railway's closure in 1959—no money for investment, improvements in the local road system and a relatively small catchment population—pretty much held true forty years later. Frankly, modern Donegal had more chance of becoming the world headquarters of the International Monetary Fund than it had of acquiring a railway system like Japan's.

To the DJ's credit he didn't laugh in his interviewee's face. Like everyone else in Donegal he was prepared to listen to any idea, however ridiculous, so long as it held out the prospect of a few precious jobs. These were desperate times.

Earlier that morning the county's largest employer, an American T-shirt company called Fruit of the Loom, had announced the closure of a factory with the loss of fifty jobs. It was moving its machinery to Morocco, where labor costs were cheaper.

Fifty people losing their job in, say, London would scarcely have merited a paragraph in the *Evening Standard* but in a Donegal village it spelled the virtual collapse of the local economy. The news was doubly worrying because the T-shirt company had seven factories in the county. Many people feared (accurately, as it turned out) that other closures would follow. It didn't matter that this firm had snaffled £10 million in grants from the Irish government when it set up its operation in Donegal, or that it ought to have had some moral obligation to a workforce that had given it a decade of highly profitable endeavor. For the sake of saving a few quid, its T-shirts would now bear the stamp Made in Morocco.

Economists probably have some sort of fancy phrase to describe this sort of despicable behavior, like globalization of the world economy. I've got one too: absolutely scandalous. How do these people sleep at night? Is it too much to hope that they might occasionally look in the mirror and say, "God, I really hate myself."

It was hard to imagine where fifty people could find alternative employment. Traditional industries like fishing and farming were struggling to survive. The so-called Irish economic miracle had transformed Dublin but in the northwest it was nothing more than a rumor. Most people I knew were fed up reading about millionaire property developers and new factory openings in the capital. "What about Donegal?" was a popular refrain.

There was always tourism—after all, this part of the world

was nothing if not scenic—but even tourism was suffering its worst year on record: down 70 percent because of bad weather, according to the latest issue of the *Tirconaill Tribune*.

Predictably, it was pouring with rain as I drove to the office that afternoon. I tried hard to remember how many days of sunshine we'd had. There hadn't been any, apart from Creeslough sports day and the afternoon I got as far as thinking of whitewashing the cottage before finding an excuse not to (I urgently needed to play golf), it had been raining solidly for two months. Frankly, it was a surprise that any tourists came at all.

When I arrived John was on the phone.

"It's the head of the tourist board," Noel whispered excitedly, pointing at a pile of newspapers on the counter. "He's complaining about the story on the front page."

We could only hear one side of the conversation. Judging by the long silences and eye-rolling at John's end, the head of the tourist board was insinuating that the disastrous drop in the number of tourists had more to do with John's imagination than the weather. He must have made the short step from insinuation to bald assertion because John suddenly said, "Why don't you fuck off?" and calmly put the receiver back on its cradle.

It may have been unprofessional, rude even, but not for the first time I was awestruck by our esteemed editor's inability to kow-tow to anyone with a title.

The phone rang almost immediately. "Answer that, Noel," he said, disappearing off to the kitchen to make tea. "If it's that arsehole from the tourist board tell him I've gone on holiday to Spain."

If I was disloyal or a judge of the Pulitzer Prize for journalism, I'd be tempted to say John's story about the local tourist industry was a bit flimsy. But I am neither of those things, so I won't. In any case his principal source —an anonymous B-and-B landlady who told him business was so bad she hadn't had to refill her margarine dishes all summer—wasn't far wrong when she said Donegal's whereabouts must have been protected under the Official Secrets Act because no one seemed to know the place existed.

I'd been to County Kerry earlier in the summer. It had been crawling with rich Americans who had come to play golf at Ballybunion, shout loudly across crowded bars and generally behave as if they owned the place. They were obnoxious but at least they parted with armfuls of cash. I hadn't met any Americans in Donegal, apart from Newt Gingrich and Barbara, my fellow Gingrich hater.

A few towns and villages in the county did their best to drum up business by staging what they grandly describe as "summer festivals," but the staple attractions of these events were mobile chip vans, Dodgem cars and two men on the back of the lorry singing karaoke versions of Beatles hits. I'm no expert on tourism but I suspect Donegal's summer festivals were unlikely to cause much of a crush at the travel shops of Manhattan and San Francisco. Nor was the Milford Busking Festival ever likely to match the global appeal of the Grammys.

Creeslough didn't have a summer festival. I went to one at a nearby village called Kilmacrennan instead. I had a great time eating chips, dancing, drinking and trying to drive home in a Dodgem car but there was no disguising that it was little more than an excuse for an extended piss-up. All of the summer festivals were.

There was one notable exception, the Mary from Dungloe— an event I had marked in my calendar months before. The tourist board had promised to put me on the guest list. Thanks to John's outburst, I would now have to buy a ticket.

To be perfectly honest, I didn't mind paying, and for a very good reason. Two reasons, actually.

First, Daniel O'Donnell, Donegal's—hell, Ireland's—musical superstar, was performing.

I'd been following Daniel's career from afar for the last decade, partly bemused but (because I'm something of a musical snob) mostly dismayed. A former gravedigger, he had started singing in pubs and ended up selling over three million albums. Not only that, he regularly appeared in the top ten and packed out ten-thousand-seat arenas from Australia to Canada. Daniel's was truly a heart-warming story, real rags-to-riches stuff, ruined only by the inescapable fact that he made truly atrocious records.

If you are one of the select group of people who haven't yet heard Daniel singing, congratulations. Take it from me, he sounds like Johnny Mathis without the raunch or the Singing Nun without the sex appeal. Yet he was (is) a cultural phenomenon, a wet dream made flesh for a generation of menopausal women, many of whom make the annual pilgrimage from all over the world to the Mary from Dungloe Festival just to see him perform.

This year they would be joined by every tabloid journalist in Ireland. Sensational news had just leaked out that Daniel had finally found a girlfriend. In normal circumstances "Millionaire Pop Singer Has Girlfriend" wouldn't have been an earthshattering headline but in Daniel's case it had the novelty value of "Norman Mailer in Cross-dressing Confession."

For years he had been Ireland's most eligible bachelor. No more. Word had it he was going to introduce the lucky lady to his fans during this year's festival. As Dungloe was only an hour's drive from Creeslough it seemed stupid to miss such a momentous occasion.

The other reason for making the trip was the Mary from Dungloe beauty pageant. Since moving to Ireland I'd obviously developed a physical deformity visible only to members of the opposite sex. I think the technical term is: I couldn't get laid. A night mingling with swimsuited contestants was the closest I was ever going to get to a deep and meaningful relationship with an Irish beauty.

When I arrived in Dungloe it was raining hard enough to wash the paint off the postboxes. The main street was deserted but for a huddle of people sheltering in the chip-shop doorway. Never one to miss the chance of a healthy meal, I nipped in for a fish supper and a pickled egg. The talk in the queue was of the Parade of Marys earlier in the day. It had taken place in a hailstorm and sounded awful, all windswept hair and corned-beef legs. I paid for my meal and headed for the venue, silently praying the contestants had smartened up since then.

The terrible weather must have severed all communications between Dungloe and the outside world because no one from the tourist board had phoned to remove the *Tirconaill Tribune*'s journalists from the guest list. I gave my name to a woman at the ticket desk who handed me an object that had featured in many of my teenage dreams: a backstage pass for a beauty contest.

According to the festival program the original Mary from Dungloe was a local lass called Mary Gallagher, who met a handsome gentleman in the town on a summer's day in 1861. Alas, her parents didn't approve of her new boyfriend. She wrote him a letter ending the romance. Two days later he immigrated to America, heartbroken. Nineteen years later Mary immigrated to New Zealand. She met her husband on the boat, had a baby son and died in 1883. Someone wrote a song about her called "Mary from Dungloe."

It took an enormous leap of imagination to come up with the idea of commemorating this tragic tale of emigration with a beauty contest but, frankly, who cares? Pass in hand, I dashed backstage to see if anyone needed a hand getting into their swimsuit.

It was chaotic. Men in dinner suits were barking into walkie-talkies, stagehands were running around carrying heavy black boxes. Daniel O'Donnell, compère for the evening, was fiddling nervously with his hair. Gay Byrne, Ireland's most famous broadcaster and one of the contest judges, was wandering around with a quiet, beatific smile on his face.

I, on the other hand, was crestfallen. The first person I met backstage was the festival press officer, who told me there were no swimsuits. "It's true," he said, in response to my disbelieving face. "Come and have a look."

He ushered me into the room where the contestants were getting ready. Everyone was dressed in evening gowns, making last-minute adjustments to their makeup and slipping on white satin sashes announcing who they were: New York Mary, Melbourne Mary, Scary Mary, Hail Mary, Mary Mary, Hairy Mary, etc., etc.

No one chased me out so I hung around in a corner for five minutes—to soak up the atmosphere, as they say in evangelical circles. It was nothing like I'd imagined the dressing room at a beauty contest would be. (Believe me, I'd done a lot of imagining.) There was no hair-pulling or cat-fights, just mountains of makeup and a mist of hair lacquer so thick it was like breathing candy-floss.

My grasp of the competition rules was tenuous but it appeared that the only qualifications for entry were Irish descent and a high embarrassment threshold. A series of heats had been held in towns and cities around the world. The winners traveled to Donegal, where they got the once-in-a-lifetime chance to parade down Dungloe main street in a hailstorm, meet the staff at McGinley's Motors in Letterkenny and visit a crockery factory in Donegal town.

Strangely, the competition for places in some corners of the globe hadn't exactly been fierce. Having once finished last in a Beautiful Baby contest at Butlin's, I'm hardly well placed to pass judgment on other people's looks but . . . let me just say some of the girls were comely.

Others were jaw-droppingly gorgeous. New Orleans Mary had clearly just stepped from the pages of *Vogue*. Donegal Mary is, was and forever shall be the girl of my dreams. Marys Cardiff, London and Dublin could take comfort from a report in one of the local papers which said that the Mary from Dungloe pageant was about more than looks. It was about personality, attitude and "showing a special talent."

I went out into the front of house just as the first contestant was about to show off her special talent, Irish dancing. She was a beautiful woman but about as graceful as a rugby scrum. A few others also did Irish dancing, some sang, one girl read a poem by W. B. Yeats.

New Orleans Mary came onstage bearing a lantern and a hammer. She read a poem she'd written about an Irish relative who was once a blacksmith. W. B. Yeats could rest easy. It was heartfelt but terrible (she rhymed "horseshoe" with "I'll remember you"). I found myself falling out of love, especially when she asked Daniel if she could say a "special hello to my boyfriend Stevie" and a seven-foot giant with pectorals the size of bowling balls stood up to take a bow.

Donegal Mary made the tin whistle sound like the New

York Philharmonic conducted by Bernstein. I wanted to marry her straight away until she, too, broke down under fierce questioning by Daniel and confessed there was "someone special in my life called Michael." I was crushed. There is only so much disappointment a man can handle on one night. I took my unrequited love to the backstage bar for a half of Guinness.

I was taking my first sip when a couple of Marys came up to the counter.

"Give me a fuckin' large gin, I'm going to get off my face," one said to the barmaid, a trifle less demure than I remembered her onstage.

"Did you hear that silly cow singing?" said the other, nodding in the direction of a rival.

Her friend shook her head in disgust. "Whitney Houston, eat your fuckin' heart out."

I watched the rest of the show on the TV in the bar. Eventually, the judges went off to a room at the other end of the building to choose a winner. All the contestants mingled nervously around backstage for half an hour. The atmosphere was as convivial and sisterly as the convent in *The Sound of Music* before the Nazis showed up. Addresses were being swapped, promises of lifelong friendships exchanged—not with me, sadly. By midnight my initial enthusiasm had crumbled into something beyond boredom.

I couldn't leave, however. John was adamant that Daniel's girlfriend was the big news. "Speak to Daniel. I want the whole story," he barked at me before I left, sounding for once in his life like a proper newspaper editor.

Luckily, the great man came into the bar as I was about to go home.

Only once in my life have I been in the presence of musical genius, at a recording studio in London. I was playing pool with Lloyd Cole and the Commotions' guitar roadie when David

Bowie walked into the room. This is a true story. I was breathing the same air as Ziggy Stardust, the man who recorded "Heroes." In my tiny little universe Bowie was God. I remember what happened as if it happened this morning. My brain frantically issued instructions to the rest of me to remain cool but my cheeks turned the color of ketchup and my mouth said, "Excuse me, Mr. Bowie, can I have your autograph?" I believe the medical term is starstruck.

Daniel didn't have quite the same effect on me, although I did get quite a fright when he fixed me with his big, staring blue eyes.

"Excuse me a minute, Mr. O'Donnell, could I talk to you about your girlfriend?"

"If you could give me just a moment, I have to speak to someone," he said, with a smile that couldn't have been cooler if it had been painted on a stainless-steel mask. He walked out of the bar.

The next time I saw him he was onstage, crowning Sydney Mary with a fake tiara and handing her a check for a thousand pounds. She was undeniably beautiful but, frankly, the wrong choice, not least because she'd said in her interview that Celine Dion was her favorite singer. Donegal Mary had been robbed. I thought briefly of mounting the stage and denouncing the whole event as a sham but headed for the exit instead.

Daniel's concert wasn't until the following night. I had planned to book into a hotel in Dungloe but it was raining harder than ever, my clothes were damp and the town felt about as festive as a pauper's funeral. The lure of sleeping in my own bed proved irresistible. I drove back to Creeslough, disappointed that I would miss the concert after all. But not that disappointed.

• • •

"Did you see Daniel, then?"

"Sure I did."

"What did he say about his girlfriend?"

"Eh, not much."

John shifted his pipe from the left side of his mouth to the right. "Not much," he said, slyly. "How much is not much? Is it enough to fill two pages I've set aside in this week's paper for the article you are going to write about the life and times of Donegal's greatest living man?"

I shook my head and yawned. This was a big mistake. It provoked John into a long and tedious lecture about how Daniel was worth ten times that shower of bluffers at the tourist board, how he had single-handedly set out to sell Donegal to the world and how he ended every single one of his concerts by urging the audience, "Come and visit my beautiful homeland."

"I'm surprised there's anyone left in the hall at the end of his concerts," I sneered, not that John cared. He was still droning on about the first time he ever saw Daniel in concert, "In a pub in Ramelton," and Daniel's hotel, "Ireland's busiest hotel," and Daniel's mother, "He loves his mammy."

When he finished he said, "Now put all that in, get a few words about the girlfriend, and you'll have quite a good article. And while you're at it I don't want any of your metropolitan sneering either. He might not be The Pulp or a Beastie Boy but Daniel is the best thing that has ever happened to this place."

"Pulp," I said, weakly. "They're called Pulp, not The Pulp."

Francis came with me to Dungloe to take photographs. We left the office early and made a detour to have a look at Daniel's hotel.

Called the Viking House, it overlooked the Atlantic at the singer's home village, Kincasslagh. It wasn't much of a hotel, more of an oversized B-and-B bungalow, really, but John was right: it was the busiest hotel in Ireland, the busiest building in Ireland in fact. The car park was jammed. The license plates were from all over Ireland, Glasgow, Manchester, even London.

Inside, the reception hall was a seething mass of wrinkled flesh and blue-rinse hair-dos. The walls groaned under the weight of platinum and gold discs.

We had hoped to have tea with Daniel. (All pop stars have gimmicks—biting heads off chickens, shooting up onstage and so on. Daniel's was serving cups of tea to his fans.) Alas, the great man wasn't around. I joined the queue for the restaurant anyway. Francis spotted a merchandise stall and went off to buy a pair of Daniel O'Donnell pot holders for his granny.

He was only gone a minute. "Sold out of oven gloves." He sighed. He wasn't alone in his disappointment. A group of women in front of us in the queue were talking about their hero's girlfriend. Never had the metropolitan world of the *Guardian* seemed so distant as it did as I stood there eavesdropping.

"I hope it's not true. She'd change him," one said firmly. "We'd never see him anymore."

"Aw naw, he'd still be oor wee Daniel. He'll always love us, even if he had a girlfriend," said her friend, who had clearly prepared for the discussion as if she was appearing on *Question Time*.

She reeled off a list of Daniel facts that made him sound as saintly as, possibly saintlier than, St. Peter: his unannounced visits to the hospitalized; the endless charity work; the hymn singing in the local church; the number of jobs created in this corner of Donegal by the Daniel O'Donnell industry; the Mary from Dungloe Festival would have crashed without his support. Then there was his own Kincasslagh Festival, which generated £750,000 for the local economy every year.

Admittedly, this isn't the kind of responsible behavior I like in my pop stars but it was hard not to be impressed. If medals were ever struck for service to Donegal's economy Daniel would be at the head of the queue, way in front of the tourist board and a T-shirt company that had taken the £10 million grant from the government and pissed off to Morocco. It's just a shame about his records.

The concert was the aural equivalent of fur-lined slippers. It lasted three hours. I hated every minute, except for a joke Daniel told about an Irishman called Neilly Dunn who went to London and didn't get in touch with his mother to tell her how he was getting on. I've forgotten most of it now but the punch line involved a knock on a cubicle door in the toilets at Victoria station and someone asking, "Are you Neilly Dunn?"

"I am," said a voice from inside. "But there's no paper in here."

"Sure, but that's no excuse for not writing to your mother for two years."

That was as good as it got.

Of course, the audience of pensionable women and their doting husbands loved it. If old age means developing a fondness for Daniel O'Donnell's voice, I'll take premature death anytime.

I didn't even find his new girlfriend. She must have been there, though. Her picture appeared in most of the Dublin-based tabloids the following morning. Her name was Rose. She looked like, well, Daniel O'Donnell's girlfriend—pretty in a girl-next-doorish way. But how she had managed to snare Ireland's most eligible bachelor was destined to remain a mystery, at least to the readers of the *Tirconaill Tribune*.

"Don't worry about it, she'll not last long anyway," Francis said, with spooky prescience, as we headed home. Two months later, Daniel's fans had him to themselves once again.

Francis thought he knew a shortcut back to Creeslough. We got lost and ended up on a nighttime tour of Donegal's wilderness. I might have enjoyed it if I'd been able to take my eyes off the fuel gauge, which hovered alarmingly in the red for three-quarters of the journey. Civilization seemed to end at the outskirts of Dungloe. There were weeds growing through cracks in the road. If the car had run out of petrol we'd have been old enough to be Daniel O'Donnell fans by the time we got a lift from a passing motorist.

We stumbled across Creeslough purely by chance. I crawled into my bed just after 3 A.M. I would happily have written off the experience as one of the worst nights of my life but for a chance meeting at the back of the concert hall just as Daniel started his encores.

I had come back from the café to find Francis talking to a small, silver-haired woman.

"Lawrence, you haven't met Sarah Hunter." He introduced me, saying, "Sarah, talk to this boy, will you? He's obsessed with that friend of yours, Bernard Lafferty. His name's Lawrence Donegan."

He then turned to me and said, "Sarah knew Bernard quite well when he lived in America."

Sarah seemed to take mild offense at this introduction. "Knew him? I was the one that found him dead in his bed." She cut herself off when she saw my eyes light up. "But I can't talk about that."

We listened for a minute or so to Daniel's version of "Rivers of Babylon." Incredibly, it was worse than Boney M's. Sarah leant over to me and said, "Aw, you should have seen him lying there, looking so peaceful with his blond hair all over the pillow . . ." She stopped herself again.

"Put your hands together . . ."

"Poor Bernard, I was only taking him his morning glass of water. He looked so peaceful. He had his blue Versace night-shirt on. He looked lovely in that nightshirt."

Even with Daniel's racket drowning out half of what she was saying it was obvious that Sarah Hunter was the world's leading authority on Bernard Lafferty: the will, Doris, the "murder," what he thought about Creeslough, the helicopter flight, why he never came back.

There were a thousand questions I wanted to ask her but she clammed up before I had the chance to ask one. "Come on, Sarah, please," I pleaded.

"Sorry, but I really can't talk about it," she said, with the beginnings of a smile playing on her lips. I could tell she was wavering.

"How about Friday?" I replied.

"I'm going to Australia on holiday with my mammy."

"How long are you away?"

"Six weeks."

"I'll phone you when you get back, okay?"

"Fine. Have you got my telephone number?"

"ALL TOGETHER NOW . . . By the rivers . . ."

Public Enemy No. 1

In the cacophony of words marking the first anniversary of Princess Di's death I heard just a solitary squeak of dissent. Actually, it was a poem of dissent (to be read while holding a candle in the wind, according to the asterisked instruction at the bottom of the newspaper page) and it went:

Good-bye, Princess Di,
Though I didn't know you at all
Gosh, I really liked your hair
And the clothes you used to wear
But it seems to me that you fell in
With a crowd of queers,
Phil the Greek, his wife Liz,
And that bloke with big ears.

Good-bye, Princess Di,
Even now my hanky's wet
'Cause I cried for twenty days
Then I cried for twenty more.
But it seems to me, though I could be wrong,
  that climbing in a Merc
With a drunk behind the wheel,
  you really were a jerk.

But despite Panorama, *despite all your fame*
Your candle snuffed out a year ago
Alas, the monarchy remains.

I've never seen such a lethal combination of bad poetry and bad taste. It was the anniversary of her death, after all. As soon as I saw it in the *Tirconaill Tribune* I wished I had never written it.

John, though, could hardly contain his excitement. Standing in the car park in Letterkenny flicking through freshly minted copies of the paper, he looked happier than I'd ever seen him or expect I ever will.

"Holy fuck," he said proudly. "Look at this poem, will you? It's brilliant."

He held open the page for Bridie and Tommy to read. They looked genuinely disgusted. Francis laughed, wanly. Declan had a more-in-sorrow-than-anger expression on his face that I decided to interpret as mild amusement. There was no mistaking what Noel thought. "Jesus, I can't believe you wrote that. Don't get me wrong, I think it's brilliant, but there are folk around here that will go fuckin' crazy."

I looked again half hoping that the page had been printed in invisible ink and had faded to white.

The complaints started about an hour after we had finished delivering the papers. John was denounced in the grocery store for "dancing on the grave of that poor girl." Francis was asked by a woman he met on Milford's main street to tell me she hoped God would forgive me because she sure as hell wouldn't.

Kathleen said she was seriously considering resigning from the *Tribune*.

"But I didn't write it," I lied. "A reader sent it in. John put my name on it when I wasn't looking."

"Don't talk rubbish. I sat and watched you typing it out, Mr. Donegan, sniggering away. There was me thinking I was going to have a nice article for my collection," she said, in a low, furious whisper. (How were we to know she'd been keeping a Princess Diana scrapbook since the Royal Wedding?)

The phone calls started the following morning. The first letter arrived the day after that, from a doctor at the hospital in Letterkenny. The words FOR PUBLICATION were angrily scrawled across the top of the page. Even now, months later, it is burned on my memory. "I thought the *Tirconaill Tribune* was supposed to be a family newspaper. Mr. Donegan, you are an utter disgrace to your profession and your so-called poem was the foulest piece of excrement I have ever read in my entire life . . ."

The president of Donegal Christian Women's Association wrote to say she had met Diana at a function in Belfast just before her death. The Princess was a lovely person, she said, unlike me who was a disgraceful human being and "foul to the very core."

A couple of the lads from the Gaelic football team said they thought the poem was hilarious. I momentarily convinced myself that the silent majority, the ones who had better things to do with their time than write letters, were on my side. But I was kidding myself.

For the next two weeks I was Public Enemy No. 1. Every time I arrived in the office Noel complained about having spent most of the day on the phone apologizing to people and trying to persuade them not to cancel their subscription to the paper.

If John was worried about the loss of income he hid it well. "This is the most number of complaints in the history of the *Tirconaill Tribune*—ever!" he announced triumphantly, while we were all sitting in the kitchen drinking tea a few days later. "If I could afford to give you a pay rise, Lawrence, I would."

He printed every letter of complaint in the next issue under the headline "UP THE ROYALS!". To add some balance he spent the best part of a night composing a letter from a Mr. James Wishborne-Ashe, of Somerset, England, congratulating "your correspondent Lawrence Donegan, who managed to strip away the legend, the myths and the absolute hypocrisy of the class system which continues to divide and distort British society. He clearly has a big future in poetry circles."

Francis thought this was pushing it a bit for a poem that rhymed Merc with jerk. I thought it was, without question, the most transparent fake since the Turin Shroud.

A couple of days later an outraged letter arrived from an organization called the Irish Monarchists' Association. John thought it was a spoof at first. He refused to believe that an organization called the Irish Monarchists' Association actually existed until Francis telephoned the Dublin number on the headed notepaper and got an answer-machine that played (so he claimed) "God Save the Queen."

John was wide-eyed with disbelief. "The Irish Monarchists' Association. It's like saying there's the Gerry Adams Loyal Orange Supporters Club."

I didn't care. I just wanted the whole episode to end. Royalty, Republican, Gerry Adams, Loyal Orange, Ian Paisley . . . These were highly charged political words that I'd hardly heard since moving to Donegal. Frankly, the mere mention of them made me feel nervous. They spoke of a dangerous place I vaguely recognized from the BBC *Nine O'clock News* as having wrecked town centers and people who settle their arguments about constitutional issues with a spot of freelance baseball-bat surgery.

It often amazes me how supremely ignorant some people are about things around them. Take me, as a random example. How on earth did I get to my advanced stage of life and know so little about Irish history and politics? Where on earth did I get the daft idea that everybody who lived in the Republic of Ireland hated the British Royal Family and would heartily congratulate anyone who chiseled out a few laughs at the expense of poor dead Princess Di?

The flow of vitriol dried up after the letter from the Monarchists' Association, thankfully. But the experience taught me a couple of valuable lessons: don't write poetry, and avoid contact with Irish politics at all costs.

But, of course, you can't avoid contact with politics in Ireland, even in Creeslough.

As if the village's admiration for Diana wasn't a startling enough revelation, John mentioned in passing one night that an arms cache had once been found in a field behind St. Michael's parish church. Admittedly, it happened twenty years ago and it was only a couple of rusty rifles, but I was startled. This was the closest brush I'd ever had with terrorism.

I heard other tiny echoes of the Troubles as the weeks and months passed. It turned out that the Irish police had searched my cottage for guns in 1980; a member of the IRA's Balcombe Street Gang was born and raised in one of the local villages. One afternoon I was driving through Milford with a friend when he pointed at a stocky, gray-haired man walking down the street.

"See that fella there? Do you know he was a crew member on the famous ship, the *Eksund*?" Of course, I had no idea what he was talking about.

The *Eksund*, he explained, was a boat that had been seized off the Brittany coast by French customs in the early nineties. Once on board they found twenty SAM-7 missiles and four thousand AK-47 rifles hidden in the hold—weapons donated to the IRA by Libya's Colonel Gaddafi. It was the biggest arms seizure in the history of the Irish Troubles. The five-man crew, including our friend across the street, spent the next few years in a French jail. It was impossible to reconcile such a terrifying, horrible story with this shambling figure dressed in dirty wellies and a gray sweater with a hole in the elbow.

"And do you know what?" my friend said. "He's a lovely lad—one of the best electricians you will ever meet in your life."

"He's not, is he?" I made a mental note to do my own electrical repairs, no matter how dangerous.

Don't get me wrong, Donegal wasn't crawling with terrorists. Nor was everyday conversation given over to debating the merits of Loyalism, Republicanism and any other ism. In fact, it was surprising how little attention people paid to events just over the border in Northern Ireland. Sure they cared but only in the way that they cared about what was happening in Kosovo or Rwanda.

Only once did I hear mutterings of discontent, when there was a rumor that the Orange Order was planning to march through one of the local villages. But it never happened. I was secretly disappointed. I had never seen grown men wearing embroidered orange sashes and bowler hats dancing around in broad daylight, which is why I took myself off to Derry one Saturday afternoon to see the Apprentice Boys' Parade.

If ever a group of enterprising young men deserves a parade in their honor it is thirteen Protestant apprentice boys who closed Derry's gates in the face of the Earl of Antrim's Catholic army. It was December 7, 1688. The city's Protestants were petrified. A few days earlier an anonymous letter had been found at a place called Comber, County Down, that suggested they were about to be massacred.

There were thirty thousand people inside the city's fortress wall when the gates closed. Within days, ten thousand had left voluntarily. The remaining Catholics were expelled.

On April 18, 1689, the Catholic King James II brought his army to this troublesome Irish outpost expecting a meek surrender. Instead he was met with gunshot and cries of "no surrender." History records that the King flounced back to Dublin "very much mortified." Three days later his troops began the bombardment of Derry. For the next six weeks repeated attempts to storm the city walls were repelled. Eventually the besieging army decided to starve the garrison into surrender.

The survivors had now been hemmed inside the city walls for seven months. Living conditions were unimaginable so I won't ask you to imagine them. Instead I will simply reveal a price list of what was available in the city's shops by this stage of the siege:

Quarter of dog	Five shillings and sixpence
A dog's head	Two shillings and sixpence
A cat	Four shillings and sixpence
A rat	One shilling
A mouse	Sixpence
Horse blood (1 qrt)	One shilling

Relief—and it must have been some relief after a dinner of boiled dog's head, deep-fried mouse and a glass of horse's blood—came on July 28, with the arrival of English warships on the River Foyle. Three days later the demoralized Catholic troops decamped and left.

In the frankly surprising words of a spokesman for Sinn Fein (the main Irish Republican party with links to the IRA), the victory won by the thirteen young apprentice boys was "an act of truly revolutionary self-determination which can only be admired."

The man from Sinn Fein must have hated saying that but he

was right. The apprentice boys and those who endured the siege of Derry were immeasurably brave. Eight thousand people died on either side of the wall. I just wonder how the survivors felt at the end of all the suffering when it was discovered that a massacre of Protestants had never been imminent at all, that the Comber letter was a fake.

I arrived at Derry early, bought a copy of *The Illustrated Orange Song Book* at a street stall (I wanted to learn the words to "The Pope's a Darkie" just in case I ever needed to ingratiate myself with the Reverend Ian Paisley) and bagged a prime viewing spot on the Craigavon Bridge across the River Foyle. The parade set off toward the city center just after noon. There were ten thousand marchers, from middle-aged men wearing their Sunday best suits, to families on a day out and half-drunk young men in preposterous outfits. It was a festival of bad tailoring—yellow suits with red piping, orange jackets with blue trousers, lilac suits with red epaulettes.

I had planned to stay the whole day but felt a migraine coming on after fifteen minutes. It wasn't just the kaleidoscopic clothes. The shrill racket of a thousand flute bands playing a thousand different tunes at the same time made me want to lie down in a darkened room for a fortnight.

I walked alongside the marchers as far as the city's war memorial. We were met there by a line of riot police and armed vehicles. Beyond them was a small group of Nationalist protesters who started hurling abuse and, more worryingly, rocks. This only acted as a spur for the flutes to become shriller and the bass drums to become louder and even less rhythmic.

By now the atmosphere was deeply unpleasant. I don't mind admitting I was scared, although march aficionados insisted it was all passing off relatively peacefully. I nipped into a newsagent's to buy a copy of the *Guardian*. "Bad day for business," I said, waking up the man behind the counter.

"You should have seen it last year." He smiled. "There was a war going on outside the door."

I hadn't seen my old paper for months now. I was relieved to discover the loss of my skills hadn't led to a massive circulation collapse and rapid closure. I headed off to the nearest café to see what my ex-workmates had been up to. I was only gone for twenty minutes but such is my uncanny journalistic instinct that I still managed to miss a mini-riot, not to mention a police officer shooting his gun into the air in an effort to dissuade some youths from kicking him to death. Another triumph for Scoop Donegan. No wonder the *Guardian* was getting along pretty well without me.

Calm had been restored by the time I wandered back to the war memorial. I'd read somewhere that over 170 bands were taking part in the march. Judging by the noise heading in my direction about half of them were still to pass. Given the choice of listening to "The Sash" eighty-five times or an afternoon playing golf in Donegal, I headed straight for the car and home.

I was glad to get out of Derry, frankly. I felt like a ghoul for going there in the first place. If the Apprentice Boys' Parade and the attendant aggro had been happening at the bottom of my garden I would have gone on holiday for a week to make sure I missed it. Yet here I was cursing my luck because I had missed all the action. No doubt everyone who'd lived in Derry for the last thirty years was cursing their luck because they hadn't.

I made a silent promise on the way home that, once and for all, I would keep my nose out of Irish politics.

And I did, except for an article I wrote later that week about the attitudes in rural Ireland toward the troubles in Northern Ireland. I wrote that terrorism was hardly more than a faint distraction from everyday life in Donegal. It wasn't that people were indifferent, they were just happy that an accident of history had left them on the side of the border where killing and maiming weren't a daily occurrence.

In passing I mentioned the *Eksund* arms shipment. I said it was a measure of people's desire for normality that the presence in their midst of a man convicted for trying to import four thousand AK-47s from Libya was remarked upon by my friends only because he was the best electrician in the county. I did, I confess, make a mild joke at his expense—that it must have been a real come-down from shaking hands with Colonel Gaddafi to fixing the fuse box in some oul fella's house in the hills of Donegal.

A few days after this throw-away line appeared in print John, Francis and I were in the kitchen debating whether or not I should go to Tory, a small island off the Donegal coast.

Work had just finished on the island's new streetlights. This was a hugely significant event for the community. It had spent the last thirty years resisting the Irish government's efforts to force them to live on the mainland. To have that same government stumping up the cash for brand-new streetlights must have been the sweetest kind of victory.

I would have loved to have witnessed the occasion but I wasn't sure if I could face the ferry trip. I get seasick stepping into a bath. The eleven-mile stretch of Atlantic ocean between the mainland and Tory was a notoriously rough crossing, even when the weather was good. By the time I reached the island I suspected I would have vomited enough to fill a coal-sack.

Reluctantly, I decided to phone a couple of islanders instead, interview them and write the story with my feet planted firmly on the office desk. Or at least that was the plan until a slightly scruffy figure appeared at the kitchen door, ostensibly to speak to John. But for some reason he kept staring at me. I thought this odd but smiled back, picked up a copy of the *Farmers' Journal* from the table and started flicking through the pages.

I was halfway through a fascinating article about sheep dip when it dawned on me: it was the man from the *Eksund*. He was standing three feet away, looking at me as if he was measuring me for a coffin. I kept my head down, staring straight at the page. But I didn't read a word. I could sense his eyes boring into the top of my bowed head. He was there for two minutes. It felt like forever. When he finally left, I looked up. John was sucking up air through his pursed lips.

"Jesus, boy," he said tightly, "that guy hasn't been in this office for a few years at least. Did you see him checking you out?"

This was not what I wanted to hear, frankly. My sphincter started flapping like the front door of an abandoned wooden shack in a strong wind. I could just about handle the disapproval of the Irish Monarchists' Association and assorted Princess Di fans. Getting on the wrong side of an IRA man—even if he had retired to the less intimidating profession of electrician—was a different matter altogether.

There might have been a moment when I had been more petrified but for the life of me I couldn't recall it. I tried hard to hide this from Francis and John. "Don't be daft. What would he be checking me out for?" I said, with a watery smile. "He wasn't. Was he?"

"Holy fuck. I'm telling you he was checking you out." John looked deadly serious.

Francis shook his head. "Jesus, John, will you calm yourself? You're scaring the life out of the boy. Can't you see he's shitting himself?"

"I'm not," I squeaked, sounding like Aled Jones with his balls in a vice.

Francis tried his best to calm me down. No one ever got

bumped off in Ireland for making a joke, he said. "There's a peace process, these days—the violence is over."

"Is that right, Francis? What about the punishment beatings?" John interrupted. He was clearly enjoying this. "You know, baseball bats with a few six-inch nails through them and the like. You can do a lot of damage with those boyos."

"Very fucking funny, John," Francis said. "Just ignore him, Lawrence. He's only pulling your leg."

"That boy will do more than pull your leg if he takes a notion." John bent down and scratched the dog under its chin. "Wouldn't he, my wee Bouncer?"

It was just about then that a nauseating boat trip, followed by a week on a remote Irish island, suddenly seemed like a great idea. I went home and bolted the front door for the first time since moving to Creeslough. I threw some clothes into a hold-all, ready for a quick escape in the morning. The weather forecast was bad. I packed a coal-sack.

The ferry for Tory left the mainland at a place called Magheraroarty, an hour's drive west of Creeslough. I went to bed early. I couldn't sleep. Instead I kept perfectly still with my eyes closed in the hope that anyone who burst through the front door carrying an AK-47 might decide I looked so peaceful it would be best not to disturb me.

Never had I been so glad to see dawn break.

When I got to Magheraroarty a crowd of middle-aged men was milling around. Every one of them was wearing khaki trousers, waistcoats with a phalanx of pockets and a baseball cap. They all had two pairs of binoculars hanging from their necks and enough photographic equipment to kit out a NASA space probe. I recognized the uniform. They were bird-watchers.

I bought a ticket from the white fisherman's hut at the end of the quay and sat on the wall outside waiting for the ferry to arrive. The weather was misty and dull but nowhere near as bad as forecast. There was very little wind, thankfully.

Whatever had tempted all these people to this remote corner of the planet on such a gray day must have been hugely exciting. They were squawking away like hungry seagulls. I thought about asking but that would have broken one of my golden rules for a happy life: never get trapped in a conversation with a bird-watcher.

The ferry, *Tormor*, appeared out of the mist and anchored in the bay. Passengers were relayed out by dinghy, six at a time. I hung back to avoid the bird-watchers. I went out on the last trip along with a man from the electricity board, an elderly woman, a French couple and a German hippie in a hand-knitted jumper.

The journey lasted a minute but was action-packed. The French couple were clearly on honeymoon and had some unfinished business from the night before. The electrician and the hippie were delighted to discover that ringside seats for a sex show had been included in the price of the ferry ticket. Meanwhile, the old woman blathered away to me in Gaelic. She sounded censorious. "Would you look at that filthy French bastard with his hand up that girl's skirt—disgusting!" she said. Or at least she might have done, I couldn't understand a word.

Thankfully, both she and the French couple had calmed down by the time the *Tormor* gently eased out of the bay. Even the bird-watchers had run out of things to say and were becalmed. A watery sun appeared through the haze. I started to relax for the first time since the encounter with Mr. Eksund. As we skimmed across a flat sea into the great wide open, the world was suddenly at peace. It was going to be a good crossing.

It wasn't. As soon as we hit open water the swell started to rise. Pretty soon my breakfast was doing the same. I thought reading a book might take my mind off the sickness then remembered I'd packed Sebastian Junger's *The Perfect Storm*, a terrifying account of six men whose trawler went down in mountainous seas. I tried to go to sleep instead. That didn't work. Eventually I went outside and hung over the rail, waiting for the inevitable.

When it came it was multi-colored and violent and seemed to last for an age. My breakfast hit the big black ocean in a series of tiny plops. Afterward I sat back, closed my eyes and hoped the breeze on my face would somehow soothe my turbulent guts. I must have fallen asleep momentarily because I woke with a jump to find one of the bird-watchers sitting next to me.

"Are you not feeling well?" he said.

"Not at all, I'm feeling fantastic," I replied sourly, hoping that my vomit breath would send him scarpering to the other end of the boat.

"Yeah, I'm a bad sailor too but I took some seasickness pills before we got on."

"Many congratulations."

Either he didn't hear me or decades of bird-watching had made him immune to sarcasm: he didn't take offense and move to another seat. I knew then that I was trapped. I was still feeling lousy and weak but I promised myself I wouldn't surrender easily.

We sat in silence for five minutes until he rubbed his hands together excitedly and said, "Oh, it's going to be a very big day today."

"Mmmmm." I closed my eyes. Incredibly, he took this as a signal of heightened interest.

"Yeah. One of the guys back there was saying it's the first live recorded sighting of this particular bird since 1957."

I opened my eyes again. The heat from the sun had started to burn off the haze. It was possible to see the outline of Tory on the northern horizon. Looking back toward the mainland I guessed we were about halfway through the crossing. It had taken half an hour to get this far. Another thirty minutes to go.

"Yeah. There was a dead one of the same species found in Cork about five years ago and another in Wexford seven years before that."

It was far too early to give in. In any case the effort involved in ignoring him was taking my mind off the nausea.

"But a real live one . . ." He whistled through a gap in his teeth. "As soon as a friend telephoned to tell me the news I jumped in the car. I left Dublin last night around midnight. I came all the way on my own. Got here this morning about six. The worst thing is, I forgot to pack some sandwiches and a flask of tea. Of course there's no chance of a cooked breakfast in Magheraroarty. I'm bloody starving . . ."

As he wittered on it was obvious why he'd chosen to sit next to me: even his bird-watching mates thought he was the most boring man on earth. He had no one else to talk to but me. My resolve started to crumble. I stopped feeling sorry for myself and started feeling sorry for him. Tory was growing bigger on the horizon. I figured we would be there in fifteen minutes.

"Do you think there's a café on the island?" He was almost down on his knees at this stage.

"All right, all right," I said, making it clear I was doing him the biggest favor of his life. "What kind of bird is it? And do tell me, because I'm fucking dying to know, what are its principal distinguishing markings?"

Ballybeg

Imagine a municipal art gallery where the *Mona Lisa* was on permanent display. Then imagine the outrage if it was secretly decided that Leonardo's masterpiece had to go because it was costing too much to heat and light the exhibit room. One night a janitor took the painting off the wall and threw it on a bonfire. By the time the vandalism was discovered it was too late, the *Mona Lisa* was gone forever.

Of course, it couldn't happen. No one would be stupid enough to destroy a priceless treasure just to save a few pounds on the electricity bill. Would they?

Now, imagine that the priceless treasure was not a painting but a living culture, an island with its own language and traditions and people whose ancestors first moved there in the sixth century. Imagine a secret plan to force these people to leave their homes because if they did, it would save the government money. Imagine if that same plan involved turning the island, host to some of the most important archaeological sites in Ireland, into an army firing range.

Imagine . . . actually, don't imagine anything. It's unnecessary, because all of this really happened. In 1978 a secret plan was drawn up for Donegal County Council to "evacuate" an island and sell it off for target practice. The island was called Tory.

It might have gone ahead too but for the islanders' stubborn refusal to let their community die. With the help of the local Jesuit priest, Father Diarmuid O Péicín, they alerted the world to what was going on. The campaign to save the island eventually forced the Irish government to stump up money for a running water supply, sewage facilities, a half-decent road, good

schooling for the local children, street lighting—in short, everything most people take for granted but that the Tory islanders
had been deliberately denied in an effort to force them to move
to the mainland.

I can't begin to tell you how pleased I was that the islanders'
campaign succeeded and that Tory is now thriving. If it hadn't I
would have missed out on one of the most perfect weeks of my
life.

As soon as the ferry docked I ran away from my new bird-
watching friend. The island had a handful of B-and-Bs but I
decided to splash out. I booked into the hotel at the pier, partly
because it was Tory's biggest employer and I wanted to do my
bit for the local economy. If that meant spending the night in a
room with a color television—a clear violation of my self-
imposed ban on TV—then it was a sacrifice I was prepared to
make.

There were only two other guests. The receptionist took me
upstairs and told me to pick a room. I chose one with a king-size
bed and a television that didn't work. When I phoned Reception
to complain I was told someone would come straight away to
fix it. I detected an end-of-summer-season weariness in her
voice that said, "Dream on, Sunshine." Rightly, as it turned out.
After half an hour I gave up waiting, slipped on a pair of shorts
and set off to do some exploring around the island instead. The
television could wait. It probably still is. I got the distinct
impression that TV repair wasn't a priority in this part of the
world.

Everything I'd read about Tory's rugged beauty and isolation
was true. Creeslough seemed like downtown Tokyo in comparison.

I wandered along the island's only road. There was evidence
of the long struggle for survival everywhere: traditional Irish

cottages that had lain empty for years, with boarded-up windows and gray walls where the paint had flaked away; rusting car axles; an abandoned tractor or two. There were a few people around. Old women sat out on kitchen chairs enjoying the afternoon sun. Weathered men fixed boats. Their sons dragged bales of seaweed home for drying. Kids splashed around in the water at the quayside. I felt as if I'd stepped back into a simpler, more innocent age.

I went into the craft shop to ask when the streetlights were due to be switched on. The woman behind the counter had the radio tuned to a broadcast of Bill Clinton's grand jury testimony about his affair with Monica Lewinsky. (Perhaps I'd been a bit rash on the simpler, more-innocent-age front.)

"What do you think? Is he guilty?" I asked her, marveling at the global media village.

"Of course he did it. But who cares?" she said, with a wink and a toothless grin that suggested the presidential charm would have been just as effective in this part of Donegal as it had been in the Oval Office.

There was bad news. The streetlights had been switched on a couple of days earlier. I was genuinely disappointed at missing it, which is something I never thought I would say about a streetlight ceremony. Still, it meant I could concentrate on enjoying myself. I hired a bike and cycled to the far end of the island, which sounds impressive but took me all of five minutes. I spent the rest of the afternoon sunbathing at the edge of a precipitous sea-cliff and read a copy of *Islanders*, Father O Péicín's book about Tory's struggle to survive.

Saving islands rather than writing was his forte but it was a great yarn and should be required reading for anyone writing a thesis about the cultural stupidity of some politicians. I discovered later that *Islanders* was going to be turned into a film starring Paul Newman as the priest and a sack of cabbages as the Donegal County Council.

I had intended to return to the hotel, have a shower then eat in the bar, but on the way back I stopped to admire the view at the harbor and became hypnotized by the sound of water gently lapping against the rocks. Before I knew what was happening I was stripped to my boxer shorts and wading in up to my chest.

There is nothing between Tory and the Arctic except ocean. I don't know why I was surprised it was freezing but I was. I swam around for five minutes, long enough to attract a small but admiring audience of three day-trippers. They gave me a round of applause when I came out. I felt proud, if a little upset that I'd never be able to have sex again.

The rest of the week passed as if it were an idyllic dream. The locals said it was the finest September weather the island had seen for years. I swam every day, sunbathed, read, bicycled, ate dinner in the hotel bar and went out afterward to admire the stars and the streetlights. The hotel owner Pat Doohan told me that previously people walked the island in the pitch-dark in twenty-yard installments. They had to wait for the lighthouse beam to sweep across the road, then run like the clappers and stop. Wait. Run. Stop. Imagine doing that every day of your life, possibly with a few whiskeys in your belly. Only then was it possible to fully understand why people got so excited about streetlights.

This was just one of Pat's countless stories. He could talk interestingly about Tory for hours. The island's myths and legends were his particular area of expertise. Most of these stories involved people being turned into stone or slaying their firstborn grandson. It all sounded like tourist shtick to me but to be on the safe side I filled a little plastic bag with "magical" Tory clay before catching the ferry home. It had the power reputedly to ward off rats and protect fishermen at sea. I figured it could come in useful for the cottage, not to mention the ocean-going trawler I might buy one day.

John said I was the first person he'd ever known to come back from Tory with a suntan. He also said two other things. The first made my heart flutter alarmingly: "There was a boy that came in looking for you. He was wearing a balaclava and said something about you making up the numbers in a game of baseball."

Thankfully, Francis was on hand to set me at ease and give him a stern ticking off for breaking his promise not to terrify members of staff.

His second remark was less threatening to my immediate health but to my mind far, far crueler: "Have you heard the news? Meryl Streep is coming to Donegal next week."

On nights when we were putting the paper together in the attic, I'd often spoken to John about my profound feelings for Meryl Streep: that I thought she was a terrific actress, not to mention a complete babe; and that if Buddhism was right and there was such a thing as reincarnation I'd swap my entire record collection to come back as the kid in *Kramer vs. Kramer*—anything to spend five minutes sitting on Meryl's knee with my nose tucked into her cleavage.

John knew better than to tease me about Meryl Streep. I looked at Francis for confirmation that this was another of John's hilarious jokes. This time he shook his head and handed me a fax. "No, he's not having you on. I couldn't believe it myself but it's true."

I read the fax. "Oscar-winning actress Meryl Streep and star of *Dancing at Lughnasa* will be making a personal appearance at the County Donegal premiere of the new film version of Brian Friel's play Tickets for this special event at the school hall Glenties will cost £30. All money raised will go toward the Fintown Railway and the new school sports field. Please contact . . ."

There was a telephone number at the bottom of the page and a name, Malachi McCloskey. I found it hard to believe anyone would make up a name like that. Nevertheless I was highly suspicious of the fax, for a variety of reasons:

(1) The record shows that John McAteer had a history of faking documents (i.e. Mr. James Wishborne-Ashe, of Somerset, England, and the Princess Di debacle).

(2) The idea of anyone in Donegal paying thirty pounds to watch a film was laughable. It was now possible to buy a smallholding and a flock of mountain sheep in Donegal for thirty pounds. There was a new filmed version of Brian Friel's *Dancing at Lughnasa* but it would be showing at the Letterkenny Cinema in a fortnight (tickets three pounds).

(3) We had a running joke in the office about unlikely sightings of movie stars in Donegal, inspired by one of the other local papers that clearly had a fantasist on the staff. Barely a week passed without a visit from a screen legend. Only the week before, "Hot Hollywood couple Cameron Diaz and Matt Dillon were seen in Whoriskey's the grocer's in Ramelton last week. Matt bought half a pound of brussels sprouts. Cameron had an orange-flavored lollipop, which she seemed to enjoy very much."

This was just about as believable as Meryl Streep showing up in Glenties.

(4) I'd heard of a world premiere but I'd never heard
of a County Donegal premiere.

I read the press release again and looked at John. He turned
his back. "I'm saying nothing. I've been told by Francis to keep
my mouth shut," he said, mock-huffily.

I phoned the number at the bottom of the press release, half
expecting to get a massage parlor in Dublin or the Irish
Monarchists' Association. Someone answered straight away. I
explained I was from the *Tirconaill Tribune* and wanted to speak
to Malachi McCloskey.

"That's me," a businesslike voice said. There was an authen-
ticity about his manner that was entirely out of step with a
hoax. I could see John out of the corner of my eye. He looked
extremely pleased with himself.

"I want to talk to someone about the Meryl Streep visit."

He didn't miss a beat. "Yes?"

I hesitated. "It's a joke, isn't it?"

Malachi laughed. "I hope not. We've been having committee meetings about it every night for the last month. We've
booked the hall, got our hands on a special video player and a
giant screen. We've sold most of the tickets." He gave me a
lengthy description of the logistical nightmares involved in
arranging parking for four hundred cars in a town as small as
Glenties.

I was stunned. Either John had wasted the entire week while
I was on Tory Island setting up a hoax, possibly with the help of
an old actor friend from his days working at the theater. Or
Meryl Streep really was coming to Donegal.

"Malachi, do you know a guy called John McAteer?"

"John McAteer? Who's that?"

If Malachi was an actor he was clearly in Meryl Streep's class.

He was now giving an Oscar-winning performance as someone who believed I was a crank caller. "Listen, is there something wrong? If not, I really have to go. There's a lot of work still to do on the parking arrangements."

"Actually, Malachi, it's just that Meryl Streep is my all-time heartthrob and I just can't believe that she's coming to Donegal."

The suspicion in his voice shaded to weariness. Obviously, I wasn't the first person in the last week to accuse him of being a fantasist. "Yes." He sighed. "A lot of people in the town are the same. They can't believe it either. But I've got a pile of faxes from the film company in my hand that say she is. We'd been asking them for months how can they be sure she's coming and they just kept saying, 'Trust us.' Now they're sending us her schedule—when she's arriving, what she wants on the night, all that kind of stuff."

There is a variation of an old saying—well, there is in our house—which says that if you give a monkey a typewriter it will take three days to write a Ken Follett novel and a million years to come up with the complete works of Shakespeare. This is just a way of expressing the statistical truth that anything is possible, but that some events are drearily commonplace while others are so unlikely you could wait for eternity for them to happen. Into the latter category I would have inserted the suggestion that one day I would meet Meryl Streep at a film premiere in Donegal.

When I put the phone down I was in a state of shock. Malachi gave me the film company's telephone number and promised to keep me a ticket. I arranged to meet him in Glenties later in the week to collect it and interview him about arrangements for the premiere. It turned out that he was a Meryl Streep fan too, though not as devoted as me. No one was.

• • •

The *Tirconaill Tribune*'s exclusive interview with Meryl Streep was an unlikely proposition from the outset. I phoned the film company on the off chance. The woman in the press office was very friendly but incredulous.

"The what?" she said, when I told her who I was and the name of the paper I worked for.

I repeated myself, not that it made any difference.

"The *Tri-color Tribune*?" She sounded faintly disgusted, as if she'd just found a pair of soiled knickers that had been down the back of a settee for six months.

There seemed little point in trying to correct her. I stuttered on, skirting round questions about the *Tribune*'s circulation (up to 3,007, since you ask) and the fact that the local cinemas didn't even advertise in the *Tribune*. I promised her we were "a must-read" for every moviegoer in Donegal.

After two minutes she put her hand over the mouthpiece. I heard her muffled voice say to someone else in the room, "Wait a mo', I'll just get rid of this joker on the phone."

She removed her hand. "I'm sorry, what was that you were saying?"

"I was saying that we wouldn't write anything nasty about Meryl. We'd give her a really nice spread, across two, maybe three pages with some lovely photographs. We have one of the country's top photographers working for us. Please. We would only need five minutes. An interview with the *Tribune* could be good . . ."

I only just stopped myself saying an interview with the *Tirconaill Tribune* could be good for Meryl's career.

At least she let me down gently. She said she was sure I'd understand but that Ms. Streep had a limited amount of time in Ireland. She could fit in only a handful of interviews. Naturally, these would all be with journalists from national newspapers. She needed to target her list of "key markets" (I didn't even bother asking her to check if Creeslough was on the list), I wasn't to worry, however, because Ms. Streep would be giving a press conference when she arrived in Glenties. I would have ample opportunity then to ask her a question.

The following week reminded me of those stomach-tightening days as a ten-year-old in the run-up to Christmas morning. If anything, time passed even slower and the sense of anticipation was far, far greater. I didn't mind this. Nothing, not even the lingering doubt in my mind that John wasn't teasing me about Mr. Eksund after all, could anesthetize the dreamy sense that life had never been this sweet.

For those few heady days the possibilities of life in Creeslough seemed unlimited. If Meryl Streep could turn up in Donegal, then the Velvet Underground could re-form with me on bass guitar, and the manager of Celtic FC could phone to offer me a £10,000-a-week contract. As if to prove the point, events on the Gaelic football field had taken an improbable turn.

This might come as a shock—it did to everyone who had witnessed my initial efforts to solo the ball—but it turned out that I wasn't that bad a player. In the words of the reserve team manager Liam Ferry I was "a good old-fashioned full forward."

By this he meant that when a defender stuck his elbow into my jaw I was prepared to elbow him back in the eye-socket. This sounds far more impressive than it actually was. Defenders in the Reserve League were either young lads or older guys with stunted growth and beer guts. Real men played in the Senior League—if any of *them* had elbowed me in the jaw I would never have regained consciousness.

Grateful though I was for Liam's words of encouragement, I liked to think I brought more to the team than just thuggishness. Admittedly I hadn't scored a single point in four games (something of a record for a full forward, apparently) but I turned up every week. I was fit. I ran around a lot. Most of all, I was a talisman. It was surely no coincidence that since I'd started playing regularly St. Michael's hadn't lost a game in the Donegal GAA Third Division (Reserves).

Three wins in a row had lifted the team from bottom of the seven-team league to fourth. Three days before the Meryl Streep film premiere we were due to play against Milford at the Bridge. Victory meant we would move into second place.

Somehow I knew we would win and we did. What's more, I scored my first ever point. I'd like to say it came from a forty-yard kick after a searing run from my own goal-mouth but it didn't. It was a misdirected hand pass from ten yards that drifted over the bar on the gale force wind. Still, my point was the difference between the two teams.

Liam was delighted, doubly so when I made a retaliatory lunge on someone from the other team who'd elbowed me in the face earlier in the game. "Good tackle, Lawrence," I heard him shout from the home team dugout as the referee wrote down my name in his book.

The senior team won its game against Milford too. Afterward everyone went back to the Corncutter's Rest "for sandwiches"— a common euphemism in Gaelic football circles for a post-game piss-up.

Despite the impression left by Hollywood films, not all of rural Irish life takes place in a village pub where the *craic* is good and everyone is fighting or so drunk they can hardly talk. That is a gross caricature. But on that one night in the Corncutter's Rest I would concede that Hollywood had it just about right. I staggered off in the direction of home, God, I don't know when. Late, I guess.

• • •

I'd arranged to visit Malachi McCloskey the following afternoon. I dragged myself out of bed around midday and set off for
Glenties. I'd never been there before but had been told to pre-
pare myself to be impressed. I was, and would have been more
so had I not felt like I wanted to die.

Glenties was beautiful but in the autumn sunshine its brilliant flower beds and the orange, blues and greens of the buildings on the main street made it impossible to explore for more
than ten seconds without risking sickness. I went straight to
Malachi's instead. He lived next door to the sparkling lemon
Highland Hotel in a gleaming white Georgian courthouse with
a front door so scarlet it was . . . it was just taking the absolute
piss.

I rang the doorbell and closed my eyes. When I opened them
again there was a slightly bemused figure in the door frame. I
introduced myself, saying, "Sorry, Malachi, I'm a bit hung-over."

He laughed, took me downstairs to the basement kitchen
and made coffee. I felt marginally better, although not well
enough to remember more than half of our conversation.

I seem to recall Malachi telling me he had lived in Scotland
for years. Like me, he'd recently moved to Ireland to begin a
new life. His father had been the general practitioner in
Glenties long enough to have a housing estate named after him.
"When this Meryl Streep thing came up he said to me he'd been
on committees all his life, now it was my turn," he explained.
Like me, Malachi could hardly believe she was coming.

Glenties, disguised in the play as a small Irish town called
Ballybeg, was the setting for *Dancing at Lughnasa*. Brian Friel
holidayed in the town as a boy. The play's main characters, the
Mundy sisters, were based on Friel's aunts, who'd lived in a cottage just off the main road to Letterkenny called the Laurels.

When I'd finished my fourth cup of coffee Malachi offered to take me there, then to the school to collect my ticket.

The Laurels was sadly dilapidated (it reminded me of my own cottage, actually) but Malachi said the committee was planning to spruce it up in time for Meryl's visit. She and Brian Friel were going to unveil a plaque.

From there, it was only a short drive to the school.

We had to wait in the reception hall while someone went to find the tickets. The atmosphere was euphoric. Pupils were dashing around on last-minute assignments. The bare corridors amplified already noisy conversations. Teachers attempted to calm everything down but it was obvious their hearts weren't in it. They were excited too.

Malachi smiled. "Well, who can blame them? It's Hollywood coming to Glenties. It'll probably never happen again in the lifetime of these kids."

"Or their kids' kids," I said.

I was jealous. I couldn't remember ever being this happy when I was at school. Mind you, the most famous people who ever came to our school were a punk rock group called the Cosmic Pancakes and an actor from *Coronation Street* whose name I can't even remember.

"I wonder what she'll be like?" I sighed.

"Who, Meryl?" Malachi shrugged, trying his best to look as if he'd been dealing with Hollywood stars all his life. "I bet she'll be great."

She was better than great. From the moment her chauffeur-driven Audi pulled up at the door of the Highland Hotel she was fantastic, charming, gracious, good-humored, warm, and any other word you'd care to select from a thesaurus of gushing compliments.

More memorably, at least to a shallow person like me, she was astonishingly beautiful. The most beautiful person I have ever set eyes on. Honestly. If you have never seen a proper movie star in the flesh keep it that way, otherwise you will never look in a mirror again without seeing Quasimodo with a skin complaint.

After a few introductions in the hotel lobby, Meryl disappeared off to her room. She came downstairs an hour later for a brief press conference in the hotel bar. Everyone had the chance to ask one question, a stricture that left me with a dilemma: how could I cram twenty years of devotion, admiration and pent-up sexual desire into a single exchange?

I toyed with "Can I have your babies?" but in the end settled for a pathetic "Could you tell us, Meryl, what are the things you like best about Donegal?"

She looked straight at me when I spoke and smiled. For a moment it felt as if the world was just the two of us. "Oh, God, everything about this place is so beautiful I hardly know where to start," she began. I didn't hear the rest. I was lost in the tender folds of her voice.

I snapped out of my trance just in time to dash up to the school for the screening. Unfortunately, the film was crap. Why can no one in the movies do rural Ireland? Even Meryl's Donegal accent had traces of the Italian farmer's wife from *Bridges of Madison County*. One of the other sisters sounded suspiciously Cockney.

Not that any of this mattered. Everyone loved the film, or said they did. Afterward, the entire town crammed into the hotel ballroom for a buffet-cum-party. I saw Malachi roaming around. He looked great, dressed in his bow-tie and dinner suit.

"I told you she would come, didn't I?" he said, when I finally caught up with him. "What's she like?"

"She's a star. A total star."

When the buffet finished, a troupe of local dancers and musicians staged a show based on the mythical festival of Lughnasa. Meryl sat on the floor at the front of the hall, drinking a glass of Bailey's and leading the applause. When it finished, she got onstage and made the sweetest, most gracious thank-you speech.

"I just wanted to say I'm grateful to everyone who has made me feel so welcome here in Glenties," she said. "It's a wonderful place, with wonderful people. Please accept my apologies for any indignities I have heaped upon your accent but I hope I have portrayed one of the Mundy sisters, Kate, as well as Brian Friel intended."

"Don't worry about the accent, Meryl, we forgive you," I shouted, when she finished, but the cheering was so loud I don't think she heard me.

The Meryl Streep film premiere party wasn't a life-changing experience but it was a great night out and it taught me this: I had to do something about my social life.

Sure, the whole point of moving to Creeslough was to enjoy a quieter, simpler existence but somehow I'd turned into the most boring man on earth. The highlight of my week was a quiet beer in the Corncutter's Rest on a Saturday night while watching *Match of the Day* on the pub's big-screen television. The highlight of my highlight was a conversation with Danny Lafferty, who was usually finishing off a sixteen-hour working day with a quick burst of bar-tending and didn't really have time to talk.

Me: "Hi, Danny. A glass of Guinness, please. What's the news?"

Danny: "There's no news."

Me: "Oh, well."

Danny: "Can't stop. There's people to serve."

No offense to Danny—it wasn't his fault that I was boring and he was busy—but once upon a time I was a happening man about town. It wasn't so long ago that I was going to a nightclub every night of the week and dancing until dawn. My disco days were over but I was damned if I was going to live like a hermit. Most people I knew in Creeslough had a pretty good social life. Why not me? The Meryl Streep film premiere was a perfect example of a good night out. If Meryl couldn't make it to Donegal every week then I determined I was going to make my own entertainment.

I started going to Letterkenny one night a week. I met up

with friends at an "Irish" theme bar on the main street. It wasn't so long ago that "real" Irish pubs in Ireland were closing because no one wanted to drink in them but this place was always packed. Nowadays people couldn't get enough of wooden beams and rusty Woodbine signs, provided their bottled lager came with a wedge of lime. There was an interesting psycho-sociological debate to be had on this phenomenon but somehow we never got round to it on our nights out. We were usually too busy making pathetic attempts to chat up women or listening to the house band.

My friend Joseph and I were standing at the bar one Thursday night when the band started playing a Lloyd Cole and the Commotions song called "Lost Weekend."

"I wrote this tune," I said, just to fill a space in the conversation.

"Sure." Joseph laughed. "And I'm a fucking brain surgeon."

"No, I did. I wrote this song in my bedroom in July nineteen eighty-five. Well, I wrote the music."

(When I say "wrote the music" what I mean is I took the basic chord structure from Iggy Pop's song "The Passenger" and rearranged it into a pale imitation.)

"Bollocks."

I finally convinced him by reeling off information that only the editor of the *Guinness Book of Obscure Hit Singles* or the composer of such an insipid 1980s hit would know: highest chart position (number 17, November 1986), number of radio plays in the Czech Republic in 1998 (6), size of last royalty check (£8.74).

Joe shook his head. "Jeez, you're a pop star. Why did you never mention it before? I used to really like Lloyd Cole."

"And the Commotions."

"Sorry. And the Commotions. Which one were you?"

"Scary Commotion."

The house band was halfway through "Lost Weekend." To be perfectly honest the song sounded better than it ever did when we played it.

"You know Lloyd Cole is playing in Dublin next month, don't you? I saw the advert in the *Irish Times* the other day," Joseph said, pausing for a moment's thought. "You don't fancy making the trip, do you?"

Of course I did. This was exactly the kind of excursion I'd had in mind when I told myself I had to get out and do more. Dublin was only five hours away. We could drive down in the morning, book into a cheap hotel, have a look round the city, go to the concert and then to a nightclub. I hadn't seen a Lloyd Cole gig since May 1988 at Wembley Arena. It was terrific but then I'm probably a bit biased, I was standing behind him playing bass guitar. I wondered what his concerts were like now.

I wondered, too, what Dublin would be like. I hadn't been there for years, since Lloyd Cole and the Commotions were nominated in the Best International Group category of the Irish pop music industry awards in fact. We lost—to REM (whatever happened to them?).

Joseph and I had the arrangements for our Lloyd Cole weekend made by the last chorus of "Lost Weekend." He said he'd book a hotel. I said I'd make a few phone calls and get us on the guest list for the concert, maybe even backstage to meet Lloyd afterward.

Joseph couldn't make it in the end. He had to go shopping with his new girlfriend. I could hardly believe that someone had fallen for one of his pathetic chat-up lines ("Excuse me, I'm a stranger here. Can you direct me to your bedroom?") but it happened in the pub a week later. Within another week they were

inseparable and the week after that I was making the long journey south on my own.

Francis had been to Dublin earlier in the summer to see the
Tour de France cycle race and said it was a "crazy place." Even
allowing for Francis's unspoken assumption that anyone who
didn't live in beautiful Donegal was by definition crazy, there
was more than a sliver of truth in what he was saying.

Hardly an edition of the *Irish Times* was published without
details of a new survey that had found Dublin to be the fastest-
growing/richest/trendiest/most attractive/most youthful/
most crowded/most expensive/slowest moving/sexiest city in
Europe. Added to this were countless other stories about the
tourist boom, the crime boom and the financial-sector boom.

Most of all, there was the property boom. This had reached
its apotheosis earlier in the summer when a terraced house in
Dalkey, a picturesque fishing village to the south of the city, was
sold for £6 million. Admittedly, it came with a nice sea view and
Bono for a neighbor but this was an extraordinary sum of
money, even for Dublin. "Is someone mad?" asked the *Times*, as
a national debate raged. Viewed from Donegal (where £6 million would have bought most of the county's housing stock),
the question mark was superfluous, the sentence in need of
only a minor rearrangement.

I set off from Creeslough half expecting to be turned back at
Dublin's outskirts by the fashion police for failing to have a sufficiently flashy car. Fortunately, the journey passed without a
hitch.

At first glance the familiar parts of the city center hadn't
altered since I was last there, architecturally at least. Trinity
College hadn't been flattened to make way for a multiplex cinema, Grafton Street was still a thriving shopping precinct and
not an eight-lane motorway. The Georgian squares and terraces

remained largely intact. However, the population appeared to have multiplied ten-fold. So, too, had the number of beggars by the roadside. And the traffic. Especially the traffic.

It took me half an hour to drive the mile from O'Connell Street to the south side of St. Stephen's Green, where I was staying. With a great deal of difficulty, I'd managed to find a hotel room. It cost me seventy pounds. I could have gone for a cheaper B-and-B on the city outskirts but I wanted to relive the hotel-gig-hotel routine of my "pop star" days. The room was second-rate and scruffy. It fitted the bill exactly.

I dumped my bag and went off to explore Dublin. Lloyd was playing at 8 P.M. This left me just five hours. I had planned to go to Dalkey and gawp at the £6 million house but with the traffic so bad it would have taken too long to get there and back. I wouldn't have had time to do anything else. I settled instead for a taxi ride to a place called Ballymun followed by a quick tour of the city center shops.

Ballymun is a high-rise housing project on the north side of the city. Rightly or wrongly, it has a reputation for being one of the worst slums in the country. In the thirty-odd years since it was built it had sunk to the bottom of every deprivation index ever devised. Naturally it wasn't on the Dublin tourist route, except for members of United Nations' delegations investigating abject urban poverty. I would never have thought of going there but I wanted to write an article about it for the *Tribune*.

The project had been built by a politician from Donegal called Neil Blaney. He was long dead now but he had been born and raised in a thatched cottage at a beautiful village called Rossnakill, near John's house in Fanad. (When I say "built" what I mean is that Blaney was the government minister who approved its construction, a decision he came quickly to regret bitterly.)

I thought I could usefully spend an hour at Ballymun gathering information around the project for a "Blaney's legacy" story that would contrast his rural background with life on a Dublin sink project. I intended to make a few trenchant points about £6 million houses and Ireland's current obsession with money. I wanted to remind *Tribune* readers about an economically deprived place I'd decided to rename for my purposes as "forgotten Ireland." If nothing else it would stop Francis filling the paper with more pictures of the Fanad Community Band.

I abandoned the idea five minutes after the taxi driver dropped me off. For a start I couldn't find anyone to interview. When I eventually saw some people they were scurrying home or standing on the other side of the dual carriageway that—a masterly stroke of urban planning, this—had been bulldozed right through the middle of the project.

I hate to say this, because most of the people living there probably did their best in impossible circumstances, but Ballymun looked even worse than I imagined it would: an ugly mess of discolored concrete and boarded-up flats. There was graffiti everywhere, most of it targeted against drug dealers.

A biting wind snaked between the tower blocks. I thought about approaching a knot of young men standing at the entrance to the Ballymun shopping center but they looked more interested in mugging me than dishing up interesting insights on forgotten Ireland. The Ballymun Citizens' Centre was closed, as was the Ballymun Horse Owners' Association office. What could I have asked them anyway? Is that Shergar over there? How would you feel if I told you the politician who built this dump once lived in a pretty thatched cottage in Donegal? Isn't it ironic? Do you want to smash me in the face for trying to exploit your misery for cheap journalistic purposes?

I waved down a taxi and headed back to the city center. A

few weeks later I read that there were plans to demolish Ballymun but that some residents didn't want to leave. They must have been off their fucking heads. I couldn't get away quick enough.

Grafton Street wasn't just busy, it was a seething mass of humanity. I couldn't walk five yards without bumping into someone or falling over their children. I'm not the most coordinated person in the world but I can usually manage to negotiate a street without too much trouble. Clearly something was wrong. And then it dawned on me: I wasn't used to being among people. For months I'd had whole beaches, entire moors and mountains all to myself. Now I had one cubic foot.

The adjustment took a little while but I got used to the bedlam. The queues, the noise, the crush—suddenly they seemed vibrant and exciting. Even the Grafton Street buskers weren't too irritating, except for a Japanese art student chalking Roger Dean album covers on the pavement. I didn't mind stumbling into him. In fact, I did it deliberately. I gave my pound coin to an enterprising tramp who was drumming on his knees with two empty plastic Coke bottles.

The newspapers were right. Even Francis was right. Dublin —at least this one small corner of Dublin—was booming and crazy. The shops were packed. Young, old, male, female, tourist, local. Everyone was rushing round with fists full of carrier-bags, as if they had one hour to spend their life's savings before the world ended. The city was spilling out, like a corpulent belly trapped in a tight waistcoat. I suspect it will all go horribly wrong and Dublin will wake up one day to discover it's bloated and overblown and no one loves it anymore.

Swept along in the general consumer madness, I spent a fortune on books and records. Afterward, I went into one of the countless trendy cafés just off Grafton Street and paid seven pounds for a cappuccino and a stale mixed-pepper sandwich. I didn't even flinch. The craziness was infectious. The shopfront shutters were going down when I came out again. The city was taking a well-earned breather before the Saturday night bedlam. I walked across St. Stephen's Green and back to the hotel to do likewise.

Lloyd was playing at a club near Dublin Castle, about half an hour's walk from my hotel. I showered, changed and headed out into the early evening. I was bursting with curiosity. He had played at the same venue the night before. There was a review in one of the evening papers describing him as a "legendary singer" and the concert as a "blatant foray down Memory Lane."

It was very complimentary but disconcerting too. Legendary? Memory Lane? I thought you had to be Johnny Cash's age before you became legendary or on the Gerry and the Pacemakers Merseybeat Revival Tour to qualify as any sort of foray down Memory Lane. I was fairly sure Lloyd wasn't that old and I knew *I* wasn't. It was only a decade since we were onstage together at Wembley. Now the newspapers were describing us as legendary. Or, rather, they were describing Lloyd as legendary. (I wondered how they would describe me—the man who went from Wembley Arena to the *Tirconaill Tribune*, by choice? Mad, probably.)

I rummaged through my memories of that previous life. I'll admit to discovering some things that I missed. When I was in the band, the hour before a gig was always my favorite time. All the traveling for the day was over, the sound check was done, you didn't have to be nice to anyone from a record company. All that was left was the quiet thrill of anticipation: Will we be any good? Will there be any good-looking women in the front? How many will even notice the bass player? Going to a club afterward? Groupies? (Sometimes. Plenty. Hardly any. Always.

None . . . Okay, one. She was German, her name was Nicky, and she had enormous pointed breasts.)

I ambled through the city, imagining myself to be Leopold Bloom. I stopped for five minutes at College Green to watch the hordes of raucous young men in shirtsleeves, their hair carefully gelled, heading toward the pubs in Temple Bar. The women were no less raucous and, if you ask me, a lot better-looking. Everyone looked so fresh and so very, very young. For a moment, I felt very old and very alone.

There was a queue outside the venue when I arrived. I breathed a sigh of relief. Thankfully I'd managed to make a few phone calls and get on the guest list.

I could have walked right up to the door and collected my backstage pass but that would have been showing off. In any case, the queue appeared to be moving quickly. I tagged on to the end of the line.

Here's a little rock and roll history. For a short spell in the mid-1980s it would have been true to say that a Lloyd Cole and the Commotions album was, like a Che Guevara poster and an unread copy of Jean-Paul Sartre's *The Age of Reason*, an essential item in the life of any self-respecting student.

All modesty aside, the music was good. (Julie Burchill described it in the *NME* at the time as "a country-and-western Velvet Underground.") But the main appeal was undoubtedly Lloyd's lyrics. It wasn't every pop songwriter who had the imagination to rhyme "Norman Mailer" with "get a new tailor," or describe a character in a song as "looking like a friend of Truman Capote."

Of course, some people said his lyrics were too clever. *Melody Maker*, I recall, was particularly poisonous. More to the point, the nation's students were hooked. Our first album *Rattlesnakes* (still available from all good record stores, incidentally) stayed in the charts for four months.

At least half a dozen of those students had stayed loyal, only now they had grown up and were standing behind me in a queue reminiscing about a concert Lloyd Cole and the Commotions played in Dublin years ago. We were great, I was pleased to discover. I'm ashamed to say the thought—the thrill!—crossed my mind that I might be recognized.

"What was that Tom Verlaine cover version they did that night?" someone asked. I would have volunteered the answer but it was my turn at the ticket booth.

"I'm on the guest list," I said to the woman behind the glass. "The name's Donegan."

She ran her pen down the sheet of paper, then flicked over to the next page, shaking her head as she reached the bottom. "I'm sorry I don't see it. What was the name again?"

I smiled. "Donegan. Lawrence Donegan."

She looked again and smiled back. "Sorry."

I felt the first stirring of panic, and embarrassment. I hoped I wouldn't be recognized by one of the grown-up students. "But you don't understand, I have to be."

I could see the two bouncers twitching. "Okay." I sighed. "It looks like I'll have to buy a ticket then. How much are they?"

She waved her pen at the neighboring ticket booth. There was a sheet of A4 paper scrawled with the words SOLD OUT Scotch-taped to the window. I could sense the grown-up students beginning to get impatient.

"Please, I've come all the way from Donegal."

She could see I was helpless. The look on her face softened. "Listen. Can you stand to the side just now, let these people collect their tickets, then we'll try and sort this out." She clearly thought I was some dopey hick from up the country who had never been to a concert in his life.

Once everyone else had got their tickets I attempted to

explain how it was possible to be both a dopey hick from up the country and on the guest list for a Lloyd Cole concert in Dublin. It was a complicated story about phone calls to London and the Commotions' ex-drummer Stephen and booking agents and tour manager. She seemed skeptical. I might have broken through her resistance if one of the bouncers hadn't chipped in to say that they couldn't let anyone else in because of fire regulations.

In the end I had to deploy the nuclear option, the sad-loser-reminiscing-at-the-end-of-bar alternative to an even sadder walk back to the hotel and night in watching *Match of the Day* on the TV. But the fact was she wasn't going to let me in. The bouncers were cracking their knuckles, getting ready to shoo me away. I did a quick calculation. It meant humiliating myself but, on the other hand, I was never going to meet these people again.

"But . . . but you've got to let me in," I whined. "I used to be a Commotion."

Whether she genuinely believed me or was just overwhelmed by a vast wave of pity I don't know. But a brief phone call was made from the ticket booth. Five minutes later a woman in a cream suit came to the door. She asked me who I was, made a daft joke about me promising never to cause a commotion at her club again and waved me through.

"There's no seats left. You'll have to stand at the back," she said. I took this to mean a backstage pass was out of the question, not to mention the touching reunion with Lloyd.

Much as I'd love to say the concert was terrible, that it lacked the meaty bass-guitar throb that hits an audience in the gut like a Mike Tyson punch and leaves it gasping for more, I can't. For a start it was all acoustic instruments. There was no vast

PA, no bank of computer-controlled lights, no backdrop, no hairy-arsed roadies shouting, "CHECK! One, two," into the microphone. The stage was adorned by two yellow floral arrangements at either end of a row of guitars and a couple of small speakers.

Downstairs was a sit-down cabaret, have-a-glass-of-wine-and-appreciate-the-singer-songwriter's-art kind of place. Upstairs was a tough-shit-you-should-have-bought-your-tickets-earlier cattle pen. I squeezed into a tiny space on the balcony next to a Grace Kelly look-alike in a green baseball cap. The lights were already dimmed. A couple of minutes later Lloyd wandered on to the stage.

He played some of his own newer songs, a few well-chosen cover versions (Bob Dylan's "You're a Big Girl Now," the Velvet Underground's "New Age") and a lot from Lloyd Cole and the Commotions' back catalog. I know I'm probably biased but the latter went down best with the crowd.

The Commotions had a song called "Are You Ready to Be Heartbroken?" The guitar intro is instantly recognizable and when he played it Grace Kelly grabbed my arm and started squealing, "I love this song, I love this song." I thought she was about to have an orgasm. Including encores, he played for just over an hour. During every single minute I would have happily stuck a dagger in my thigh to have been onstage with him.

I worked out years ago that pop concerts are either dutiful—choreographed and hence lifeless—or joyful. This was definitely joyful. It wasn't really like a concert, more like having a party at someone's house. The audience didn't want it to end. One vast girl, who looked alarmingly like Nicky the Zeppelin-chested German groupie, even climbed onstage and grabbed Lloyd's leg in an attempt to stop him leaving.

When the lights finally went up Grace Kelly sighed. We

looked at each other. "God, that was amazing," she said, in a beautiful Irish accent.

"Wasn't it?" I replied, totally smitten.

The house-lights came up. She had a gorgeous, open smile and looked even more beautiful than I'd thought. Her bobbed fair hair was hooked behind her ears. She gathered her bag and slipped on her coat, getting ready to leave. I didn't want her to go. I racked my brain for something to say that could keep her there, even for another minute. "Are you a big Lloyd fan?"

"I've loved him for years," she said. "Ever since he used to play with the Commotions. They were amazing too."

What!

I had two options. I could either let this remark pass, accept that my music career was over a long time ago, walk out of the venue, maybe stop off at a pub for a solitary pint on the way back to the hotel. Or I could attempt a blatant foray down Memory Lane.

No contest. She hadn't made a single step in the direction of the exit when I heard myself say: "I used to be a Commotion, you know."

Annie

"Can we just take this moment . . ." a woman wearing what looked like a giant doily with sleeves lifted her hands in the air and took a deep, exaggerated breath. *Ssssnnnifff. Aaaaaahhh.* ". . . to appreciate the beauty of the ceremony we are about to witness?"

Francis rolled his eyes and whispered, "Welcome back to the wacky world of the *Tribune*."

We were standing on a beach near Creeslough. Francis had been tipped off about an open-air wedding. The bride was from an island somewhere in the Pacific, the groom from Ireland and the presiding minister—Ms. Doily-Dress—was from San Francisco. The Haight-Ashbury district, judging by her vocabulary. She was probably the live-in evangelist at the Grateful Dead house.

The sun was shining but the sea breeze had blown out the "symbols of our spiritual life" (candles, to you and me). The happy couple had that beatific look that came from knowing they were about to embark on a long and loving journey through life together, the first fortnight of which would be devoted to vigorous sex.

I ought to have been ashamed of myself for sneering at them. It was such a sweet idea—to be married against the backdrop of a rolling ocean, among family and friends—but since I'd returned from Dublin I couldn't stop myself feeling sour about everything.

It wasn't that Grace Kelly's rugby-playing accountant boyfriend had been waiting outside the venue to collect her in his shiny black Mercedes 2.8XXL FastAction SmugGit Coupé.

Quite the reverse. I was relieved to see her disappear into the night. Even if she had been the type to throw herself at an ex-Commotion (she wasn't) I don't think I'd have been able to have a relationship with anyone who'd knowingly French-kissed an accountant.

Once she had gone I toyed briefly with the idea of hanging around at the backstage door for Lloyd. In the end I decided I'd suffered enough humiliation for one lifetime and headed back across the city. On the way back to the hotel I dropped into a bar just off St. Stephen's Green and had a few beers. It was packed and noisy and I loved every minute.

I loved it so much that when I woke up at noon the next day I decided to stay in Dublin for more of the same. I phoned John to ask him if the *Tribune* could struggle along without me for a few more days. "Oh, aye," he said. "I'll just get Bouncer to write your stories. No one'll notice the difference."

I spent the three days doing touristy things like visiting the Dáil, touring the museums and spotting celebrities. Dublin is awash with stars. I saw Gabriel Byrne walking down Grafton Street and Roddy Doyle in a bookshop. I took a bus to Dalkey to have a look at the £6 million house and ended up seeing Maeve Binchy and Damon Hill. At night I went to pubs. I even took out a mortgage and bought a drink in the salubrious Shelbourne Hotel. I had a wonderful time.

That was the problem. Arriving home in Creeslough was like stepping into a world drained of noise and excitement.

I know what you're thinking: But hang on, that's why you went there in the first place, you clot. And you're right. But when I was in Dublin I bought a book called *Downshifting: The Guide to Happier, Simpler Living* and nowhere in its 379 pages did it say you weren't allowed to have second thoughts.

I was having a few second thoughts, that was all. Being in

Dublin was like meeting a childhood sweetheart again and discovering that she'd turned into Gwyneth Paltrow—gorgeous, sexy, exciting, fun, glamorous. To make matters worse, I felt like I'd ended up married to the cast of *Emmerdale*.

I hoped it was a passing phase. But there had been countless times since coming back from Dublin—standing on a beach listening to a hippie Christian taking deep breaths was only the latest—that I had seriously contemplated going back to the cottage, throwing my worldly possessions in the back of the car and heading east, to anywhere but Donegal.

Fortunately, I had a Gaelic football match to play that evening. I could release some of my frustrations by pretending my marker was Ms. Doily-Dress and elbowing him in the face a few times. With that happy thought I left Francis to take some wedding photos and join in the *al fresco* version of "Amazing Grace" and went home to get my sports kit.

We won by a mile. I scored another point, a thirty-yard kick straight between the posts. On the downside, I failed to score a goal. This was beginning to trouble me greatly. St. Michael's reserve team now had two games left in the league season and I was in danger of being the first full forward in the history of the club—possibly in the history of Gaelic football—to complete a season without scoring a goal.

There were two phone messages when I got home. The first was from Stephen, the ex-drummer of Lloyd Cole and the Commotions. I called him back straight away. He'd bumped into the band's old booking agent, they'd got talking—"idly speculating" were his exact words—and he wanted to know if I would be interested in signing up if the band re-formed to play some concerts.

Interested!

"Calm down," he said. (Stephen was like a big brother to me when we were in the band together. He spent most of the time trying to calm me down.) "We were only having a chat about it. It'll probably never happen. These things never do. But I take it from your squealing that you might be keen if it did?"

I know that I left pop music because the thought of being onstage, aged fifty, wearing a gray ponytail and brushed denims horrified me. But that was before it occurred to me that one day I could be standing on a beach, aged fifty, watching a Californian hippie christening her married friends' seventh son, or turning up for the AGM of the Donegal Christian Women's Association and being assaulted with an umbrella, or writing an offensive poem about the death of the Queen Mother at the age of 146.

I gave up pop music—I gave up the *Guardian*—but that was because I never imagined I could end up living in a Donegal village, aged fifty, promising myself that I would fix the roof and whitewash the walls as soon as the weather turned good. Aged fifty, I wouldn't even have the consolation of getting a game for a Gaelic football team—not even St. Michael's reserves.

When I thought about my life in Creeslough like that, playing in a band at fifty sounded like a lucky escape, even if it did mean wearing a gray ponytail. (Not brushed denims though— I'd have to be a hundred years old and ga-ga before I'd wear brushed denims.)

"You're right, Stephen. It'll probably never happen," I said. Meanwhile, I was mentally compiling my dream Lloyd Cole and the Commotions reunion tour itinerary: Paris, London, Berlin, Oslo, New York, Sydney, Dublin, of course, and maybe a secret gig at the Corncutter's Rest. "It'd be great if it did, though."

All this talk of getting back together made the two of us nostalgic. We swapped band-era reminiscences. "Remember that fat German groupie you went off with one night." Steve laughed. "What was her name again?"

"What fat German groupie? I don't remember any fat German groupie."

He promised to phone me with any news about the reunion as soon as possible. I promised not to die of excitement before rehearsals started.

The second message was from John. I didn't have time to call back. The phone rang as soon as Stephen and I hung up.

"I've got some news." John's voice was as flat and monotone as ever. With the benefit of hindsight I would have said it lacked its usual sly, sardonic tinge. I blundered on. "You've got news. I've got some news as well."

"Before you go any further," he said, with a seriousness even the most insensitive dolt couldn't miss, "it's my mother. She collapsed tonight. She's in the hospital."

"What? No way."

When I was at the house in Fanad the previous day Annie had been in top form. Our relationship had recovered since I'd given her the pornographic Maeve Binchy novel for her birthday. We were great friends now, bound together by our love of Ireland's favorite TV soap opera, *Glenroe*, and a mutual appetite for making fun of John and Francis.

"She's going to be all right?"

"Nope." The years John had worked at the hospital had stripped his vocabulary bare of equivocation in matters of life and death. "She's dyin', Lawrence. And that's the reality."

"Donegan, would you look at them two," Annie said, with her Saturday-night smile. John and Francis were in the kitchen cleaning up after dinner. "Remember that program *The Odd Couple*? What were their names again?"

"Oscar and Felix, Annie."

"That's it. Oscar and Felix. Ha! *The Odd Couple.*"

She was still laughing when I said good-bye to her that night for the very last time.

Annie lived for five more days. The family—sons, daughter, in-laws and grandchildren, every last one of them—were at her bedside throughout. Francis visited the hospital a couple of times. He asked me if I wanted to go with him but I said no thanks. We all knew after that first night she wouldn't recover. I had a great last memory of her and didn't want it disturbed by the sight of tubes and machines and the smell of disinfectant.

John came home just once, to grab a couple of hours' sleep on a soft bed rather than in a hospital corridor. He dropped by the office to talk to Francis and me about what was to be done with the paper.

The next issue was due out in a week's time. So far, we had my article about the open-air wedding, a piece by John about a restoration of a threshing mill and a picture of a local priest shaking hands with the Pope. Even if Francis had been a news-paper layout genius (he wasn't) it was hard to see how he could fill thirty-two pages of white space with two overwritten stories, an overexposed photograph of John Paul II and whatever else I could rustle up in the next few days.

I made the heretical suggestion that we shouldn't publish a paper at all. Francis looked appalled. "The readers wouldn't be happy. The advertisers wouldn't either."

John shook his head. "We've gone eight years without ever missing an edition, we can't start now."

I could see where the conversation was heading. Frankly, it was a place of hard work and responsibility that I didn't want to visit, even for one week. "But we can't do it, John. You're going to be at the hospital with your mother for God knows how long."

He sucked hard on his pipe, like a man contemplating a long fall into a cold, dark sea. Finally, he said, "You two are going to have to edit the paper yourselves."

Francis looked even more appalled than before. "What would I know about editing a newspaper?"

John looked at me. "Well, Bouncer can't do it, so it's going to have to be you."

"Me? Edit the *Tribune?*"

"I know. Tragic, isn't it?" He was grinning now. "But the reality is, Lawrence, there's no other option."

John left for the hospital. Francis and I agreed that the first thing we had to do was to stop giggling like a pair of nervous schoolboys on their maiden visit to a Soho peep show. This proved difficult. The responsibility of doing something as grown-up as running a newspaper made me more nervous than I had ever been in my life. I needed to giggle, otherwise I would have cried.

We convinced ourselves that the experience would be Lawrence and Francis's Excellent Adventure. We spent the next hour dreaming up front-page headlines that would make people sit up and take notice—"Monica Lewinsky Buys Milford Pub"; "Letterkenny Nun Confesses 'I had Brad Pitt's love child' "; "Aliens Land in Gortahork." When we got bored with that, we thought of job titles we could give ourselves. Naturally, I was Acting Editor-in-Chief. Francis became Managing Editor, quickly upgraded to Executive Managing Editor as a reward for nipping over to the grocer's for a packet of biscuits.

Noel, the newly appointed Associate Editor, listened to all of this with the doomed expression of an airline passenger who has just seen the port-side engine drop off the wing. "Just don't write any poems about Princess Di—please," he said, as he headed off to football training.

When we finally stopped laughing we started panicking.

A lot of material for the paper would be easy to gather— adverts, village notes, the police report, the GAA reports and the like. But that still left us with a lot of white space.

Although I would never have admitted it to his face, John did most of the "proper" journalism on the *Tribune*. He was the one who went out and dug up stories. More often than not he was the one who came up with ideas for stories that I could do.

After spending his entire career writing out everything in long-hand John had finally succumbed to the technological revolution. He'd bought himself a laptop computer and had taken to it with the zealotry of a convert. Barely a day passed without him discovering yet another reason why he should have changed over years ago. The most recent revelation was his computer's word-count function. He took great satisfaction in telling us how much he'd written every fortnight. It was never less than fifteen thousand words and he always followed this announcement by asking me, "And how many has our international-class former *Guardian* journalist written?"

I'm ashamed to admit it but I had never written more than two or three thousand words. Nor had I ever come up with any story that remotely merited the description "exclusive." The one truly self-generated article I'd done since joining the *Tribune* was an interview with the starter at the local golf club. I only did that because it meant I could get to play eighteen holes for free.

I just couldn't see how we could possibly produce a newspaper, or anything remotely resembling a newspaper, without John. I confessed as much to Francis.

"Don't worry. We'll fill the pages up with lots of photographs," he said, without enthusiasm.

"Not the Fanad Band again, surely?"

The two of us laughed mirthlessly and stared at the floor. Looking back, I guess this was when we stopped panicking. A little iron entered our soul. Why? It may have had something to do with professional pride, or the sentimental notion that a decent issue of the newspaper could be our tribute to Annie. But, if I had to tell the truth to save my own life, it was the thought of John flicking through his beloved newspaper afterward and saying, "God almighty, what have you done? We're the *Tirconaill Tribune*, not *Hello!* fucking magazine."

Francis hardly slept for five days. If he wasn't out of the office collecting adverts, he was laying out pages or taking photographs. He even wrote a couple of stories. Noel worked extra hours. Kathleen came in for an extra night and typed up endless screeds of village notes. Declan took a couple of days' holiday from the hospital to assume his temporary role as Assistant Executive Editor (with special responsibility for writing football-match reports at twice the normal length in order to fill space).

Believe it or not, I liked being a newspaper editor. It wasn't that I had the power to boss people around, because I didn't. ("When did you get the stripes, boyo?" Kathleen snorted, when I asked her to type up a press release. "Do it yourself.") It was just that for the first time in my working life there was no one to boss me around. I could write anything I wanted and it was guaranteed to appear in print. For those few days at least I felt like Donegal's answer to William Randolph Hearst. The only limitations were Ireland's libel laws, Noel's insistence that I let Princess Di rest in peace and my own imagination.

Of the three, only the latter was an irritation. I made up for lack of inspiration by working flat out. I came nowhere near McAteer's fortnightly word-count, of course, but I still wrote more acres of copy: about council meetings, our favorite Donegal poet Frank Galligan, the former butler at Donegal country estate, a school reunion (yes, another one) and the triumphant album launch party of Ramelton's very own Frank Sinatra, Patsy Boyce.

A couple of days before the paper was due to come out I met John Donegan in Letterkenny. I'd seen him a few times since my story about him appeared. Somebody had read it to him. He'd been delighted with it, and with me. I knew this because I'd heard a rumor he'd been telling people in Letterkenny that his long-lost son from Scotland had done well for himself and found a job on one of the local papers.

John looked dark and shattered. He had a five-day growth, his hair was matted and his eyes looked as if they'd been rubbed hard with a salty rag. When I asked him what was wrong he started crying.

I've always thought the best journalists are angry journalists. Francis Wheen is angry. The American writer Joe Queenan is about as angry as it's possible for a person to get without their head exploding. I was never an angry journalist. I never had the energy, or the courage. But for once in my life I got angry as I listened to John Donegan talking about the cretins who stoned his caravan every night, about the rats crawling across his bed, about his dread of the coming winter and his deteriorating health.

"I'm gonna die, Lonnie. I know I am," he said. Now we were both crying.

We went for a bowl of soup in the nearest café. When we finished we drove round the travelers' sites and talked to people. I found an eighty-four-year-old woman who had to walk a mile to the nearest bush if she wanted to go to the toilet. Her daughter, aged thirty-seven, had never had access to a proper bath. One of the sites was ankle deep in stagnant water, another didn't have even a cold water supply until the day before the last general election. We went to a housing project in the town and met a family of fourteen, all travelers, who had been sardined into a three-bedroom council house. Six of the children were sleeping in one room.

Afterward, I dropped John off at his caravan and went home to write some angry journalism.

In the middle of the night the telephone rang. I staggered out of bed, three-quarters asleep. My head felt as though it had been stuffed with cotton wool. Even so, I knew who would be calling and why.

"Are you sitting down?"

"I'm so tired I can hardly stand, Francis. Just tell me—she's died. Right?"

"Fifteen minutes ago. John just phoned to tell me."

"Shit."

"There's a mass at the hospital at lunchtime, then the body is going back to the house in Fanad for the wake tomorrow night."

"But we're supposed to be doing the paper in Fanad tomorrow night."

"So."

In circumstances other than the death of a spirited old woman I'd grown to like and admire very much I might have been quite excited. I had never been to a proper Irish wake before. What's more, I'd never been to a proper Irish wake and simultaneously edited a newspaper—under the one roof, with the body in the bedroom and a couple of computers in the attic, plus hundreds of people crammed into two downstairs rooms and hundreds more gathered outside under a starry sky.

I know this sounds like a caricature of life (and death) in Ireland. Throw in a drunk priest, a dark family secret and someone losing the coffin on the way to the graveyard and you have the plot of every crappy "Irish" comedy ever made in Hollywood. I said as much to John when I met him just inside the back door of the hospital chapel the following day.

"Of course we'll do the paper at the house. We always do," he said. "No one will mind."

"But what about the wake? What about your mother?"

"She won't mind either. Go and ask her if you like." He pointed me toward the front of the church, where mourners were filing past Annie's open coffin.

I knew John wasn't being callous, or disrespectful, or heartless—I knew he loved his mother deeply. But I had to wait for a few weeks before I could ask him exactly how he had been feeling. The answer he gave me was this: Death in rural Ireland isn't like death anywhere else, except in the biological sense. People are more reconciled to it. Religious faith is so deeply ingrained in a place like Fanad that even the most lapsed Catholic—John volunteered himself as an example—can find themselves taking temporary comfort in the belief that the deceased has gone to "a better place." "Another thing is that it's not like the city, where most people wouldn't know their neighbor was dead until the hearse turned up at his door," he explained. "Here, people live on top of one another. We're in and out of each other's houses all the time. The bonds are stronger, the community is stronger. We share everything, even death. There's not a week goes by when I'm not at a wake or a funeral. We're used to death in rural Ireland. In fact, sometimes I think we're bloody obsessed with it."

• • •

When the mass finished I went home to type up the last of my stories and have a quick nap. I woke up about nine and drove to John's house in a panic. I was late. It didn't help that I got caught in the Fanad road system's inaugural traffic jam. But just as I was denouncing God for making me late I crested the journey's final hill. The curses froze at the sight of the perfectly lit, perfectly choreographed scene below.

Cars were streaming from every direction toward John's. It was a beautiful, windless night. The headlight beams speared into the violet sky and meshed together into a translucent cloud above the house, like a halo. Silhouetted figures spilled out into the garden and gathered in the glow of the windows and the open front door.

I parked the car and went inside, trying hard to remember the tips Francis had given me on how to behave at a wake: (1) Offer condolences to eldest brothers. (2) Remember to view the body. (3) Don't get drunk (no one else will).

The house smelt of pine air freshener and floor polish. Most of the furniture had been moved out to make space. It was strange to find someone I didn't recognize sitting in Annie's old chair, beneath the flickering ten-watt bulb of her electric Eternal Flame. John's nieces toured the throng carrying plates of cakes and cigarettes. I lifted a cup of tea from the tray in the kitchen. (Not that anyone was keeping a strict count but a few days later John's sister Peggy told me at least two thousand cups of tea were drunk that night. That is a lot of mourners.)

John was in the hallway talking quietly to Harald Schimdle, the Austrian émigré who wrote with such enthusiasm about messy bodily functions in his *Tribune* medical column. Like everyone else in the house, they were talking about wakes they had attended over the years. This is the only topic of conversation at wakes. I wasn't surprised to learn there were no wakes in Austria, only death and funerals.

"What did you expect—a rave?" John said, when I told him the atmosphere was more subdued than I imagined it would be. "Someone's died, you know. We like to show a bit of respect in Ireland when that happens."

Just before midnight everyone filed into the front room for the rosary. Afterward, I slipped round the back of the house and clambered up the ladder to the attic window. Francis had been working on his own all night. He looked glad of the company. He grabbed me by the shoulders and hauled me in. I tumbled on to the floor.

"Shhhhhhhhhh." He pointed downward. "The coffin is in the room right below."

We both started laughing.

"I bet this never happened at the *Guardian*."

"Now that you mention it, I don't think it did."

We ran the front-page headline TRAVELERS' CONDITIONS A DIS-GRACE TO HUMANITY, above a picture of John Donegan in his caravan. I wrote a long rant about the treatment of Donegal's traveler families that finished with the ringing declaration that "it was time for the official bullshit—there is no other word that fits the circumstances—to stop. The time for action has come."

Leaving aside the clichés and the slightly pompous tone, it was a decent piece of journalism. At least we'd given John Donegan and his friends the chance to have their say, which to my mind made all the worrying about editing the paper seem worthwhile.

It was also the first time in the history of the *Tirconaill Tribune* that John McAteer hadn't written the lead story. Not that he cared. His mother had just died, after all. The day after the paper arrived in the shops he got an anonymous phone call from someone telling him that he was no better than the fuckin' gypsies for allowing his newspaper to print such a pile of garbage; that he should be ashamed of himself.

On the contrary, he was delighted. "Well done, Mr. Editor," he said, when I arrived at the office the next day. I can't say for certain but I think this was the first compliment he had ever paid me.

Riot in Kerrykeel

By now I knew enough about life on the *Tirconaill Tribune* to realize the Bernard Lafferty story would end over tea and biscuits in a terraced house in Donegal rather than an all-expenses-paid trip to Los Angeles and the startling discovery that Doris Duke had indeed been killed by her beloved butler. Sure enough . . .

Sarah Hunter phoned to say she was back from Australia. She wanted to talk about a friend of hers she insisted I interview, an artist. I didn't want to talk about her artist friend, I wanted to talk to her about Bernard Lafferty, her dead butler friend. The last thing she said before hanging up was, "And I'm not going to say a word about Bernard, God rest his soul."

Half an hour later I rang her doorbell. The door opened straight into a tiny sitting room. There was a blown-up photograph of a middle-aged man propped up on the settee. His dyed blond hair had been pulled back into a ponytail. He was wearing a gold lamé jacket, a white collarless shirt with black stud buttons and a diamond in his left ear. The shot had a no-expense spared feel, from the soft lighting to the makeup and beautifully even dental work.

"Bernard Lafferty, I presume." I shifted the picture to make room to sit down.

"Aye. That was the very picture displayed at his funeral. I asked if I could bring that and some of his ashes back home to Donegal. They would only give me the picture," Sarah said. "It was blown up from the one he used in his passport. But I told you I don't want to talk about him."

"Of course you want to talk about him."

"Don't."

"Do."

"Don't."

"Then why have you got his picture out? Does it always have pride of place on the settee?"

Sarah chatted for a while about her artist friend. I dutifully took a few notes and waited for the chance to change the subject. She disappeared into the kitchen. There was a pile of photograph albums lying on a coffee table. I picked one off the top and flicked through its pages. I came to a sequence of pictures of a stout, black-haired woman in a tentlike white dress. They had been taken from above, through a dirty window-pane, and were slightly blurred. But the subject was unmistakable.

"Is this Liz Taylor?"

Sarah stood in the doorway, holding a tray of tea and biscuits. "Of course it's Liz Taylor," she said, as if everyone in the world had pictures of Liz Taylor in their family photograph album. "She came to visit Bernard's house in Beverly Hills after he died. She wandered round for a while like a ghost. We were there on holiday, me and my mammy. We weren't supposed to take pictures but . . . Tea? She rang Bernard seven times in the days before he died. She knew he was ill. Biscuit? They were like mother and son, those two."

I heard no more about her painter friend.

Bernard Lafferty didn't murder Doris Duke. Of course he didn't. Detectives at the Los Angeles Police Department concluded after a year-long investigation that there was "no credible evidence" of criminal homicide. The only mystery is why it took them so long to reach such an obvious conclusion.

Consider just a few points of the "damning" evidence against the butler:

When a package containing large amounts of morphine arrived at Doris Duke's house in Los Angeles the night before she died Lafferty seized it and with a loud chuckle supposedly announced to the other staff, "Ah-ha, Miss Duke is going to die tonight." He then disappeared upstairs to his mistress's room. Twelve hours later she was dead.

Come on. I'm hardly Philip Marlowe but even I could work out that if someone was planning to inject their billionairess employer with a fatal dose of morphine the last thing he would do is start cackling like a pantomime villain and tell everyone what he was up to. Agreed?

Bernard Lafferty stood to gain a fortune if Doris Duke died.

This is true. But he stood to gain a fortune regardless of when she died, unless she had made her mind up that she wasn't going to die after all. This was unlikely. Immortality is hard to arrange, even for a woman with Doris Duke's money.

Tammy Payette, the nurse who accused Lafferty of murder, claimed Doris Duke wasn't suffering any pain when she was injected with morphine. She also said that Duke was suspicious about the medication she was receiving.

Ms. Payette's evidence was largely discredited when she was convicted a few months later for theft of jewels and other valuables from the homes of wealthy patients, including Doris Duke's.

The undertakers had been telephoned by someone in the Duke household the day before she died and told their services might shortly be required.

This is exactly the kind of efficiency that landed Bernard Lafferty a plum job with Doris Duke in the first place.

After Doris Duke died Bernard Lafferty didn't exactly behave like the grieving ex-employee that many people thought he should have been.

Three days after Doris Duke died, he went out shopping with

her credit card and spent $3,128 on clothes. This was the first stop on an Olympian spending spree at some of the world's most famous designer shops. For the next two years barely a day seemed to pass without Bernard spending thousands of dollars on Louis Vuitton, Neiman Marcus and Gianni Versace. This only proves that he was a shopaholic with bad taste in clothes and luggage, not that he was a murderer.

He started drinking a lot and behaving irrationally after Doris Duke's death.

For instance, he lost control of a $54,000 Cadillac on Sunset Boulevard, hit a curb, became airborne and crashed into three other cars. "To be airborne in West Hollywood—the traffic is so heavy—you have to be out of your mind," remarked one eye-witness, with seemingly intimate knowledge of the mindlessness he was describing. Incidents like this, however, proved only that Lafferty was a bad driver. Again, this is not the same as being a murderer.

I could go on.

As I was saying, Bernard Lafferty didn't murder Doris Duke. She was simply an old woman whose hedonistic past finally caught up with her and she died, aged eighty-one. Not a bad inning, as my grandmother used to say.

When Duke bequeathed him control of her billion-dollar fortune she left him with an army of enemies—embittered lawyers, grasping relatives and former staff—who couldn't believe they had been usurped by her butler. The way his foes told it, Lafferty wormed his way into Duke's affections by devious means and, once his position was secure, took her life. It was a fantastic story that generated thousands of newspaper articles, two prime-time documentaries, at least three books and a television mini-series starring Lauren Bacall (as Doris) and Richard Chamberlain (as Bernard).

If only the story had been true. No one, apart from Camilla Parker-Bowles, got a worse press than Bernard Lafferty. "'The 'butler' word they liked because the butler always did it," was his weary but perceptive answer whenever quizzed on the subject.

Just as it didn't take Philip Marlowe to work out that the murder theory was nonsense, it didn't take a doctorate in semiology to detect the snobbery and contempt that drove Lafferty's enemies. They refused to believe that a man from a village called Creeslough could be anything other than a cartoon Irishman, a "thick Paddy." As far as these people were concerned he was an alcoholic, uncouth, stupid Irish slob, who was unfit for anything other than $200-a-week servitude.

Admittedly, Lafferty wasn't a saint. He had a weakness for firm young male buttocks, Grand Marnier and driving airborne down Sunset Boulevard in $54,000 Cadillacs. No, his problem was that he was reckless. Doris Duke's legacy allowed him to indulge his recklessness.

There was a messy court case over the will. The judge called Lafferty a profligate, illiterate drunk with a cavalier approach to money. Surprise, surprise, he lost the case. He appealed. Everyone settled out of court. As part of the deal, control of Doris Duke's charitable trust passed from her butler into other hands. Lafferty was left with a lump sum, an annual stipend and a handful of friends who liked him for himself rather than his money. Elizabeth Taylor was one, Michael Jackson another. Sarah Hunter, retired secretary at the electricity board in Letterkenny, was a third.

For a woman who had taken a vow of silence on the subject Sarah was surprisingly reluctant to let me leave the comfort of her front room before telling me everything there was to know about the last days of Bernard Lafferty, a subject she knew better than anyone. He died while she and her mother were on holiday at his Beverly Hills mansion.

It was all in her photograph albums: the three-thousand-dollar silk bedspreads, the Hollywood memorabilia, expensive lawyers sitting round dining-room tables, exterior shots of the Beverly Wilshire, the fourth-division actresses, the Melrose Avenue shopping trips in Lafferty's favorite car, a black Rolls-Royce (reg. BL100). I turned the pages while Sarah provided the running commentary: "Those bedspreads came from Napoleon's bedroom—the one he took to war . . . Those two urns came from the movie *The King and I* . . . It's not everyone who can have lunch seven days a week at the Beverly Wilshire. That gorgeous one with the blonde hair was in *Baywatch*. No, no, it's not Pamela Anderson—Oh, you should have seen us, me and my mammy in the Rolls-Royce, we were like the Beverly Hillbillies . . ."

It was a fascinating insight into a world as far away from Creeslough and Sarah's front room as it was possible to imagine. We talked for hours, disturbed only by the occasional appearance of Mammy, a stooped, shuffling figure with a voice like a carton of Capstan full strength, and the magnified smirk of Bernard Lafferty in his passport photograph. Every once in a while Sarah would gaze longingly into his eyes and wish aloud that he was still alive.

"I found him dead in his bed, you know." She sighed.

"You told me."

"Did I?"

"Yes. At the Daniel O'Donnell concert, remember? I think you told me he was wearing a blue Versace nightshirt."

"God, he looked great in that blue Versace nightshirt," she said, her thoughts drifting off elsewhere. Her mother shuffled through the room on her way to the toilet. "Bernard loved having Mammy around. The two of them used to sit and talk for hours together. Bernard loved her. He said she reminded him of his own mammy when they were living in Donegal. Didn't he, Mammy?"

"Oh, aye," Mammy rasped.

"All he ever talked about was coming back to Donegal for a holiday, you know. He wanted to have a look around the place, to see how Creeslough was doing."

She went quiet for a moment, then picked up a photograph of funereal black limousines parked outside a church. "He hadn't been well for a couple of days. He said he had a chill. There was only three of us in the house that night, me, him and Mammy. I took him up a glass of water at about a quarter to six in the morning and there he was—sprawled over the bed with his hands out, a big smile on his face . . ."

"Stone cold dead?"

She nodded. "I wish I'd taken a photograph. He looked lovely."

So much rubbish was written about Bernard Lafferty in the days after he died (and ever since) that it's hard to know where to start. *He was murdered!* He died of a massive heart attack, actually. *His ashes were flown back to Ireland and scattered on his parents' grave in Creeslough!* Close. They were dropped in the ocean off Los Angeles. "I asked the Hawaiian housekeeper if I could bring some ashes back to Donegal and she told me Bernard wouldn't have wanted them to be split up," Sarah said.

People in Creeslough were ashamed of him! "We were proud of him. We were always proud of him—we would have welcomed him with open arms if he'd come home," one church-going pillar of the community told me.

The most ridiculous piece of nonsense, however, was the headline *Butler's Lady Pal May Get Fortune!* The story referred to Sarah.

"The *Sun* printed that on the front page," she said, with a snort, fishing out the cutting from a desk drawer. "Look at this. Every word a lie. God, I didn't even *want* his money. It all went back to the Doris Duke Foundation. I didn't want anything from him. He used to hand me all sorts of beautiful stuff and say, 'Take it.' I never did, well, except . . ."

She disappeared into another room for a minute and returned wearing what I can only describe as a mink poncho. She twirled around the room and laughed. "I keep it in a ball on top of the wardrobe. Daft thing that it is."

Of all the many things I know nothing about my ignorance is perhaps the most complete on the subject of fur coats. But even I could tell this was a Rolls-Royce of a fur coat. She spread it out on the floor, like a giant fan.

"It must be worth a fortune," I said.

"I couldn't even afford the insurance on it."

"And Bernard gave you this as a present." I ran the back of my hand across the fur. It felt like gold dust slipping through my fingers. "Where did he get it?"

She smiled enigmatically.

"It belonged to Doris Duke, didn't it? You've got Doris Duke's fur coat."

She put her finger on her lips. "How many times have I told you? I'm not going to say a word."

For all I know Sarah might have had a mountain of Bernard Lafferty memorabilia on top of her wardrobe—clothes, jewelry, a couple of old boyfriends—and a thousand more secrets to tell. But she really did mean it this time. She wasn't going to say a word. I got ready to leave. It would soon be the second anniversary of Bernard's death, I promised to write an article about his life and times for the *Tribune*.

"Make sure it's a nice article. I don't want to read any of that tabloid rubbish," Sarah shouted, as I walked toward the car.

"Of course." I really meant it. From everything she had told me about Bernard, I'm sure I would have liked him. I would have thought twice about sharing a Jacuzzi with him, sure, but he sounded like great fun. A complimentary article wouldn't be difficult at all. Driving home, I even thought of a headline: "Deathbed Secrets of Sordid Butler!—*Tribune* reveals the shocking truth."

I went out for a beer that night with Liam Ferry, manager of the St. Michael's Gaelic football reserves. I mentioned my day with Sarah Hunter. Liam had been brought up a couple of miles from Bernard Lafferty's family house in Creeslough but didn't know of him until he became famous as a millionaire butler. There was a twelve-year age difference between them. "Jesus, but I wouldn't have minded some of his money," he said, getting out of his seat. "Do you want another pint?"

As I watched Liam standing at the bar it occurred to me that if you ranked every person in the world in any category—happiness, heterosexuality and so on—it was guaranteed that he and Bernard would have been at opposite ends of the line. Stop me if this sounds a little like Jeffrey Archer, but once upon a time they were both ordinary young lads growing up in Donegal. Look what happened: one left and ended up in Los Angeles, a millionaire, accused of murder, unhappy and dead; the other stayed put and ended up working at the Muckish sand quarry, not rich, shaved, wearing a pressed lime green shirt, happy and standing at the bar waiting to get his round in.

There had to be a lesson in there for me, right? Stay in

Creeslough and end up like Liam. Leave Creeslough and end up like Bernard. Rural = Good, City = Bad. The *Tirconaill Tribune* forever . . . or the Lloyd Cole and the Commotions reunion tour? *The Quiet Man* or, I don't know, some horror film that hasn't been made yet about an innocent schoolboy from Creeslough who buys an airline ticket to America and ends up being diverted to Sodom and Gomorrah?

If only the choice was as stark as that. The ridiculous thing is, I used to think it was—that's why I decamped to Creeslough in the first place. I knew better now. Visiting Dublin, the Lloyd Cole concert and the idea of re-forming the band had reminded me that the life I had had before wasn't entirely awful, just as living in Creeslough had taught me that life in rural Ireland wasn't "opting out" at all.

When I thought about it, the only thing John Connolly and his father had opted out of when they chose to try to make a living out of the farm was an easy life. Danny Lafferty and everyone else who slogged their guts out to make sure Creeslough was a thriving community hadn't opted out of anything. They had opted in. Working for the *Tribune* definitely wasn't opting out. In fact, working for the *Tribune* was opting in—to John McAteer's never-ending war against the council and the tourist board and Newt Gingrich and dead whales lying on the beach.

So what would I be doing if I left Creeslough and went back home to Glasgow on the off-chance that Lloyd Cole and the Commotions might get back together again? Opting out of opting out? Or opting out of opting in, or opting back in again after almost a year of opting out? I didn't know and, to be honest, it hurt my brain even trying to figure it out. All that I knew was I had made up my mind what I wanted to do.

• • •

Liam and I spent most of the night talking about Gaelic football. St. Michael's was due to play against a team from Downings in the Donegal Third Division (Reserves) League the following Sunday. The match was a title decider.

For reasons mainly connected to a lack of natural athleticism the trophy cabinet at home has remained empty throughout my sporting life except for a fifty-yard swimming proficiency certificate and a charity fun run medal. Naturally, I was beside myself at the thought of actually winning a prize rather than simply getting one for turning up. Liam, on the other hand, had been involved with St. Michael's long enough to know that winning the Donegal Third Division (Reserves) League was down there with swimming proficiency certificates in the genetic soup of sporting achievement. "Oh, aye, it is the biggest game for the club since God only knows," he said distractedly, and changed the subject.

But eventually the conversation came back round to Gaelic football. It always did in rural Ireland. One minute you were sitting in a pub chatting about the weather or the relative merits of Led Zeppelin and AC/DC and the next you were caught up in a passionate debate about the great games, the great players, *the legends*. I never had a clue who or what anyone was talking about but usually joined in the argument anyway. The story of my life, really.

My excitement about the Downings game must have been infectious because before too long Liam was reminiscing on the great St. Michael's matches down the years. The 1967 Under-16 County Championship final, the Tommy Ryan Cup final, the Gaeltacht Cup, the 1983 Junior Championship. "Now, that was a big game. Do you know what the score was?" he said.

"Remind me again."

"We played Milford in the final at Ballybofey, beat them 1–15 to 0–6. Tony Wilkinson, Mickey McColgan—what a great player he was, Colm McFadden, John McGinley, Tommy Doherty, Tommy McGinley. God, Tommy McGinley played that day and he had a few broken ribs. What a team we had."

The 1983 Donegal Junior Championship was St. Michael's finest moment. Liam was too modest to mention his own name in such select company but I happened to know that he played in that game too.

"Not forgetting Liam Ferry." I laughed. "I heard he was a bit of a player in his day."

"Me?" He shook his head. "I could tackle a bit. I refused to be beaten but I didn't have much skill. I was a bit like you, in fact. I was a trier."

With that ringing endorsement from my team manager I drained my glass, declined the offer of another beer—"No thanks, I'm in training for Sunday's game"—and headed home. It was late and I had to get up early. John McAteer was going to war again in the morning and he needed someone to carry his knapsack.

I woke at 6 A.M., threw a handful of cold water in my face and headed off to Kerrykeel. Dawn shimmered silver on Mulroy Bay as I drove. I knew the village well. It was five miles north of the *Tribune* office, a picture-postcard version of Ireland: thatched cottages, thick hedgerows, a place where life proceeds with a slow, rhythmic swing. But not today.

I crested the incline on the approach to the village and saw the police roadblock ahead. Twice in the last two months the villagers had stopped the mobile phone company erecting its radio mast at the police station, next to the local primary school. John had been tipped off that it was coming back a third time—with the riot squad for protection. "Get there early and bring a tin helmet," he said.

He was excited and I could guess why. If ever there was a story that the *Tirconaill Tribune* existed to cover then this was it. In one corner there was the police, the mobile phone company and its precious mast. In the other stood the people, brandishing alarming scientific reports that mobile phone masts caused cancer in children and a sense of injustice that no one had asked them if they wanted the damn thing. Guess whose side John was on?

I got to the roadblock, rolled down the window and flashed my press card. "What paper are you from?" one of the officers said.

"The *Tirconaill Tribune*."

It would be fair to say that the *Tribune* wasn't the favorite publication of the local police. John never missed an opportunity to portray them as a Gaelic version of the Keystone Cops.

"Well, there won't be much for you boys to write about today. Not that you will be bothered—you'll write it anyway, no doubt."

"And a good day to you too, Officer, you miserable old goat," I said, although not until I'd driven a hundred yards down the road.

A crowd of about a hundred and fifty had already gathered outside the police station. Some of them had been there all night. John arrived just after me. As he climbed out of his car, camera hanging from his neck, an extraordinary thing happened: people started cheering.

I couldn't believe it at first. I'd heard of journalists turning up at the scene of a story and people throwing basins of cold water from first-floor windows, or releasing large and fearsome dogs. But never cheering. No one had ever cheered me when I turned up at a story. If they had I would have retired instantly on the grounds that life as a journalist couldn't have got any better.

"Did you hear that?" I said to John. He flashed me a secret smile, like a content hen sitting on a warm egg. "Well, they know they'll get a fair and balanced report from the *Tribune*."

A few minutes later someone at the far end of the village shouted a warning. As she did a trailer carrying the phone mast moved slowly into view, flanked by black-clad police carrying riot shields and batons. Some protesters ran toward them, others lay down in the road. As they did, scores more police spilled out from behind the station.

I'd been caught up in riots before, but that was in London and Paris and Rotterdam, at football matches and poll-tax protests. This was Kerrykeel. This was picture-postcard Ireland. The two sides met in the middle of the road. Police batons started swinging. Protesters were dragged away by the hair, screaming and kicking. The trailer inched ever closer to the school. I was terrified someone was going to be crushed under its wheels.

"Welcome to rural Ireland," John said, getting ready to dive into the mêlée with his camera. "Let's go."

"Wait for me," I shouted. As we ran toward the line of Perspex riot shields it occurred to me that life was never like this in Ballykissangel.

Either John had missed his vocation as one of the great Irish actors of his generation or he really didn't care less that I was leaving. Francis took the news in the same way he took any news.

"That's good," he said, with a quiet smile. "Eh. What I mean is, that's good for you. It'll be good fun. Jeez. On tour with a rock band. Brilliant. Good."

I put him out of his misery. "I know what you mean, Francis. Thanks."

The three of us were sitting at the kitchen table. John slapped a lump of ham on his thickly buttered bread. "So you're leaving us for the pop world." He took a bite of his sandwich. "My mother said the first day she saw you that you wouldn't last, you know."

"How could I not know? Every time I walked into the house her first words were 'You still here, Donegan?'"

I missed Annie. We all did, of course. The evenings in Fanad hadn't been the same since she'd died. Hordes of family and friends still came to the house but it was as if someone had turned down the volume and brightness. It was impossible to tell how much her death had affected John. He went back to editing the paper, wrote just as many words and remained as inscrutable as ever. Only once, about a week after she died, when he told me how he had gone home one night and for the first time in twenty-seven years there was no light on in the front room, did I detect even the merest hint of emotion.

"She only spoke to you like that because she liked you. There was a fair number of people she couldn't stand, you know. She wouldn't even speak to them," he said.

Francis said, "When are you thinking of going?"

"I don't know. Anyway, it's not definite."

This was only half true. What I should have said was that the great Lloyd Cole and the Commotions reunion tour wasn't definite. I hadn't heard another word from Stephen since the idea had first been floated. I didn't even know if I was that keen any more. I spoke to a friend of mine who was still involved in the music industry. He laughed when I told him my plans, saying, "God, it's like the last scene in *Spinal Tap*."

(For the uninitiated, *This Is Spinal Tap* is a spoof documentary—rockumentary, if you will—about a terrible heavy-metal band. It ends with them contemplating getting back together after their single "Sex Farm" has entered the Japanese charts at number five. It is a great film, one of my favorites. I just wasn't sure it was a great template for my life.)

What was definite was that I was leaving Creeslough. Why? A psychologist might have diagnosed a mild case of Bernard Lafferty syndrome, a mental condition recognizable by the patient's delusions of international stardom. But the truth was more prosaic. I was lonely. When I looked in the bathroom mirror in the morning I didn't see me but someone who was beginning to resemble the Unabomber, with mad eyes and hair to match. I'm ashamed to admit this but it had been four months since I had last ironed an item of clothing. If my personal hygiene was bothering me what must other people have been thinking? Call me shallow and pathetic but I wanted a telly. I needed to watch *Brookside* three times a week, just like I needed to know I could walk down the street and buy a book, the new Blur record on the day it was released, or a ticket to a Celtic match.

Don't get me wrong. I loved Creeslough. How could anyone walk through the village on a sunny July afternoon and not love it? I only had to spend an hour in the Corncutter's Rest or slip on a red St. Michael's jersey to know I had made friends and sporting allegiances that would last me a lifetime. And living in the village didn't mean I couldn't watch television or buy as many books and records as I wanted. I hadn't been transported back to the Middle Ages. But . . . but . . . but . . . I wanted to go home.

If that makes me sound like a big baby, then I plead guilty. In mitigation let me just say this: life in rural Ireland isn't some cinematic fantasy. It's hard, or at least it was too hard for me.

My mind was made up. I was packing my bags and going home. I used to have a girlfriend there. I wondered if she would have me back. At least I could honestly tell her I'd been celibate since moving to Ireland. She didn't have to know this had been an involuntary state.

From there, who knows what? If it wasn't on tour with Lloyd Cole and the Commotions, then something would turn up. I could write a begging letter to the editor of the *Guardian* asking for my old job back, or get a position as a footman in a country house and work my way up to butler. Maybe I could sell cars. ("What color of car would you like, sir?" I could do that.)

"I'll miss this," I said.

John and Francis answered in unison. "What?"

"This. Sitting in the kitchen with you two like this every day, sorting out the world, putting things to right."

"Holy God. Francis, get me a violin. He's gonna start crying in a minute."

I would dearly like to say that St. Michael's last match of the season was decided in injury time when the team's rookie full forward, his head heavily bandaged after an off-the-ball incident earlier in the game, soloed the length of the field and smashed home his first goal of the season to win the match and the Donegal GAA Third Division (Reserves) League for the parish.

But, as I said, life in rural Ireland isn't a cinematic fantasy.

We were beaten by thirteen points to ten. The score flattered St. Michael's. If I was sitting in a television studio with Des Lynam and Alan Hansen I could dress it up and say Downings were fitter, faster, hungrier and more organized. But the truth was that most of our players (me included) were out late at the pub the night before. As for Donegan's individual performance? I would have to admit to Des that it was disappointing, especially as the Scottish lad had laid aside the traumatic memories of his pilgrimage to Knock earlier in the season and went to mass on the morning of the game. So much for the power of prayer.

At least I was picked to play. This was a victory of a sort after the shock of arriving at the ground to discover our dressing room was crowded. I couldn't believe it. It was usually a struggle to find fifteen to make up a team. The prospect of playing in the biggest match of the season had brought out a lot of players who hadn't turned out for months.

Liam was more used to rustling up a team than selecting one. He looked slightly embarrassed at having to leave some of them out, especially the older guys who had given years of service to the club. Instead of one last, victorious hurrah they were facing an afternoon spent freezing on the touchline without even the consolation of watching a decent game of football.

When I heard my name being called out I felt a slight shiver of embarrassment too, though it passed in a nano-second. So what if I'd only given a few months' service to the club? Tough. This was my last hurrah with St. Michael's. I was prepared to die for the cause, which was just as well because the Downings' defense looked like just the sort who might kill me given half an excuse.

In the event they didn't have to. Not for the first time in my sporting career there was a chasm between desire and execution. I was—there is no other word—hopeless. The harder I tried the more hopeless I became. I touched the ball twice in the first half and not at all during the first ten minutes of the second half.

Being substituted in any sport is humiliating but the rule-makers in Gaelic football have devised a particularly cruel method of delivering the humiliation. What happens is this: the team manager decides that a player is embarrassing both him-self and the good name of the club. He writes the offender's name on a scrap of paper and gives it to the substitute. The sub-stitute walks across the field, hands the scrap of paper to the referee and then, like the Angel of Death, runs slowly toward the man he is replacing to deliver the verdict: "You're off."

I've never committed a criminal offense in my life. I have never experienced what it is like to stand in the dock as the jury returns after its deliberation. I would imagine it is very like the moment on a Gaelic football field when it is obvious that the substitute is heading in your direction. You don't want to believe it, you want to claim extenuating circumstances or a miscarriage of sporting justice. "I've been framed," you want to cry. "It's not my fault I was born with the physical coordination of a pantomime cow."

I felt like doing all of these things when Noel McGarvey shouted, "Lawrence, you're off." I even felt like punching him in the face but of course I didn't: Noel was a gentleman, and it wasn't his fault I'd played so badly. Plus, he was bigger than me. Punching him in the face could have been dangerous.

I trudged off and took my place in the dugout next to Liam.

"Well played, Lawrence," he said.

I thought momentarily of asking him why, if I'd played well, he had substituted me. What was the point? Instead I just buried my head in my hands. Liam could see I was upset. He patted me on the back and said sympathetically, "Don't worry, there's always next season."

That was the point. There wasn't going to be a next season for me. My career in Gaelic football was officially over. My statistical record was now complete and it didn't make inspiring reading: Career points—3; Goals—0; GAA All-Ireland Championship winner's medals—0; Appearances for County Donegal—0; Donegal Club Championship winner's medals—0; Donegal GAA Third Division (Reserves) Championship winner's medals—0; Miscellaneous awards (player of the year, etc)—0.

It was all right for Liam to go around patting people on the back and telling them not to worry. The historians of St. Michael's GAA club will look upon him kindly forever. He had played in the 1983 Junior Championship winning team. His place in the pantheon of club legends was secure. How were the football aficionados of the parish going to remember me in ten years' time? As the only full forward in the club's history to finish a season without scoring a goal, that's how.

At least I had made more of an impact on the fortunes of the *Tribune*. That's not me being big-headed, it's a statistical truth. According to Francis, sales had gone up by about three hundred copies an issue since I started working for the paper. Even John conceded that I had been, on balance, a worthwhile addition to his staff. He couldn't quite bring himself to say he would miss me but a fondness had crept into his manner, if not his words, that hinted he wouldn't have minded too much if I'd decided to hang around for a few years at least.

In retrospect it all seemed like a great adventure. A lot of the time it was—the visits from Meryl Streep and Newt Gingrich, the trips to Tory Island and Dublin. Even the visit from Mr. Eksund was now funny rather than terrifying, and the Princess Diana poem a startling piece of satire that provoked the people it was meant to provoke. ("We were too bloody kind to her," was John's final word on that subject.) As for the endless school reunions, the brain-numbing council meetings and the Samaritans AGM? Suddenly, they seemed like fun, fun, fun.

We spent a lot of time in the kitchen drinking tea, converting bad memories into good ones, transforming the boring moments into necessary periods of rest between bursts of world-changing journalism. The mood was valedictory, as if we were looking back on a glorious military campaign in which there had been no deaths, only minor bruising and scratches.

It was during one of these kitchen sessions that I persuaded John and Francis that the *Tribune* should be "relaunched."

A relaunch is newspaper marketing jargon to describe that annoying day when you buy your favorite paper only to discover it looks different from the day before and you can't find the TV listings. There is always a new lifestyle section, hundreds of new columnists and a message from the editor on page two that includes the phrase "Welcome to our new-look paper for the new millennium." And the price goes up 5p.

John and Francis desperately wanted to turn the *Tribune* into a weekly but couldn't. For all sorts of boring, complicated reasons that I never quite understood, Francis insisted a weekly paper needed its own printing press and an army of journalists. This would cost fifty thousand pounds, he said, although he might as well have said fifty million for all the difference it would have made. If I had been able to produce fifty thousand from my back pocket I would have done so in an instant, both as a token of my appreciation for what they had both done for me and for the simple pleasure of seeing their faces when I produced the check.

I figured a relaunch was the next best thing to going weekly. As the only person in the kitchen who appeared to have any great enthusiasm for the idea, it was decided I would take responsibility for making it a success. I didn't mind. It would be my gift to the *Tribune*, my legacy. At least it wouldn't cost me a penny.

There was to be no new lifestyle section, no message from the editor—he told me, "Go away, I'm busy," when I asked—and no new columnists. In fact we were losing one: Harald Schimdle was moving to Germany, taking his healthy lifestyle and his healthy lifestyle column with him. *Tribune* readers would have to work out how to solve flatulence on their own in future.

John found a replacement of sorts on the Internet, a feature called "Strange But True" in which two brothers from America posed, and answered, questions such as "Any Truth in the Wild Tales of Gerbil Stuffing?", "Are Humans the Only Ones Who Get Cancer?" and "When German Biologist August Weismann Cut Off the Tails of 22 Generations of Mice He Discovered Their Offspring All Still Had Full-sized Tails." Why did he bother?

I am not making this up. I only wish I was. I begged John not to run "Strange But True." I suspect this made his mind up. It was going in.

At least I extracted a promise from Francis not to have more than three pictures on a single page. He also made a few changes to the way the pages were laid out. John said he would try to make sure the first paragraph of every story he wrote had less than a hundred words; and together we designed a new *Tirconaill Tribune* masthead. It was hardly the new-look paper for the new millennium but as publication day approached I was quietly confident that it would look better than it ever had.

The drive from Creeslough to Milford, the last I would make as a *Tribune* journalist, was melancholy. I stopped by the roadside, got out of the car and went for a walk along the shore of Mulroy Bay. A half-moon cast silver shadows across the narrow ribbon of water. They were soon gone, as a sullen sky rolled in from the north. For the first time since I'd made up my mind to leave Donegal I wondered whether I was doing the right thing. How could anyone walk away from such beauty? Suddenly it started to rain. As big black globules bounced off my head I thought, Bugger this, and ran back to the car.

By the time I arrived at the office sheets of water were rolling down the empty street. I'd never seen rain like this before, not even in Donegal. I sprinted the twenty yards from the car to the back door and I still got soaked.

John was alone in the kitchen tapping away at his laptop. "Terrible night," he said, without looking up. As he did the lights flickered. "Lightning."

I dried myself off, made some tea and went through to the office.

Francis was working at the computer. Harald, making a rare appearance, was typing out village notes on another computer. Declan was reading through rough copy and some pasted-up pages, correcting spelling mistakes.

It was definitely shaping up to be a new, improved *Tribune*. The pages were tidier: there were fewer pictures. Francis had done wonders with the layout. He showed me the new masthead on the computer screen. It looked magisterial, like the

New York Times crossed with *Time* magazine. With the exception of "Strange But True," the content was good. Great, even.

John had written an obituary of Stinky the whale. He'd been at the cliffs earlier in the week and discovered that the carcass had been washed away by the high tides. He'd also written a fantastic lead story about the riot over the phone mast under the headline "Kerrykeel Gardai Row Deepens—Officers 007 and Jack Straw Sought." The first paragraph read:

> There is serious public disquiet that the Gardai acted outside the law and there have been a catalog of complaints that protesters were kicked, abused, assaulted, elbowed in the mouth and dragged on the ground by officers who refused to identify themselves and one of the five people arrested in the incidents told the crowd afterward that two of the officers involved said their names were Jack Straw and 007. Dramatic eye-witness accounts of the police behavior before they marched into the village told of the officers being psyched up by a sergeant and suggested they were shouting, screaming and acting like lunatics. "It was like a Vietnam war movie," one source said.

I made that 115 words—fifteen more than were allowed under the new rules—but I wasn't going to argue. It was angry stuff. The readers would love it. The police wouldn't, which I guessed was the whole point.

John came through from the kitchen just as I finished reading.

"Is this what you call a fair and balanced story?" I laughed.

Before he got the chance to answer, the sharpest, loudest,

most terrifying noise I had ever heard in my life exploded across the room. The lights went out, flickered and then came back on again to reveal five ghostly faces, all of them fixed in horror as they tried to work out whether they were still alive or not. Even now, months later, there is a ringing in my ears.

John recovered first. "Don't touch anything," he shouted. The computer screens were blank. He started rummaging around in the spaghetti of electrical wiring under the desk.

"Lightning. We've been hit by lightning." He held up a computer box. It was blackened and shattered. A bolt of lightning had come down the telephone cable and blown up the computers.

"Is it serious?" someone said.

Stupid question. I knew it was serious because Francis was beating his hands on the desk and wailing, "What about the paper? It was all in the computer. God, John, we're fucked."

John shook his head. "What's the problem, Francis? You're still alive, aren't you?"

We drove in convoy through the storm to Fanad. John, who was bringing up the rear, ran out of petrol. Declan had to turn back and pick him up. Francis arrived at the house first. His initial diagnosis on the lightning strike—"the worst disaster in the history of the *Tribune*"—was slightly pessimistic. Some material was lost—adverts, village notes, the new masthead, the fancy new graphics that he'd found on the Internet—but more than half of the pages had already been finished. There was still enough time to produce a paper for the printers in the morning.

"Photographs, we'll use plenty of old photographs," he said, when I asked how we'd fill the empty spaces.

We worked until dawn—or, at least, John and Francis worked

until dawn. Harald and Declan both had early appointments the next morning and went home to get some sleep. I hung around. It was my last edition of the *Tribune*, after all. There was nothing for me to do except make tea and annoy John by asking him every five minutes if there was anything I could do to help.

I sat on the floor in the corner, petting Bouncer and watching John and Francis silently piecing together pages out of whatever stories, photographs and adverts they could find. The last thought that crossed my mind before I fell asleep was that this was how it must have been when they started the *Tribune* all those years ago; just the two of them and a steely, white-lipped determination to publish a paper.

I woke up about 6 A.M., just as they were finishing off. They both looked exhausted, but content too. I looked through the pages they had managed to throw together. The paper looked exactly the way it always did: messy layout, and rambling opening paragraphs and photographs everywhere (Francis had even slipped one in of the Fanad Community Band, for old times' sake). So much for the great relaunch. I don't believe in karma, or kismet or the crazy idea that a Greater Being is at work in the universe but if I did I would have said that someone (something?), somewhere was telling me to leave the *Tribune* alone, it was a great paper just the way it was before I started trying to interfere.

Francis went downstairs for a shower. He was driving to Derry in a couple of hours and needed refreshing. John started tidying up. "Here," he said, sliding the pasted-up back page along the desk. "Since it's your last paper I kept a space for you to write a bit about the lightning strike."

I started typing:

An Apology

Late on Tuesday night the *Tribune* offices were struck by lightning. This resulted in complete computer failure. Unfortunately, this has meant we are unable to publish some articles, adverts and local notes in this issue. We regret the inconvenience caused but at least we are all still alive—though only just.

When I finished I handed the printout to John. He stared at it blankly for a few seconds, as if he had suddenly forgotten how to read. Eventually, he shook his head and picked up a pen. "How long have you worked here now?"

"Eight months."

"Exactly," he said, scoring out the headline. "Long enough to know that the *Tribune* never apologizes for anything."

I stayed in Creeslough for another week, packing bags and clearing out the cottage. I took a scythe to the garden and whitewashed the walls. The place had never looked better than on the sharp, blue morning I closed the door for the last time.

On the way out of the village I passed Connolly's farm. Young Johnny was at the front of the barn forking hay into feed trays. I parked the car by the roadside and went over to say good-bye.

"Terrible," he said, when I asked how life was treating him. But he was smiling. "Where are you going?"

"Home."

"You don't want to take these bloody animals with you?"

"I would, Johnny, but there's no room in the car."

We leant on the fence. There was a lot of news to swap. A couple of calves had arrived unannounced in the night. Cattle feed was up in price again. I was going off to become a pop star. Possibly. Time passed. In the distance the white houses of Creeslough sparkled in the winter sun, like a handful of scattered pearls.

"Look at the village," I said. "Beautiful, isn't it?"

Johnny sighed. "Can't stand around here all day admiring the view. There's work to do."

Author's Note

All events portrayed in *No News at Throat Lake* actually took place. I have changed the names of a handful of people involved, either at their own request or where I felt their interests were best served by anonymity. I have taken a few liberties with the timing of certain events in relation to others in an effort to improve the narrative flow of the book.